Greek Mythology

DAVID STUTTARD

Greek Mythology

A Traveller's Guide
from Mount Olympus to Troy

Drawings by Lis Watkins

Thames & Hudson

To Mark Grant, Emily Jane Stuttard and Alex
Zambellas, whose warm companionship has
so greatly enhanced my own travels in Greece.

Note: All translations are by the author unless
otherwise stated.

Title-page: The birth of Dionysus from the thigh of Zeus.

First published in the United Kingdom in 2016
by Thames & Hudson Ltd, 181A High Holborn,
London WC1V 7QX

*Greek Mythology: A Traveller's Guide from Mount
Olympus to Troy* © 2016 Thames & Hudson Ltd, London

David Stuttard has asserted his moral right to be
identified as the author of this work

British Library Cataloguing-in-Publication Data
A catalogue record for this book is available from
the British Library

ISBN 978-0-500-51832-8

Printed and bound in India by Replika Press Pvt. Ltd

To find out about all our publications, please visit
www.thamesandhudson.com. There you can subscribe
to our e-newsletter, browse or download our current
catalogue, and buy any titles that are in print.

Contents

	Map	6
	Introduction: Greek Mythology in Context	8
1.	Mount Olympus: Dion & the Home of the Gods	14
2.	Sunium: Poseidon's Cliff-Top Temple	29
3.	Eleusis & the Mysteries of Demeter & Persephone	36
4.	Delos: Sacred Island of Leto, Artemis & Apollo	45
5.	Delphi: Seat of Apollo's Oracle, Haunt of Dionysus	53
6.	Ephesus: Artemis & the Cult of the Mother Goddess	64
7.	Paphos: Garden of Aphrodite	77
8.	Pylos: Where Nestor Ruled & Hermes Hid the Cattle of Apollo	87
9.	Olympia: Pelops & the Games	96
10.	Thebes: City of Dionysus, Oedipus & Heracles	104
11.	Tiryns & the Labours of Heracles	121
12.	Iolcus & Mount Pelion: Centaurs, Weddings & the Voyage for the Golden Fleece	136
13.	Corinth & False Promises of Love	150
14.	Argos: Land of Hera, Home of Heroes	159
15.	Athens: Prize of Athene, Kingdom of Theseus	169
16.	Knossos: King Minos & the Labyrinth	184
17.	Calydon: A Boar Hunt & Golden Apples	193
18.	Sparta & the Haunts of Helen	200
19.	Mycenae & the Curse on Agamemnon's Family	209
20.	Troy: A City Contested by Gods & Men	219
21.	Ithaca & the Wanderings of Odysseus	236
22.	Hades: Ephyra & the Gateway to the Underworld	249
	Acknowledgments	261
	Recommended Reading	262
	Index	263

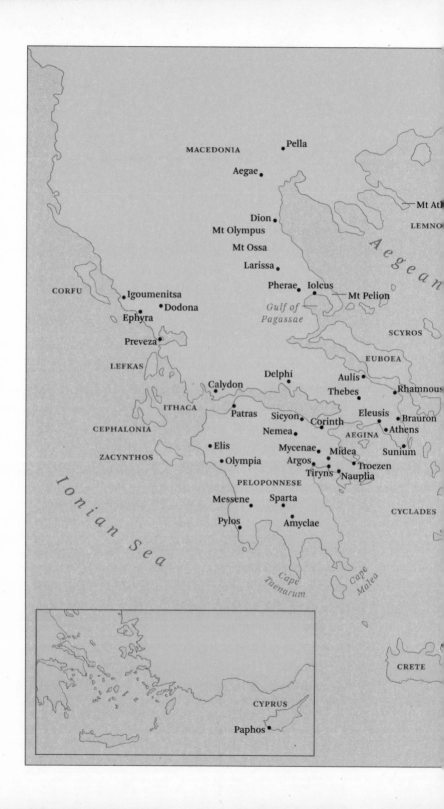

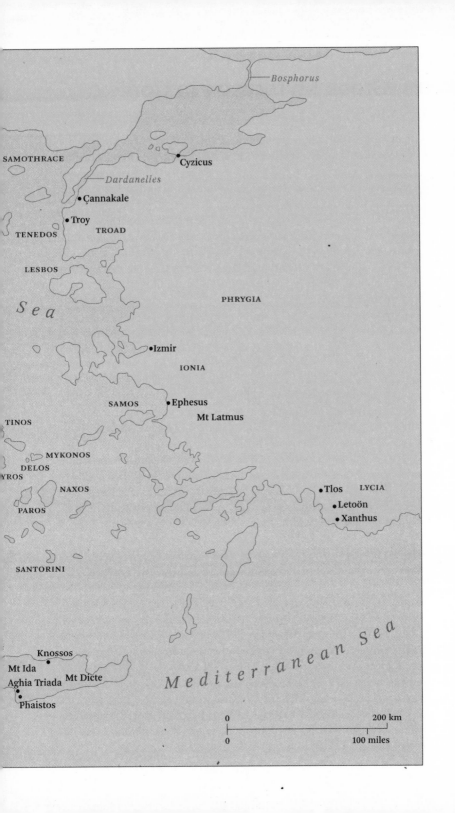

SAMOTHRACE

Bosphorus

Cyzicus

Dardanelles

Çannakale

Troy

TENEDOS   TROAD

LESBOS

S e a

PHRYGIA

Izmir

IONIA

SAMOS   Ephesus

Mt Latmus

TINOS

MYKONOS

DELOS

YROS

NAXOS

Tlos   LYCIA

Letoön

Xanthus

PAROS

SANTORINI

M e d i t e r r a n e a n   S e a

Knossos

Mt Ida

Aghia Triada   Mt Dicte

Phaistos

0   200 km

0   100 miles

Greek Mythology in Context

Greek myths have a universal quality. Populated by characters who are as recognizable today as they were in antiquity, and who frequently find themselves in dire, unenviable situations – the stuff of our own nightmares – they speak to us directly across millennia. Embraced by the Romans and never forgotten even in the Dark Ages, these myths have exercised a profound influence on literature, art and music since the Renaissance, taking root in continents undiscovered by the ancient Greeks. Today, Greek mythology is so embedded in modern culture, including film, television and computer games, that it has become part of the everyday world of many who may otherwise care relatively little for antiquity.

In ancient Greece – even after writing was introduced in the eighth century BC – most people heard the stories of mythology as children from parents, grandparents and nannies. As adults in the Iron Age they thrilled to bards who recited epic poetry at banquets. In Classical times they heard professionals declaim the *Iliad* and *Odyssey* at public festivals, while praise-singers spun legends into paeans celebrating athletes' victories and lyre-players sang love songs rich with memories of a lost heroic world. And in theatres citizen-choruses danced to hymns which celebrated fabled deeds and tragic actors took on the role of heroes. The sheer abundance of opportunities for telling and listening to myths was breathtaking.

Already in Homeric epic (which for the first time wove Greek oral myth into literature) we can witness such situations: in the *Iliad* Achilles sings of the 'famous deeds of men' as he sulks in his tent at Troy; while in the *Odyssey*, the Phaeacian bard Demodocus entertains listeners with tales of not just Troy, but the Olympian gods.

Heroic Myths

Demodocus' songs reveal two strands of mythology. The first deals with heroes – mortals or semi-mortals – who inhabit and interact with the 'real' world. Archaeology confirms that these myths contain more or less accurate reflections of the late Bronze Age world (*c*. 1500 – *c*. 1200 BC). Towns and cities such as Troy, Mycenae, Sparta, Pylos, Calydon and Knossos were thriving in precisely the period when they are imagined as playing an important role in mythology. Since the decipherment of Linear B tablets in the mid-twentieth century we have even discovered that Bronze Age peoples spoke an early form of Greek, and that the place-names of mythology corresponded to those of real settlements. Sadly these tablets were used only for bureaucratic record-keeping, not literature, and give no real evidence even for the names of kings. Hittite tablets from Anatolia, however, do connect names such as Priam and Alexandros with Wilusa, which can reasonably be identified with Troy.

Some myths resonate so closely with the evidence of archaeology that there are those today who passionately believe in their 'historical' accuracy. In antiquity, too, no one doubted that the Trojan War really happened. Historians such as Herodotus and Thucydides accepted it as fact, while from the fifth century BC it assumed even greater significance when it was seen as a precursor of the Greeks' victory over the Persians. As a result, historical figures such as Xerxes and Alexander the Great made sacrifices at Troy – the one praying to avenge the Trojans' defeat, the other to outvie it.

Prominent Greek (and, later, Roman) families traced their lineage back to heroes of the Trojan War, just as some English people today boast of ancestors who came to Britain with the Normans, or Americans profess connections with the Founding Fathers. Thus Alexander claimed descent from Achilles (and Heracles), while Julius Caesar and Augustus counted Aeneas and Anchises among their forebears.

Creation Myths

Demodocus sang, too, of the gods, and an important body of Greek mythology takes place in a wider cosmic setting. Some myths describe the creation of the universe. Hesiod summarizes them in his short epic poem, *Theogony* ('Birth of the Gods') – a fusion of Greek and Near Eastern traditions. Here the world is born from the void of Chaos, generations of gods vie for supremacy, and sons castrate or otherwise weaken fathers to seize ultimate control. A bewildering array of gods and goddesses populates this early world, many the personifications of abstract concepts such as Vengeance, Lawlessness, Fate and Harmony.

Such creation myths have their roots many millennia before Hesiod in early man's attempts to explain his environment and his place within it, and many of their themes are shared across different cultures. For example, the story of a great flood sent to punish (or annihilate) mankind, whose only survivors, a pious couple, subsequently repopulate the world, appears throughout the Near East, while common to many of the world's great religions is the patriarchal explanation that a woman (be she Eve or Pandora) caused all human misery.

Universal Myths

Even myths that at first seem quintessentially Greek contain universal folk-tale motifs as three examples show. The first involves a baby abandoned to die, who returns to claim a throne. Central to the myth of Oedipus, this theme plays an important role too in the tale of the Trojan

Paris, as well as of Pelias and Neleus, respectively king of Iolcus and founder of Pylos. A variation is the story of Perseus, set adrift in a casket with his mother Danaë. In certain circumstances throughout antiquity babies *were* exposed to die, and the motif of a child surviving to grow up and wreak deliberate or accidental vengeance no doubt reflects real fears.

A second example betrays another anxiety, this time about the written word, which for early Greeks must have seemed both magical and sinister. Letters written by rejected women wrongly accuse two mythological characters of rape: Hippolytus, who is killed as a result, and Bellerophon, who lives to be exonerated.

In a third motif an adventurer overcomes adversities and wins the love of a foreign princess. Sometimes (Perseus and Andromeda) the outcome is benign; sometimes (Jason and Medea; Theseus and Ariadne) it is disastrous. Occasionally it turns expectations on their head. Rather than journeying to an unknown land, Oedipus unwittingly returns home to defeat the monstrous Sphinx and claim the hand not of an exotic princess but of his own mother.

Causation, Local Myths & Variations

There are also aetiological (causation) myths. Many explain specific phenomena, either natural or man-made. One tells how, when Apollo inadvertently killed the beautiful youth Hyacinthus, he caused the letters 'AI AI' (representative of wailing) to appear on the petals of the hyacinth; another recounts how the same god's anger caused crows to have black feathers.

Cities used local myths to proclaim their own status or the origins of rites. Thus Thebes boasted of its foundation by the legendary Cadmus, while Athens claimed that it was so loved by the gods that Poseidon and Athene fought one another to possess it. Elsewhere, mythology was used to bolster sanctuaries such as Delphi, Delos and Eleusis, while hymns performed there heightened ties between worshippers and mythology.

At its peak the Greek world stretched from Spain to India and from the Black Sea to the Nile. A common language and shared religious beliefs provided a sense of unity, but travel could be difficult and the world was physically fragmented. So it is not surprising that localized legends and variations of more widespread myths sprang up – made possible not only by a combination of chauvinistic pride and vivid imagination, but by the fact that throughout much of antiquity there was no concept of religious (or mythological) orthodoxy. No one version of a story – even of a god's birth – took precedence over another.

Equally, myths could be reshaped and revised, and new versions coexisted happily with old. Thus the sixth-century BC lyric poet Stesichorus (from Metaurus in South Italy) could write in his *Palinode* that the Spartan

Helen never went to Troy, but instead the gods hid her in Egypt and sent a phantom in her place. A century later the Athenian Euripides used both this and the older, still more common version of the myth interchangeably in his dramas.

Mythology in Greek Literature & Art

For the Greeks mythology was all-pervasive, richly diverse and constantly developing. For us, however, our knowledge is confined to surviving literature and art (such a small fragment of what was originally produced that we can never be certain how representative it is). The Greeks had their own views about the relationship between mythology and literature. The fifth-century BC historian Herodotus (who was familiar with Egyptian, North African and Near Eastern mythology as well as Greek) wrote:

> How each of the gods came into being, whether they existed for all time and what they look like – these are things about which no one knew until yesterday or the day before so to speak, since I imagine that Hesiod and Homer both lived no more than 400 years before my time. It was they who instructed Greeks about the gods' birth, gave gods their names, assigned their honours and skills, and described their appearances.

Herodotus was wrong on several levels. Homer and Hesiod were closer to him in time, the origins of mythology much more distant. But he was correct that it was early epic poets who helped crystallize details of mythology and the gods. Homer assumes an easy familiarity with a wide range of myths, clear evidence that they were common currency. But there were many other early epic poems, only fragments of which survive. Some told of the Trojan War, others of Thebes, still others of the adventures of Jason and the Argonauts.

From the seventh century BC, lyric poets such as Sappho from Lesbos, Tyrtaeus and Alcman from Sparta, and the Theban Pindar peppered their verses with mythological allusions, sometimes so obscure that modern readers find them almost incomprehensible. From the sixth century BC, mythology provided material for hundreds of tragedies, written and performed in Athens and throughout the Greek world. In the Hellenistic period (following Alexander the Great's death), mythology was studied, developed and transformed at the Library of Alexandria by scholars and poets including Callimachus, whose *Aetia* catalogued causation myths, and Apollonius of Rhodes, whose *Argonautica* was self-consciously modern in its learned references. Prose authors, too, such as the second-century BC Apollodorus, collated and streamlined myths, often tying themselves in knots, while Latin poets such as Vergil and Ovid adopted and adapted Greek mythology to suit their Roman ends.

In the second century AD mythology fascinated the traveller Pausanias. His *Description of Greece* provides useful evidence for local variations, as well as for many now lost artworks that played an important role in the understanding and dissemination of Greek myths. One was the Throne of Apollo at Amyclae near Sparta, whose sculptures represented myths as diverse as the Calydonian boar hunt and the Judgment of Paris. Another was the Chest of Cypselus in the Temple of Hera at Olympia: perhaps dating to the seventh century BC, its richly carved sides and lid showed scenes from the Trojan War, the Voyage of the *Argo*, the Labours of Heracles, the voyage of Odysseus, the Seven Against Thebes and the adventures of Theseus and Perseus.

Myths in a Landscape

Sometimes sculptures helped link location with mythology. The east pediment of the Temple of Zeus at Olympia showed preparations for Pelops' chariot race, which was supposed to have begun close by, while the subjects of the west pediment and west metopes (self-contained sculptural blocks) of the Parthenon at Athens were myths set on the Athenian Acropolis. Natural phenomena provided another link. Also on the Athenian Acropolis an olive tree and three grooves in the rock, apparently made by a trident, reinforced the reality of Athene and Poseidon's contest. In Magnesia in Asia Minor a cliff shaped like a weeping woman was identified with Niobe, turned to stone, still mourning her children slain by Artemis and Apollo. At Delphi another rock, positioned at what for the Greeks was the centre of the earth, was venerated as the stone Cronus swallowed in mistake for his son, Zeus.

For many, the very landscape was alive with myths and mythical creatures. Dryads lived in oak trees, oreads in mountain caves and nereids in ocean waves. Breezes, pasturelands and meadows, fountains, springs and rivers, all had their resident spirits. In many places, too, mythology and landscape were inextricably linked – the boar hunt to the wooded glens of Calydon, the birth of Aphrodite to the sparkling sea at Cyprus or the slaying of the Minotaur to the palace at Knossos.

A Traveller's Guide

Greek landscapes shaped Greek myth, which in turn influenced Greek history. So, to try to link myth and history with their associated sites, this book takes readers on a journey through the Greek mainland, as well as to some of the Aegean islands and sites in Turkey which once were Greek. All the locations are accessible today, and visitors may use this book as a companion. For armchair travellers, the brief evocations that begin each chapter are intended to capture something of their modern atmosphere.

Travel is instructive, but not essential, for Greek mythology still thrives wherever there are receptive minds, as a poem first published by the present author's Humanity professor, Robert Ogilvie, makes clear:

> When I was one, in Shillingstone,
> June afternoon you spent
> In reading Homer. Twenty now
> Homer I read in Ghent.
>
> From Ghent to Shillingstone is far.
> It's twenty years away.
> But clear-seen Ithaca is near.
> I'll meet you there today.

1

Mount Olympus: Dion & the Home of the Gods

They say that Mount Olympus is the everlasting home, immutable, of the immortal gods. Gales cannot shake it, nor rainstorms drench it, and no snow clouds come near; but, rather, the high air opens out, serene and cloudless, bathed in the purest light. Here every day for all eternity the blessed gods lead lives of happiness.

Homer, *Odyssey*, 6.41f.

On the fertile plain between the sea and Mount Olympus, Dion thrums with life. Tall clumps of trees – oak, ash and poplar, cypress, plane and agnus castus – chitter with the busyness of birds that flit between the branches with a sudden chirr of wings before alighting on a cluster of bamboo. Doves murmur in the tree-tops. Distant crows abrade the air. Iridescent dragonflies hover over the flat surface of the lake or dance around the pillars of a sunken temple, where water flows clear over weathered stones and tortoises loll, lazy in the sun. Straight paved streets stride off with an initial confidence, only to be overcome by lush vegetation, distracted by wild roses and entangled in a sea of asphodel. Elsewhere, anemones and poppies stud the rippling meadows as they flow towards the theatre. And rising up behind the ranks of benches – so close and yet remote, at once forbidding and apparently benign, its high peaks crowned with clouds, its slopes already burgeoning with grapes – is Mount Olympus, the legendary dwelling place of Greece's gods.

In the Beginning

For the Greeks, Mount Olympus was the ultimate seat of power. The gods whose home it was controlled the earth and skies, and all that lived there. Theirs was an extended ruling family, often beset by arguments and egos, sometimes capricious, sometimes fiercely loyal, but always jealous of their own authority and merciless against any who opposed it.

But the Olympians did not always rule the cosmos. Nor was there always a cosmos to rule. At first there was only Chaos, a yawning void, infinite and empty, a lifeless place of endless darkness. Hesiod described the process of creation:

> In the beginning came Chaos; next full-bosomed Gaia
> [Earth], an ever-safe foundation for all the deathless gods,
> who live on snowy Mount Olympus; and misty Tartarus
> in the bowels of the broad-pathed earth; and Eros
> [Desire], the most beautiful of all the deathless gods, who
> loosens limbs, seducing even the most clever minds and
> spirits of both gods and men.

Now that there was form and animating spirit, other entities quickly came into being. From Chaos came Night (Nyx) and Day; from Earth came 'Ouranus, star-speckled sky, her equal, that he might cover her entirely'. Earth, too, was evolving. Hesiod tells how:

> She gave rise to long mountain chains, the lovely home
> of Nymphs, who dwell high in the mountains' wooded
> glens. With no recourse to pleasant lovemaking, she

bore Pontus with its rolling waves – the barren sea. But
afterwards she lay in love with Ouranus and so gave birth
to Ocean with deep-drifting currents.

The fundamental cosmic form was now in place, imagined by early Greeks as a flat discus-shaped earth surrounded by the freshwater stream of Ocean. Beneath lay Tartarus or Hades, the Underworld, soon to be home to the dead, while above stretched Ouranus, the sky.

The Birth of the Titans

Impregnated by Ouranus' rains, Earth gave birth to a succession of primal beings, called Titans ('Stretchers' or 'Strainers'). Some, personifications of abstract ideas such as Themis ('Divine Tradition') and Mnemosyne ('Memory'), would play an important role in Greek religious thought. Others, such as Rhea, brought forth future generations; still others were ferocious and malformed creatures. Such were the Cyclopes: 'Arrogant and boastful ... who gave Zeus thunder and forged his lightning-bolt. In all else they were like gods, but they had just one eye set in the middle of their foreheads. And so they called them Cyclopes ['Round-Eyed']...'. But deadliest of all was Cronus 'of the twisted mind, his father's bitterest enemy'.

But none of the children of Ouranus and Gaia had seen the light of day. No sooner were they born than Ouranus secreted them beneath the earth. So many offspring were returned into her womb, that Gaia stretched and strained in agony. At last in desperation she forged a sickle of the strongest stone and demanded which of her sons would help her. Only Cronus volunteered. Placing the sickle in his hands, Gaia instructed him to wait till nightfall, when Ouranus covered her, intent on making love. Hesiod imagined Cronus reaching out his left hand, 'holding in his right the saw-toothed sickle, while he eagerly sliced off his father's genitals and flung them far behind him'. From the gouts of blood were born the Giants and the avenging Furies, while from the genitals themselves, which splashed into the sea, came Aphrodite, goddess of sex and love, who in time was washed ashore near Paphos on her favoured island, Cyprus.

Now other gods appeared. Night gave birth to terrors: Old Age and Famine; Wars and Killing; Quarrels, Falsehoods, Blame; unerring Nemesis, who punishes wrongdoers; the ruthless Fates, 'who at birth assign both good and bad to mortals, who hunt down the transgressions of both gods and men, goddesses whose anger never stills until they wreak a dreadful justice on the criminal'.

Some of Pontus' children were more benign: his firstborn was Nereus (sometimes called 'The Old Man of the Sea'), whose daughters, the Nereids, could calm the 'sea-swell on the misty sea and soothe the screaming winds'. But others were truly terrifying: Briareus with a hundred hands; the Harpies ['Snatchers'], bird-women who conveyed dead souls of heroes down to Hades; Echidna, half 'fair-cheeked girl', half blotchy, bloated snake; the Sphinx, the Hydra, the Chimaera, creatures who would plague the earth until heroic mortals killed them. Streams and rivers bubbled up. The breezes blew. Helios, the sun, came into being, and the moon, Selene. And the first Dawn broke.

The Coming of the Olympian Gods
Amid this welter of creation, Cronus forced himself incessantly on his sister Rhea. She bore five children – three daughters (Hestia, Demeter and Hera) and two sons (Haides and Poseidon). But as soon as each was born, Cronus ate them. For it was prophesied that his own son would overthrow him. Advised by her parents Ouranus and Gaia, Rhea, pregnant for a sixth time, fled to Crete. Here on a mountain top (identified in antiquity with both Mount Ida and Mount Dicte) she bore a son and hid him in a deep cave, around whose mouth she set Curetes, armoured youths, to mask the baby's cries by clashing spears against their shields. Then she wrapped a stone in swaddling clothes and presented it to Cronus as his child. Without a glance, he gulped it down.

Gods quickly grow to adulthood, so it was not long before the boy left Crete and came disguised into his father's court to serve as cupbearer.

The gods (with Themis in her chariot drawn by lions) fight the giants on the north frieze of the late sixth- / early fifth-century BC Siphnian Treasury, Delphi.

With cunning guile he made the old god violently drunk. Retching, Cronus vomited first the swaddled stone, then each of his five (mercifully undigested) children. Only now did he realize the truth. Even he could not trick fate. His sixth child – Zeus – had come to topple him.

Battle was joined. On Cronus' side were the Titans, with Atlas as their general. Against them stood Zeus, his five siblings and the Cyclopes, whom Cronus had imprisoned deep in Tartarus, but Zeus had since set free. Only after ten years did Zeus prevail. Most of the Titans were consigned to Tartarus, though some say Cronus, pardoned, was allowed to rule the blessed dead in the Elysian Fields.

But the Titans had powerful cousins – twenty-four Earth-born Giants – and in time they sought vengeance. As the Giants tore up mountains, piling Mount Pelion on top of nearby Ossa in an attempt to scale Olympus, another war engulfed the cosmos. It was only with the help of Heracles that the gods defeated their gross rivals. No more attempts were made to overthrow them.

The Olympian Gods

In popular Greek imagination there were twelve gods and goddesses specifically associated with Olympus, each living in a palace of their own built on bronze foundations in the high mountain valleys. For the most part they were imagined in human form – which prompted the late sixth- / early fifth-century BC philosopher Xenophanes to observe: 'If oxen, horses or lions had hands, with which they could draw and work as men do, horses would draw gods like horses, and oxen like oxen, and each would make their bodies like their own.'

The gods possessed human emotions and their hierarchy reflected that of Bronze Age Greece – with an autocratic king, a queen, lords, princes and princesses; but they were as far removed from mankind as the most powerful mortal ruler from his lowest slave. There were other differences, too. Most crucially the gods were immortal. *Ichor* (divine blood) pulsed through their veins. They dined exclusively on *ambrosia* (literally, 'not mortal [food]'), washed down with *nectar* ('deathly [drink]'). And they could assume whatever shape they liked – bird or animal, man or woman – travelling effortlessly across the earth, interacting with humankind for good or ill.

In the imagination Olympus, too, could assume different forms. Mostly it was the mountain in northeast Greece, but at other times it was something altogether more remote and less substantial. In the *Iliad*, Homer pictures Hera harnessing her chariot and driving with Athene to find Zeus on a journey that appears to take them from this more ethereal realm to the physical mountain.

Raising her veil, Hera turns towards
Zeus on the frieze from Athens'
fifth-century BC Parthenon.

Quickly Hera flicked her lash across the horses, and
the gates of heaven opened of their own accord,
groaning on their hinges. The Horae ['Hours'] are their
gate-keepers, and to them are entrusted the mighty
heavens and Olympus, for they decide whether to release
the rolling clouds or close them in. So, through these
gates they urged their horses, which responded to the
goad, and they found Zeus, the son of Cronus, sitting on
his own, far from the other gods, on the peak of many-
ridged Olympus.

On Olympus the gods are often envisaged in assembly or banqueting.
Perhaps the most stunning representation of this divine assembly appears
on the Parthenon frieze (inspired by a frieze on the earlier Siphnian
Treasury at Delphi). On it, Hera receives news from her divine messenger
Iris, while beside her, seated on a throne, her husband looks on in majesty.
He is Zeus, the undisputed ruler of the gods.

Zeus

Drawing lots with his brothers, Haides and Poseidon, to see who should rule each of creation's three zones – the land (together with the heavens); the sea; and the Underworld (or Hades) – Zeus won the earth and sky. Enthroned on the ridge of Mount Olympus, which is today called Stefani, and holding in his right hand a golden sceptre, he ruled both gods and men. A passage from the *Iliad*, said to have inspired his celebrated statue at Olympia, describes the sheer power of his presence: 'Zeus, the son of

With an eagle perching on his left hand, Zeus wields his thunderbolt. (Attic red figure vase, *c.* 470–460 BC.)

Cronus, spoke, and he inclined his head with his dark brows, and the mighty king's hair, anointed with ambrosial oil, fell forward from his immortal head. And great Olympus trembled.' As well it might. For the great sky-god was armed with an all-powerful weapon, the lightning bolt, whose blast wreaked total devastation. Some imagined that the lightning bolt was Zeus' true essence – pure blazing, blinding energy, concealed and contained within his (safer) anthropomorphic form.

All gods had avatars. Zeus' was the eagle, his special messenger, which could soar so effortlessly and so resplendently. The fifth-century BC lyric poet Bacchylides encapsulates the bond between god and bird:

> Lightning-fast on tawny wings, the eagle, confident in its immeasurable strength, cleaves the vast unfathomable sky – the messenger of Zeus, the thunder-god, whose rule is wide. And all the little birds, shrill-chattering, scatter in terror. The high peaked mountains cannot check him nor the pounding storm-waves of the tireless sea, but on outstretched wings he soars across the vastness of the earth, his feathers gently ruffled in the western breeze. And all men see him.

Zeus, Hera & Their Children

Once established as the king of the newly victorious Olympians, Zeus (following Cronus' example) pursued his own sister Hera and, after seducing her near Argos, made her his wife. But although celebrated on Olympus, theirs was not a marriage made in heaven. Zeus' serial philandering wounded Hera deeply. Indeed, she was not the only god to find his rule at times intolerable. Homer tells how Hera and the other gods once tied Zeus up, and it was only when the sea-nymph Thetis summoned Briareus, whose hundred hands made light work of even complicated knots, that he was freed. Zeus' wrath was terrible. He enslaved Poseidon and Apollo for their part in the conspiracy, forcing them to build the walls of Troy, and took his revenge on Hera. In the *Iliad* Zeus reminds her:

> Do you not recall how you were hung from a great height, with an anvil suspended from each ankle, and I fastened golden handcuffs to your wrists, unbreakable. And you hung there in the misty air, and far and wide across Olympus the gods were angered. But they could not free you.

Only when the gods swore a great oath never again to rebel against him did Zeus set Hera free.

Of their three children, only their daughter, Hebe ('Youth'), was entirely undemanding. One son, Ares, was the god of war, of whom (in the *Iliad*) Zeus declares: 'I hate you more than any of the gods on Mount Olympus. Conflict is your chief delight – and war and violence. You have the harsh inflexibility of your mother Hera, which I cannot bear. Indeed, I can only just control her by my words.'

Their other son, Hephaestus, was (to his parents at least) even more troublesome. When he was born lame, Hera considered him so unattractive that she flung him from the peaks of Mount Olympus far out to sea. Two sea-nymphs, Thetis and Eurynome, rescued him and brought him up, in return for which Hephaestus made them 'beautiful bronze goods, brooches, spiral arm-bands, cups and chains, there in their hollow cave, while the roaring stream of Ocean gushed, foaming, by'. In time, Hera discovered her lost son and, appreciating his potential, reinstated him on Mount Olympus, put him to work on enhancing her jewelry collection and gave him Aphrodite as his wife. In another version of the myth Hephaestus took revenge by constructing a throne, which clamped Hera tight and held her captive. Only thanks to Dionysus' persuasive words and wine did Hephaestus set his mother free.

Zeus was even less enamoured of his son. Once, when Hephaestus took Hera's side, Zeus seized him by the foot and again threw him off the mountain. The *Iliad* describes Hephaestus falling for a whole day before crashing to earth on Lemnos. But he was reprieved. Homer imagined him working in his smithy on Olympus, assisted by golden automata formed like beautiful young women, with 'sense, mind, voice and strength', creating wheeled tripods, which could move of their own volition. (Later authors placed Hephaestus' forge in Sicily, beneath Mount Etna.) Despite his skill, Hephaestus was a figure of fun. The gods laughed 'merrily' not only as they watched him hobbling around their banqueting hall, but when they discovered that his brother Ares had cuckolded him.

Despite their feisty relationship, Zeus was susceptible to Hera's blandishments. Indeed, he magically extended their wedding night on Samos to last three hundred years, and Homer describes how Hera, having dressed alluringly in her bedchamber on Mount Olympus, later seduced Zeus on a mountaintop near Troy:

> He took Hera in his arms, and beneath them from
> the earth rose fresh young grasses and clover, jewelled
> with dew, and crocuses and hyacinths so plentiful and
> soft that they cushioned them from the hard earth.
> And they lay down together, and a golden cloud – it
> was sublime – rolled over them and drops of dew
> dripped down.

Deucalion & Dion's Altar to Zeus

On earth long generations passed – a Golden Age, free from disease, when the fields brought forth crops without the need for farming, and a Silver Age of bitter arguments. An Age of Bronze followed, when human beings were first created, but they were soon found to be degenerate. One of their number, Lycaeus, either sacrificed his son to Zeus on an Arcadian mountaintop or served him to the god in a barbaric banquet. Repelled, Zeus turned Lycaeus into a wolf, incinerated his fifty lawless sons and resolved to destroy the human race.

So Zeus amassed the inky storm clouds and rain fell in torrents. The great plains of Greece were inundated and the rivers roared. Mankind was drowning, but the Titan Prometheus was not prepared to see his mortal son, Deucalion, die. He advised him to build a chest, fill it with food and embark with Pyrrha, his wife, Pandora's daughter. The chest bobbed safely on the rising water until Deucalion and Pyrrha were the only mortals left alive. When Zeus saw them, his anger melted. Both were pious. Neither must be destroyed. So after nine days and nights the waters abated, and on the peak of Mount Parnassus the chest came to land. On Zeus' advice, the two survivors picked stones from the mountainside and threw them over their shoulders. From Deucalion's sprang men, from Pyrrha's women, and so a nobler human race was born. In time Deucalion and Pyrrha had children. One of their daughters, Thyia, bore a son to Zeus: Macednos, from whom Macedonia was named.

In thanks for their salvation Deucalion erected an altar to Zeus at Dion in the shadow of Mount Olympus – the first altar of the new age. In Classical and Hellenistic times it marked out Dion as a site of special sanctity. Indeed, 'Dios' is the possessive case of 'Zeus'. Dion quite literally belongs to Zeus.

The Muses

Other divinities, too, lived on Mount Olympus, most notably the Muses, daughters of Zeus by the Titan Mnemosyne. One of their homes was on the mountain's northern flanks, in Pieria, near Dion. Pausanias says that originally there were three Muses, though by Hellenistic times their number had expanded to nine, and specific roles were assigned to each. Thus Calliope became the muse of epic poetry, Clio of history, Terpsichore of dance and so on.

The Muses, too, were swift to punish rivals. When Hera persuaded the winged Sirens to compete with them in song, the Muses tore out the Sirens' feathers and crowned their own heads with them. Another time, the nine mortal daughters of Pieros (king of Pieria) challenged the Muses to a contest. When the Muses sang all creation held its breath in wonder; but when the mortal girls performed vast darkness cloaked the world. Triumphant, the Muses changed them into birds as punishment. Another musician, an accomplished Thracian lyre-player Thamyris, issued his own challenge: if he defeated them in song the Muses must let him sleep with each of them in turn. He lost. The Muses blinded him and removed his musicality.

Hesiod claimed to have experienced a more benign encounter with the Muses on Mount Helicon near Thebes, where they commanded him to sing of the birth of the gods (in his poem *Theogony*). He describes them:

> delighting the great spirit of their father Zeus on Mount
> Olympus, singing in harmony of things that are and
> things that still shall be and things that came before.
> Their sweet voice pours untiring from their lips, and
> the house of father Zeus the thunderer smiles, filled
> with the Muses' voice, as fragrant as a lily, and the snowy
> peaks of Mount Olympus echo back, and the palaces of
> the immortals.

The Muses' inspiration was invaluable. It was only thanks to them that poets could speak with any confidence about the gods and heroes of the distant past.

The Muses appear at many of the great communal events of Greek mythology. Accompanied by Apollo on his lyre, they sing and dance at the weddings of Cadmus and Harmonia in Thebes, and Peleus and Thetis on Mount Pelion. They regularly perform at funerals, too, most memorably mourning Achilles in the *Iliad*, while in a tantalizing fragment from Pindar's *Dirges*:

> They lulled to rest the corpses of their sons. The first
> sighed her lament for Linus; the second sang the song
> of grief for Hymenaeus, whom Fate despatched when first
> he lay in wedlock; and the third performed her threnody
> for Ialmenus, whose strength was drained when he was
> stricken by a merciless disease. But for Orpheus of the
> golden sword...

Orpheus

Orpheus was born near Dion in Pimpleia, a village with which he kept close ties throughout his life. His mother was Calliope, the eldest of the Muses. Some said his father was Apollo, others that it was King Oeagrus, the son of Pieros (whose daughters were punished by the Muses). Orpheus' musicianship was legendary. The fifth-century BC poet Timotheus tells that he introduced the lyre to Pieria, where his playing was so fine and his voice so sweet that (in Euripides' words): 'Deep in the deep forest folds of Olympus, Orpheus magicked the trees with his music, magicked the wild forest beasts with his music.' Everything that heard him followed him: trees, boulders, animals. Even mountain streams changed their course so they could listen to his singing; and in the Thracian land of the Cicones the wood nymph Eurydice ('Wide Justice') fell in love with him. Enraptured, the two married. But soon disaster struck. While Eurydice was picking flowers and weaving garlands with her fellow nymphs, she disturbed a sleeping snake. It bit her on the ankle and within moments she was dead. Grief stricken, Orpheus sang such heart-rending laments that all nature mourned with him. At last, when they could bear his anguish no longer, the Muses suggested to Orpheus that he should travel to the Underworld and beg Haides to return Eurydice to life.

Setting fear aside, Orpheus descended deep beneath the earth until he met the savage guard-dog of Hades, the three-headed Cerberus. Softly Orpheus soothed it with a gentle lullaby; and soon he was standing in the presence of King Haides. Here he sang his tearful elegy, pouring out his love for his lost wife, begging Haides to restore her to life – she had been so young. His music touched the hardest heart. The ghosts of criminals condemned to everlasting tortures swooned to hear it; the icy hearts of savage Furies melted; and even Haides was moved to compassion. He agreed to Orpheus' request. On one condition – that on the way home he must go ahead, not looking round until both reached the upper earth. As Orpheus walked on, he heard Eurydice's light footsteps close behind him. At last faint sunlight could be seen. But now Orpheus stopped and listened. Nothing. How could he be certain that Eurydice was following? Impulsively, he looked round. And there she was, a sad smile on her lips, as (true to Haides' orders) she turned and left him. And the darkness engulfed her.

For Orpheus life was meaningless. All he could do was sing of his lost Eurydice. But still his music was irresistible. Everywhere he went, women fell in love with him. At last at Dion – crazed with desire – they clawed and tore at him hysterically, until their passion faded and they found that they had ripped him limb from limb. Some said that Orpheus was rent apart not from desire, but because he worshipped Apollo and neglected Dionysus. So, Dionysus jealously unleashed his maenads (his female followers), who attacked Orpheus at sunrise on a mountaintop. Still others told that Orpheus was killed by Zeus' thunderbolt.

The Muses collected his remains and performed the last rites over them at Dion. A few miles from the city on the road towards Olympus, Pausanias saw a pillar topped by a stone urn, which (locals said) contained Orpheus' bones. Pausanias wrote, too, that at Dion the women

Still clutching his lyre, Orpheus is attacked by frenzied female devotees, one wielding a spit, the other a rock.
(Attic red figure vase, *c*. 640 BC.)

who killed Orpheus ran to the River Helicon to wash off his blood. But as they neared, the river in revulsion sank into the ground so that it might not be complicit in the murder. Today, where it sank, there is a small idyllic lake. Only Orpheus' head survived his mutilation. Still singing, it was carried by the waves to Lesbos, where it was buried with great veneration. The Muses took Orpheus' lyre to Mount Olympus, where the gods transformed it into a constellation.

In antiquity, a collection of hymns and teachings attributed to Orpheus formed the basis of a mystic religion (Orphism), whose adherents believed in the survival and transmigration of the soul after death.

Dion & Olympus in History & Today

Imbued with great sanctity, the peaks of Olympus were probably taboo throughout antiquity. We hear of no attempts to scale them. As for Dion, as one of the most sacred sites in the kingdom of Macedonia, it rose to prominence under its ruler Archelaus I in the late fifth century BC. A century before, to compete at the Olympic Games, Alexander I of Macedon had been forced to prove his Greek credentials by claiming descent from Heracles and the kings of Argos. Now, Archelaus turned Dion into a sanctuary as fine as any in the Greek world. He erected a temple to Zeus, a stadium and a theatre, and established the 'Olympia', a festival of athletics and drama sacred to Zeus and the Muses. Here may have been performed the (lost) *Archelaus* by Euripides (who as an old man joined the king's court). His *Bacchae* and *Iphigenia in Aulis* were perhaps intended for Dion's theatre, too.

In the fourth century BC Philip II staged magnificent ceremonies at Dion in celebration of victory. His own relationship with the gods was complex. In 336 BC, during his marriage celebrations, he caused statues of the twelve Olympians to be paraded in the theatre at nearby Aegae – joined by a thirteenth: of himself. It was an act other Greeks would have regarded as *hubris*. So they would not have been surprised when moments later Philip was assassinated.

In 334 BC, before his invasion of Persia, Philip's son Alexander held a lavish festival with games and sacrifices at Dion. Near the theatre he erected a magnificent tent housing a hundred banqueting couches, where he entertained his generals. Later that year after victory at Granicus he ordered a bronze statue group by Lysippus to be installed at Dion to com-memorate the twenty-five cavalrymen who had fallen in battle. In 332/331 BC, Alexander claimed to have learned from the oracle at Siwah in Egypt that he was the son of Zeus – and thus the half-brother of Dionysus and Heracles. In subsequent campaigns he caused the Olympian gods to be worshipped as far away as India. On the banks of the Hyphasis he erected twelve tall altars – one for each god – but wisely none for himself.

In 220 BC, Aetolian Greeks allied to Rome ransacked Dion, but it was soon rebuilt by King Philip V. It was from Dion that this Philip marched south to his defeat at the hands of the Romans at Cynoscephalae in 197 BC and that, in 168 BC, King Perseus marched north to be defeated by Rome's Lucius Aemilius Paulus at Pydna. In Rome itself the Olympians quickly became identified and syncretized with Roman gods, preserving (if subtly altering) Greek religion and mythology, which then spread north and west as far as Britain.

In 31 BC Dion became a Roman colony, growing into an important and thriving town. By AD 346 it was the seat of a bishop, but in AD 393 the Christian emperor Theodosius' decree banning pagan religion dealt a heavy blow – followed three years later by Dion's sack by Alaric the Goth. Earthquakes and floods did much further damage, and soon Dion was abandoned.

In 1806 the site was discovered by the Englishman William Leake, but only in 1928 was the first real investigation undertaken. One of the most significant discoveries (made in 1992) forges an exciting link with Dion's association with the Muses. In the Roman 'Villa of Dionysus' the pipes from a first-century BC *hydraulis* (water organ) were found, part of the world's oldest surviving keyboard instrument.

Dion

c. **500 BC**	Evidence of worship in Dion's 'megaron-type' temples.
c. **413 BC**	Dion becomes a major sanctuary and walled city under Archelaus I.
? *c.* **407 BC**	Euripides' *Archelaus* performed in Dion's theatre?
348 BC	Philip II's celebrations for victory over Olynthus.
338 BC	Philip II's celebrations for victory at Chaeronea.
334 BC	Alexander the Great sacrifices before invading Persia.
220 BC	Dion sacked by Aeolian Greeks, but soon rebuilt.
31 BC	Dion becomes a Roman colony.
AD 396	Alaric the Goth sacks Dion.
AD 1806	Dion 'discovered' by William Leake.

Dion lies just off the E75 motorway south of Katerini in northeast Greece. A pleasant road passes through vineyards in the lee of Mount Olympus, which towers to a height of 2,919 m (9,576 ft).

The beautifully laid out archaeological park lies close to the modern village. From the ticket office the path leads past the sacred lake (right) to crossroads. Ahead are **'megaron-type' sanctuaries** of Demeter. The right fork leads first to the (heavily reconstructed) **theatre,** then across the meadow (where Alexander pitched his tent) towards (right) the **Sanctuary of Olympian Zeus** with remains of its 22-m (72-ft) long limestone altar, the site of ancient hecatombs (sacrifices of 100 oxen). Nearby are remains of a Roman **odeon.** Partially retracing one's steps but continuing straight on, one comes first to the **Sanctuary of Zeus Hypsistos** (Zeus the Highest), with its altar and temple, originally approached through an avenue of columns topped with marble eagles. Nearby across the river is the partially submerged **Sanctuary of Isis.** From here the path leads across the modern road and through the city walls into the (partially excavated) city itself. Working clockwise, it leads past **Public Baths** and an **Early Christian Basilica** before crossing the impressive **'Main Avenue'** (site of a fine Roman façade bearing carvings of shields and breastplates) to the remains of large villas, including the **Villa of Dionysus.**

In the village, the **Archaeological Museum** houses finds from the site, including pipes from the *hydraulis*, **mosaics,** a **sundial,** and remains of a **statue of Isis** and the **statue of Zeus Hypsistos.**

2

Sunium: Poseidon's Cliff-Top Temple

With the great god Poseidon I start my song, who shakes both
the earth and the barren sea, the sea-god, who rules Helicon and the
broad expanse of Aegae. The gods have given you a double honour,
great Earth-shaker: to tame horses and save ships. Greetings,
Poseidon, dark-haired Earth-keeper! Come with kindness,
Blessèd One, and save our sailors!

Homeric Hymn to Poseidon

A fifth-century BC bronze statue of Poseidon wielding his (now lost) trident was discovered in the sea north of Sunium.

High on the headland, serene in the sinking sun, the temple beckons like a siren to the sea. As the slanting light pours through the slender columns, their marble gleaming like fresh-churned butter, it diffuses in a creamy golden glow, while across the polished rock cool shadows elongate, their fingers stretching to caress the still warm stone. Only the sudden clattering and clucking of two partridges scurrying across the temple steps disturbs the calm – a calm made more hypnotic by the rhythm of the sea below, long rollers rubbing in against the rocks to flat-line in a whisper of white spray. On the velvet of the sea the sun burns, its intense light dazzling in myriad refractions. And far on the horizon, islands arc like dolphins in the haze: the northern Cyclades, tantalizing with their promise of the open seas beyond. No wonder, then, that it was to the sea-god that the headland here at Sunium was sacred or that the temple was erected in his name: the master of horses, the shaker of the earth, Poseidon.

The Realm of Poseidon

In the division of spoils between the sons of Cronus, Poseidon received the sea. Just as Zeus could command the thunder clouds, sending light-ning bolts to crash down to earth, so Poseidon could summon earthquakes, causing solid land to roll and ripple like the sea. Perhaps it was because he was associated with such bucking, undulating motion that Poseidon acquired his third sphere of influence: the horse.

Poseidon ruled the sea's salt waters (though not Ocean, the fresh-water river encircling the earth) from an underwater palace. Traditionally this was situated north of Sunium, between the mainland and the north-west Euboean town of Aegae, which in historical times boasted a temple to the god, and after which Strabo maintained that the Aegean Sea was named. Homer describes Poseidon's palace:

> Gold, gleaming, everlasting. Here Poseidon came
> and harnessed to his chariot his two swift bronze-
> hooved horses with long golden manes. Dressed all
> in gold, he took a golden whip, fine-crafted, in his
> hand and stepped into the chariot and left to drive
> across the sea-swell. From far and wide the creatures
> of the sea came from their lairs to frolic round the
> king they knew so well. In joy the sea parted as he went.
> So the horses sped lightly on their way, and the bronze
> axle was unwetted.

As they read this description, Greeks almost certainly imagined Poseidon wielding his trident, the three-pronged spear that some Mediterranean fishermen still use today, and by which he is invariably identified in Classical art.

The Loves & Cities of Poseidon

Poseidon married the sea-nymph Amphitrite, but their courtship was unconventional. Some say that Poseidon abducted Amphitrite when he saw her dancing with the Nereids near Naxos; others that the nymph, reluctant, fled east to seek sanctuary with Atlas. But Poseidon sent a dolphin to plead with her and such was its success that the gods created a constellation in its memory. Poseidon's passion for his wife did not prevent him from straying, however, and his love-affairs were legion.

Among over a hundred lovers of both sexes, whose status ranged from gods to mortals and everything between, were Gaia (on whom he fathered the whirlpool Charybdis), and the Olympian goddesses Aphrodite and Demeter (his sister). Like many of Poseidon's conquests, Demeter was unwilling to succumb to his advances, so she shape-shifted into a mare and hid among the herds of Oncius, king of Arcadia. Her disguise was ill thought out. The god of horses, Poseidon tracked her down, changed himself into a stallion and covered her. Thus Demeter was delivered of two children: a goddess-daughter, Despoina ('Mistress'), who presided over rituals known as the Arcadian Mysteries, and an immortal black horse, Arion, swift as the wind and possessed of the power of speech.

Lesser goddesses and nymphs, too, attracted Poseidon's eye, often with unhappy consequences. Two were daughters of a fellow sea-god, Phorcys. When Amphitrite learned of her husband's dalliance with one, the lovely Scylla, she took vengeance by dissolving noxious herbs into the pool in which her rival habitually bathed. As Scylla sank into the water, she felt her body change. Though still a beautiful woman from the waist up, from her hips six dogs' heads now protruded on long necks, their jaws bristling with triple rows of teeth, while beneath them twelve dogs' legs dangled down beside a fishy tail. Devastated, Scylla took up residence in a cave above a narrow strait, where she devoted her existence to destroying sailors. (Other accounts blame Scylla's transformation on the witch Circe, who was jealous of the lesser sea-god, Glaucus.)

Another of Phorcys' daughters was the beautiful sea-nymph Medusa. When Poseidon raped her in a temple of Athene, Athene was outraged. Unable to vent her anger on Poseidon, she turned its full force on Medusa, transforming her into a gross monster with boar's-tusk teeth and writhing snakes instead of hair – and piercing eyes, which turned all who looked at her to stone. In addition, Athene prevented Medusa from giving birth. It was only when she was decapitated by Perseus, the prince from Argos, that Medusa was at last delivered of Poseidon's two children: a giant, Chrysaor, and the winged horse, Pegasus.

Cities, too, caused Poseidon and Athene to quarrel. They reluctantly shared the northeast Peloponnesian town of Troezen, but when Athens was awarded as a prize to Athene, Poseidon in pique flooded the nearby Thriasian Plain, and only Zeus' intervention restored the situation.

Poseidon was equally unsuccessful – and consequently vengeful – in his dealings with other cities. Cheated of his rightful prize for building Troy, he sent a sea-monster to devour the daughter of its king, Laomedon; and when Argos was awarded to Hera, Poseidon, unpredictable as ever, caused its rivers, which once flowed throughout the year, to dry up in the summer (as they still do to this day). Contesting Corinth, he again failed to secure a total victory. He was forced to concede Acrocorinth to Helios, though he won the lower city and the port of Isthmia, where close to his temple the two-yearly Isthmian Games were held in his honour. In antiquity only two cities were named for Poseidon: Potidea in northern Greece and Poseidonia in southwest Italy, known today by its Roman name, Paestum.

Some say it was from Sunium's cliffs that King Aegeus watched daily for Theseus' ship to return from Knossos, hoping to see the white sail, the agreed sign that his son's quest to kill the Minotaur had been successful. When, instead, he saw a black sail (left in place by a forgetful Theseus), the grief-stricken Aegeus threw himself into the sea, which ever since has borne his name, Aegean (a more common explanation than Strabo's). Later, Sunium was the scene of another death. In the *Odyssey*, King Nestor of Pylos, tells how, as the Greek fleet returned from sacking Troy:

> We came to holy Sunium, the headland of Athens. Here
> Phoebus Apollo with his gentle arrows slew Menelaus'
> helmsman, as he gripped in his hands the steering-
> oar of his swift ship – Phrontis, the son of Onetor, who
> surpassed all tribes of men in steering when storm
> winds blew in fury. Despite his impatience to be on his
> way, Menelaus stayed there to conduct a funeral for his
> companion and perform the proper rites.

Sunium in History & Today

Because of its position at the southernmost tip of Attica, Cape Sunium was of great strategic and symbolic importance to the Athenians. Herodotus tells how, by the beginning of the fifth century BC (when a temple was being built on the headland), a four-yearly ceremony was held in which a sacred ship sailed round the coast from Athens to Sunium. We have no further details, and would know nothing of the celebrations had not the islanders of Aegina (in 490 BC) 'lain in wait for the sacred ship and seized it with many of the leading men of Athens on board, whom they took and bound in chains'. Shortly afterwards, the Athenians took vengeance of a sort, when they allowed a boatload of Aeginetan exiles to settle at Sunium, from where they launched piratical raids on their native island.

In late summer 480 BC Sunium witnessed Greece's rapidly changing fortunes, when its still-unfinished temple was burned by the Persians under Xerxes. Within weeks, however, the Greek fleet defeated Persia's navy at the Battle of Salamis. In thanks the victors dedicated three enemy triremes: one on Salamis, a second at the sanctuary of Poseidon at Isthmia and the third at Sunium, where it was hauled in triumph on to the headland and displayed in the ruins of the temple.

In 444 BC, as part of Pericles' programme to restore Attica's destroyed sanctuaries, building began at Sunium. Four years later the Temple of Poseidon was complete. Although only its ruins can be seen today, its original form can be gauged from the almost identical and still complete Temple of Hephaestus in Athens' Agora. It was not the only temple built at Sunium. A Temple of Athene was constructed on the low hill to the north, whose precinct may have included a hero-shrine to Menelaus' helmsman, Phrontis.

In 412 BC, during the Peloponnesian War, the promontory of Sunium was fortified. It remained in use as a military base throughout the Hellenistic period, when ship-sheds were built at sea level beneath the temple. Under Rome, Sunium declined. In the first century AD, Athene's temple was dismantled and re-erected in the Athenian Agora. (Two of its Ionic capitals are displayed in Athens' Agora Museum.) A hundred years later, Pausanias began his *Description of Greece* with the observation that: 'Cape Sunium is on the mainland of Greece, jutting out from Attica towards the Aegean and the Cyclades. When you have sailed round the promontory you see a harbour and – on top of the promontory – the Temple of Athene of Sunium.' He meant of course the Temple of Poseidon. It is an unfortunate beginning to an otherwise excellent book.

By the late fourth century AD (when the Byzantine emperor Arcadius ordered 'any temples still intact to be demolished discretely and without ado') the majestic Temple of Poseidon was abandoned. The promontory became the haunt of pirates. When Lord Byron visited in 1810, he wrote of 'five and twenty Mainnotes (pirates) … in the caves at the foot of the cliff with some Greek boatmen their prisoners'. Their presence did not prevent him from carving his name on one of the temple's columns or eulogizing the site in his poem 'Don Juan':

> Place me on Sunium's marbled steep,
> Where nothing, save the waves and I,
> May hear our mutual murmurs sweep…

Sunium

SOME IMPORTANT DATES & REMAINS

C8th BC	Signs of occupation at Sunium.
c. **500 BC**	Tufa temple begun.
490 BC	Athenian sacred ship bound for Sunium attacked by Aiginetans.
480 BC	Unfinished temple destroyed by Persians; Persian trireme consecrated to Poseidon after Salamis.
444 BC	Work begun on new temples of Poseidon and Athene.
412 BC	Fortification walls built around promontory.
C1st AD	Temple of Athene dismantled and rebuilt in Athens.
C2nd AD	Pausanias misidentifies Temple of Poseidon.
C4th AD	Temple of Poseidon closed down.
AD 1810	Lord Byron visits Sunium.

An easy excursion from Athens, Sunium is popular with coach parties, especially in the evening when sunsets can be stunning. As a result, the compact site is often overrun. Out of season, however, its romantic isolation can still be appreciated.

From the car park and conveniently placed restaurant (with good views of the temple), a path leads from the ticket booth, from where it is possible to look across the access road to the foundations of the **Temple of Athene** (no access). Steps lead up past **fortification walls** to the **Temple of Poseidon** (no access to interior). Another path leads west down towards the bay, with a view to the **ship-sheds** below. From the restaurant, it is possible to walk to the end of the promontory, from where the view towards the temple and out to sea is breathtaking. Care should be taken as the cliffs are sheer and unfenced.

3

Eleusis & the Mysteries of Demeter & Persephone

Haides, who rules so many, harnessed his immortal horses to
the golden chariot. Persephone climbed on board and beside
her Hermes took up reins and goad, and they galloped out of
the courtyard. Swiftly they came to the end of the long road.
Neither sea nor rivers nor tall-grassed valleys held back the deathless
horses – no, nor high mountains either – but they cleared them all
on their path through the soaring air. [Reaching Eleusis,]
Hermes reined in the horses near the temple, fragrant with incense,
where fair-garlanded Demeter was living. When she saw them,
she ran out as a maenad runs through dappled woodland on the
mountainside. And when Persephone saw her mother's lovely eyes,
she leapt down from the chariot and ran towards her, throwing her
arms around her neck, embracing her.... And at Eleusis, the life-
bringing bosom of the earth ... soon in the springtime wheat fields
would rustle with long ears of corn and the fertile furrows would be
thick with wheat-ears to be bound tight-close in sheaves.

Homeric Hymn to Demeter, 374–89; 450–56

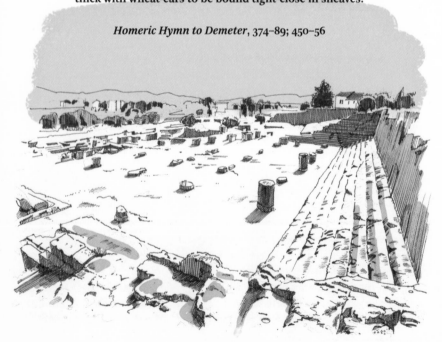

For most of its history, the plain around Eleusis has been luxuriant. From the rocky outcrop rising low above the sanctuary, the pure air loud with birdsong and the shrilling of insects, a visitor could once gaze across the sparkling bay towards the pale blue hills of Salamis, and far away the Peloponnese, its jagged mountains shimmering in haze. Inland, gold wheat fields stretched from the surrounding mountains to the sea, while by rutted farm tracks crocuses, anemones and irises splashed a raucous dance of colour.

No longer. Today the environs of Eleusis are an industrial inferno. Choking fumes rise from chemical factory chimneys, and flames from the burn-off of oil refineries; container ships and tankers loll at anchor in the bay; unlovely modern warehouses and showrooms, offices and houses sprawl across the concrete plain; and a constant whine of traffic screams from the motorway to Athens. Yet somehow the sanctuary still manages to preserve some vestige of its dignity, its sense of wonder, its lost identity as the site of perhaps the most transcendental of all rituals of the ancient world, the Eleusinian Mysteries, inexorably linked with the myth of the goddesses Demeter and Persephone.

Demeter & Persephone

Demeter was the archetypal mother goddess. (Even her name proclaimed her status: '*meter*' means 'mother', while the prefix '*de–*' may be connected either to the Cretan word for barley (*dea*) or to *dē*, the Doric word for 'earth'.) Hers was the fertile plough-land, which, so Greeks believed, the sky-god Zeus impregnated with his rain to help produce rich crops or flowers. Zeus impregnated his sister Demeter more conventionally, too, and to them was born a daughter, Persephone ('Death-Bearer'), whose name was so taboo that many called her simply 'Korē', 'Girl'.

Haides, god of the Underworld, was not discouraged by his close blood relationship with Persephone (he was doubly her uncle) and he resolved to abduct and marry her; he even persuaded Zeus to help him. Their plans came to fruition one dewy morning as Persephone: 'leaving her mother ... played with Ocean's daughters, picking flowers across a springy meadow – roses, crocuses, delightful violets; and irises, and hyacinths. And narcissus, too....'

It was this narcissus, placed there by Zeus and with a hundred scented heads, that was her downfall. As Persephone leant down to pluck it, the earth gaped open. Haides in his golden chariot rose up; he snatched the girl and, as she piteously called on Zeus to save her, galloped with her back into the Underworld.

For nine days and nights, in which she neither ate nor drank, Demeter wandered the earth searching for her daughter, demented, a flaming torch in each hand. At last she learned what had happened from Helios

Hermes runs beside the chariot as Haides abducts Persephone, in a mosaic recently found in a Hellenistic tomb at Amphipolis.

and stormed out of Olympus: 'to wander the cities and fine works of men, tearing her cheeks incessantly. No man who saw her recognized her, nor any deep-bosomed woman, until she came to the house of wise Celeus, who ruled Eleusis, fragrant with incense.'

It is here at Eleusis that the rest of the myth is set. Disguised as an old woman, Demeter sat grieving by a well until Celeus' daughters saw her, pitied her and brought her to the palace. While their servant, Iambe, cheered her up with bawdy jokes, they placed her on a chair draped with a sheepskin and persuaded her to drink a *kykeon*, a heady cocktail of fermented barley and pennyroyal. Uplifted, Demeter agreed to work for Celeus' household as nurse to his young son, Demophoön. She even tried to make the boy immortal. By day she anointed him with ambrosia, breathing her divine spirit into him, while each night, to secure her magic, she thrust the child into a blazing fire. When his mother witnessed this, she cried out in distress – at which Demeter, offended, renounced her duties and revealed her true identity. Then she ordered the people of Eleusis to build her a temple.

With nothing to distract her, Demeter gave herself over once again to longing for Persephone. The Homeric Hymn describes her:

Growing weak with yearning for her deep-bosomed
daughter. And for mankind she brought a cruel
distressing year across the all-sustaining earth: the soil
refused to send forth grain, for richly garlanded Demeter
kept it concealed. In vain the oxen pulled the curved
ploughs in the field; in vain was the white barley sown.
She would have exterminated all the peoples of the earth
with painful famine and robbed all the Olympian gods
of the honour of man's sacrificial offerings, had not Zeus
noticed and acknowledged it in his heart.

Moved by self-interest, Zeus persuaded Haides to return Persephone, but,
before he did, the god of the Underworld enticed her to eat a pomegran-
ate seed 'with the sweetness of honey'. It was a ruse, and one which
Demeter suspected, for no sooner had she and Persephone been reunited
than she asked her daughter:

My child, when you were beneath the ground, did
you eat anything? ... If you did not, then, now that
you've returned from vile Hades, you can stay with
me and your father, Zeus the storm-gatherer, whom
all the immortals honour. But if you did eat, you must
return into the depths of earth to live there for a third
part of each year, and with me and the other gods for
two thirds. Whenever the earth blossoms with all
species of sweet-scented flowers, you shall rise up
once more from gloomy darkness, a miracle for gods
and mortal men.

And so it was, and so it has been ever since: in the Greek summer the
scorched earth lies barren, only returning to life with the coming of
September. In gratitude to the Eleusinians, Demeter taught their prince,
Triptolemus (whom she had also nursed), the art of ploughing, and initiated Celeus and his sons into her Mysteries, 'which must not be infringed
or disregarded or divulged, because the greatest piety before the gods
restrains the tongue. Blessed is that mortal living on the earth, who has
witnessed them; but for the uninitiated another fate entirely waits, with-
ering in gloomy darkness.'

The Eleusinian Mysteries
What happened at the Mysteries (which in Greek means 'initiation rites')
is itself mysterious. Because the *mystes* (initiate) was forbidden on pain
of death from revealing what went on, no first-hand account survives, so

we must reconstruct the rituals and their meaning from oblique references in literature and representations in art.

The Mysteries were open to men and women, free and slaves. There were two stages of initiation. The first, the Lesser Mysteries, were held in spring in the month of the *Anthesteria* ('Feast of Flowers', roughly February/March), originally at Eleusis but from the fifth century BC at Athens. These were said to have been inaugurated by Demeter especially for Heracles, to purify him from his blood-guilt after massacring the Centaurs. At them, neophytes each sacrificed a piglet to Demeter and Persephone and ritually cleansed themselves in the River Ilissus. The subsequent rituals, a mixture of hymns, dances and instruction, helped to make sense of what would be experienced eighteen months later in the Greater Mysteries at Eleusis (it being forbidden to be initiated into both in the same year).

The Greater Mysteries took place over nine days in September and were marked by a sacred truce, which allowed participants to make the pilgrimage to Eleusis in relative safety. First, priests accompanied by young Athenian men, newly enlisted in the army, carried sacred objects in procession from Eleusis to Athens, where they were temporarily housed in the Agora in a building called the Eleusinion. The next day, participants flocked down to the sea, purified themselves by washing in the water, and each sacrificed a piglet – perhaps in the belief that the creature would absorb their sins. Three days later, initiates clothed in sumptuous robes, their heads crowned with myrtle leaves, processed from Athens the 22 km (14 miles) to Eleusis. Many danced, told ribald jokes (recalling the jokes that Iambe told Demeter) or sang hymns to Iacchus, whose wooden statue was carried in front of the procession. Iacchus was an embodiment of Dionysus, god of the grape, who already by the early fifth century BC shared the Mysteries with Demeter and Persephone. The sacred communion of bread and wine has a lengthy pedigree.

Initiation ceremonies took place two days later. Having fasted, sacrificed and purified themselves, neophytes, dressed in new clothes, entered the Telesterion, the Hall of Mysteries, a huge, many columned building, which underwent several major enlargements throughout its history. What happened next we cannot tell, but it is likely that initiates first drank Demeter's *kykeon* (the cocktail of fermented barley and pennyroyal), to enhance suggestibility and produce hallucinations. Lit by torches, and enlivened by lavish costumes designed by the theatrical impresario Aeschylus (born at Eleusis in 525 BC), the ceremony probably involved a sacred drama (based on the events in the Homeric Hymn to Demeter) in which initiates participated. It may have begun with a re-enactment of the search for Persephone, a great gong reverberating each time she was invoked by name, and ended with the goddess' epiphany, when the inner

The goddesses of the Eleusinian
Mysteries, Demeter and Persephone,
flank the young prince Triptolemus
on a marble relief from Eleusis,
c. 440 BC.

sanctum's doors were opened to reveal her bathed in blazing light. Plutarch reveals something of the atmosphere:

> Initiates into the Mysteries crowd together at the start in a pandemonium of jostling and shouting; but when the sacred ritual is being performed and the time comes for the revelation, they are at once rapt in silent attention. The same is true of philosophy. In the early stages, you will see a great multitude, much talk, much confidence, as some people roughly and aggressively compete for the good reputation it accords; but whoever has reached his goal and seen a great light – as if the sanctum had been opened – takes on another demeanour entirely, one of silence and awe.

Elsewhere, he writes of how initiation closely resembles death. At first there is confusion, then terror, shivering and trembling, before, at the blazing of a wondrous light, the traveller arrives in lush pastures, where dances are performed and sacred revelations seen.

The most sacred revelation seems to have involved raising a casket containing sheaves of corn from beneath the earth. Although cut, and therefore dead, they contained the seeds of new life. As the accompanying liturgy may have proclaimed, the initiate, who through his or her experience had passed on to a higher spiritual plane, would similarly be reborn after death. This made the Mysteries extremely potent, and many Greeks, including philosophers such as Pythagoras and Plato, believed in the transmigration of souls into many bodies, both human and animal. In John's Gospel, Christ uses the same Eleusinian metaphor to foreshadow his own forthcoming death and resurrection to 'certain Greeks' in Jerusalem for the Passover: 'Verily, verily, I say unto you, except a corn of wheat fall into the ground and die, it abideth alone: but if it die, it bringeth forth much fruit.' Initiates spent the final day feasting and performing rites in honour of the dead. Then they returned home, reflecting perhaps – in the words of an inscription discovered at Eleusis – that 'the blessed gods have bestowed on us a beautiful mystery. For mortals death is to be feared no more: rather, it is a blessing.'

Eleusis in History & Today

The site of Eleusis dates to at least the fifteenth century BC, and by the seventh century BC, when the Homeric Hymn was written down, the Mysteries enjoyed local prestige. By the mid-sixth century BC Eleusis was annexed by Athens. Although control of the Mysteries remained in the hands of Eleusinian priests, the Athenian *tyrannos* (sole ruler) Peisistratus, striving for international recognition, encouraged initiates to attend from the wider Greek world.

In 480 BC the Persians burned the sanctuaries of Attica. Eleusis was no exception. However, days later the Greeks defeated the Persian navy in the Bay of Salamis, directly opposite Eleusis – probably on the very day on which the Mysteries should have been performed. Herodotus records how before the battle 'a cloud of dust [was seen], like a cloud raised by 30,000 marching men, coming from Eleusis ... and the sound of voices like the hymn to Iacchus, sung at the Mysteries.... The dust-cloud rose into the sky and drifted across to Salamis, where the Greek fleet was stationed.'

When the Athenians rebuilt their temples, they incorporated a talismanic band of Eleusinian limestone into the bastions flanking the entrance to the Acropolis and the frieze of the Temple of Athene Polias (Protector of the City). They also proclaimed the Eleusinian message of rebirth in the Parthenon frieze. Meanwhile, at Eleusis they enlarged the Telesterion and built a wall around the sanctuary.

The Mysteries thrived. In the fourth century BC, the courtesan Phryne caused a stir by bathing naked in the sea during the purification rites. Under the Romans, initiation became *de rigeur* among intellectuals and the upper classes. Cicero proclaimed them the best and most sacred of all 'Athenian' institutions, declaring that 'from them we have gained the ability not only to live contentedly but to die with greater hope'.

Hadrian enhanced the site. Pausanias was warned in a dream against writing about its buildings. And after Costoboc tribesmen plundered and destroyed much of the sanctuary in AD 170, it was immediately restored by Rome's emperor Marcus Aurelius. The Mysteries were eventually banned by the Christian Roman emperor Theodosius in AD 392. Four years later Alaric the Goth ransacked Eleusis, and the town went into gradual decline.

By the late eighteenth century, Eleusis was once more on the map, a magnet for antiquarians and looters. Early the next century, Edward Dodwell recorded:

> The present inhabitants lament the loss of Ceres
> [Demeter]; whose colossal bust was removed in 1802,
> by Dr. [Edward] Clarke. In my first journey to Greece
> this protecting deity was in its full glory, situated in the
> centre of a threshing floor, amongst the ruins of her
> temple. The villagers were impressed with a persuasion,
> that their rich harvests were the effect of her bounty; and
> since her removal, their abundance, as they assured me,
> has disappeared.

SOME IMPORTANT DATES & REMAINS

C15th BC	Signs of habitation at Eleusis.
late C7th BC	Homeric Hymn to Demeter written down.
early C6th BC	Eleusis annexed by Athens.
mid-C6th BC	Peisistratus makes the Mysteries an international festival.
480 BC	Persians sack Eleusis.
post-449 BC	Pericles rebuilds sanctuary.
***c.* 360 BC**	Further protective walls built by the Athenians under Lycurgus.
AD 170	Eleusis sacked by Costobocs, but rebuilt by Marcus Aurelius.
AD 392	Theodosius bans the Mysteries.
AD 396	Alaric sacks Eleusis.
AD 1875	First factory (Harilaos Soaps) built at Eleusis.

Surrounded by modern factories, but ringed, too, by pleasant cafés, Eleusis (also signposted *Elefsina*) is a curious oasis of tranquillity, especially in spring, when wild flowers grow among the ruins. From the entrance, the path leads to the **Greater Propylaion**, a second-century AD gateway built into the fifth-century BC circuit wall, containing Demeter's well. Next comes the first-century BC **Lesser Propylaion**, leading to the sanctuary itself. Right is the **Plutonion**, the cave sacred to Haides (or Pluto), where Persephone was believed to have returned from the underworld. Ahead are the somewhat confusing remains of various phases of the **Telesterion**, which in its heyday accommodated 3,000 initiates.

On the rocky outcrop above the site, the **Museum** contains objects relating to the Mysteries, including a marble **votive piglet**, a *kernos* or ceremonial vessel, and the celebrated **'Fleeing Kore'**, a representation of Persephone attempting to escape Haides' clutches. Another **headless statue** is of Demeter, while the torso-less head of a caryatid from the Lesser Propylaion may represent the goddess wearing a crown containing corn, poppies and a *kernos*. There is also a copy of the **marble relief showing Demeter, Persephone and Triptolemus** – the original is in Athens' Archaeological Museum. A second caryatid (Dodwell's 'colossal bust' of Demeter) can be seen in England at the Fitzwilliam Museum, Cambridge.

4

Delos: Sacred Island of Leto, Artemis & Apollo

Queen Leto came to Delos and, addressing wingèd words, she asked: 'Delos, might you wish to be the seat of my son, Phoebus Apollo, and house him in a rich temple? Surely you can see that no one else would want you! You'll never be blessed with rich herds of cattle or flocks of sheep or goats. You'll never produce lush grapes or harvests of abundant crops. But if you have a temple to Apollo, who shoots from afar, all men will flock here with their offerings, and the heady scent of fatty sacrifice will coil into the air for ever, and you will feed all those who live here from the hands of others, since your own soil is infertile.'

So Leto spoke, and Delos rejoiced and said in reply: 'Leto, most honoured daughter of great Coeus, I shall gladly welcome your son, the lord who shoots from afar. For now my name brings no pleasure to mankind, but then I would be honoured beyond measure.'

Homeric Hymn to Delian Apollo, 49–65

At first sight, Delos is a scraggy island. Low in the sea, it crouches, the surf slapping hard against the crumbling jetty of its once Sacred Harbour, its thin soil dun and dull, the salt breeze rattling its scrawny shrubs, stones skittering unexpectedly as clacking quails take fright and scurry off, affronted, up the hillside. Follow them up the low (if strenuous) rise of Mount Cynthus, and the view from the top is unforgettable – an arc of islands: Tinos to the north; then sweeping clockwise, Mykonos; Paros; Naxos to the south; and to the west beyond low-lying Rhenea, Syros, with its narrow streets and bustling port. All are members of the Cyclades, that great wheel of more than two hundred isles and islets, which from the fourth millennium BC developed a distinctive art and civilization, and at whose hub is Delos. For Greeks of the Classical age, it was one of the most sacred sites on earth, for it was here that the goddess Leto gave birth to Apollo and Artemis.

The Delivery of Leto

Leto was a Titan, whose sister Asteria, a goddess of oracles and dreams, had once borne Hecate (goddess of ghosts and necromancy, to whom dogs were sacrificed at crossroads). Asteria attracted Zeus' roving eye, but rather than succumb to him she turned herself into a quail and leapt into the sea – at which she was transformed once more, this time into the floating island of Ortygia (Quail Island). Thwarted, Zeus transferred his attentions to Leto, according to Hesiod 'the gentlest of all goddesses on Olympus'. He found her more compliant than her sister, and soon she was expecting twins. But Hera, angry at her husband's philandering, made Leto's pregnancy as painful and protracted as possible.

Issuing a stern command to Eileithyia, goddess of childbirth, not to go to Leto's aid, Hera ordered Ares and Iris to ensure that nowhere on earth would offer Leto refuge. So, driven from mainland Greece, pursued by a savage Python, and in increasing discomfort, Leto fled to the Asiatic coast. In Lycia, as she slaked her thirst at a bubbling spring, shepherds tried to drive her off. In anger, she turned them into frogs – today the now partially flooded sanctuary of Letoön (near Xanthus in modern Turkey) pulsates with their descendants' croaking. At last, despairing, Leto turned to Ortygia, the floating island which had once been her sister Asteria. Being unattached to the earth, it was not subject to Hera's injunction. Besides, Hera respected Asteria for having rebuffed Zeus.

So by a circular lake on Ortygia Leto crouched, clutching a palm tree, in agonizing childbirth. After almost endless torment she was delivered of a daughter, Artemis, soon to be worshipped as the goddess not only of wild beasts and the hunt, but also of midwifery. For, being divine, no sooner was she born than Artemis was helping to deliver her twin brother, Apollo, god of light. As she did so, a flock of swans rose high from the

Asiatic River Pactolus to 'circle [the island] seven times, singing as the god was born, the Muses' birds, most musical of any bird that flies ... while the island's nymphs reverberating far and wide intoned the hymn of childbirth. At once the blazing sky echoed the resounding chant, and Hera felt no rancour, for Zeus had assuaged her anger. And at that moment the [island's] bedrock turned to gold, the round lake flowed with gold, the palm tree's leaves were gold, and the swirling Inopus gushed a golden flood.'

From then, too, the island changed its name. Now firmly anchored to the ocean's floor, it became known as Delos ('Clearly Seen').

At least two other places claimed to be the site of Leto's birthing: the Paximadia islands (known in antiquity as the Letoai), off southern Crete; and the city of Buto on Egypt's Nile Delta. According to Herodotus a floating island still existed there in the fifth century BC. It was not Egypt's only connection to Delos. The 'swirling Inopus' (in fact a desultory stream, which no longer flows) on the island was believed to derive from a subterranean branch of the Nile, its waters increasing at the same time as its Egyptian cousin was in flood. Perhaps more convincing is the evidence for Leto's own cross-cultural connections – in the Near East, Lat (or Allat) was a great mother goddess, while in Lycian 'Leto' means simply 'Lady'.

But it was on Delos, by the shore of the sacred lake, that Leto was most devoutly worshipped. Here she shared a temple with her twins, Artemis and Apollo. In mythology, too, the family was tight-knit.

The Vengeance of Apollo & Artemis

When Niobe, queen of Thebes, was heard boasting of her superiority to Leto – because she had borne twelve (in some versions fourteen) children, the goddess only two – Apollo and Artemis were quick to act. Nocking poisoned arrows, they let fly a fusillade of death, Apollo mowing down the sons, Artemis the daughters. Homer tells how, leaving her children 'lying nine days in their own blood', Niobe fled east to Lydia. There on Mount Sipylus she sat and wept so long she melded with the mountainside, 'brooding on the pain gods gave her'. As the 'Weeping Rock' near Manisa in Turkey she can still be seen today.

Like Artemis (sometimes called Cynthia after Delos' Mount Cynthus), Apollo, ever young, athletic, golden haired, was highly strung. Both were masters of the bow; Apollo, in addition, was virtuosic on the lyre, which had seven strings because at his birth the swans had circled Delos seven times. But like the taut-stretched bow- or lyre-string, the twin divinities could suddenly snap, and when they did they brought destruction – especially when honour was at stake.

In Phrygia on the mainland east of Delos, when the satyr Marsyas boasted of his prowess on the *aulos* (an oboe-like wind instrument)

Artemis and Apollo unleash a deadly volley of
arrows against the children of Niobe. (Athenian red
figure vase painting, fifth century BC.)

Apollo challenged him to a competition. As both were consummate musicians, the lyrist Apollo could win only by suggesting that each should sing while playing. For Marsyas this was impossible, and, triumphant, Apollo had the satyr flayed alive. Marginally more fortunate was Midas, the king who famously changed all that he touched to gold: when he expressed his preference for Pan's piping, Apollo gave Midas ass' ears as punishment.

Apollo's rage could also be unleashed against mankind through plague. At Troy, at the opening of the *Iliad*, Apollo, angered because his priest has been insulted by the Greeks 'descended from Olympus, his bow and quiver at his back, and, as the god swooped down in fury like the night, his arrows clattered at his shoulder. There by the ships he stood and fired, and his silver bow sang chillingly. He first shot mules, then dogs, then men. And well-packed pyres burned constantly.'

Like many gods, Apollo embodied a unity of opposites. In Sophocles' *Oedipus the King*, when Thebes is ravaged by a mysterious plague (provoked in part by a misunderstanding of the god's oracle at Delphi), the citizens call on the 'Healer from Delos', Apollo, to cure it. Indeed, one of the most common hymn-forms sung to Apollo (whose name the Greeks linked to the word *apollumi*, 'I destroy') was the *paean*, literally the 'cure song'.

Apollo's Festivals on Delos
On Delos, Apollo was the focus of worship especially by Ionian Greeks, who flocked here from Athens and many of the islands and the coastal

cities of west Asia to take part in two festivals: the four-yearly Delia and the annual Lesser Delia. For the latter, Athenians garlanded their sacred trireme with Apollo's laurel leaves and sent it to Delos, where sacrifices were made, while Athens itself was purified. (Meanwhile no executions could take place – in 399 BC, the condemned Socrates had to wait until the ship's return before drinking the hemlock that would kill him.)

The quadrennial Delia were spectacular. Addressing the god, the Homeric Hymn to Delian Apollo proclaims:

> Your greatest joy is Delos. Here, to honour you, Ionians
> in long flowing robes assemble with their children and
> their modest wives; in boxing and in dancing and in song
> they call you to their minds, delighting you in contests.
> To see the Ionians thronged there, you would think them
> ageless and immortal, gazing on their beauty, delighting
> in the men and the deep-bosomed women, in their sleek
> ships and in all their treasures. And another marvel, too,
> whose fame will never die – the girls of Delos, handmaids
> of Apollo, who shoots from afar! When they have first
> sung praise-songs to Apollo and to Leto and the archer-
> goddess Artemis, they recall the deeds of men and
> women long ago in praise-songs to delight the throngs,
> imitating every voice and accent of all regions so that
> each man would believe that he himself was singing:
> so cleverly is their praise-song conceived.

In the music and dances of the Delian festival, Apollo's role as Mousagetes (leader of the Muses) was supreme. From the sixth century BC onwards (the beginning of Delos' heyday), artists often showed Apollo holding his lyre in the company of two or more musician Muses, while at the Delia the dancing girls in some way may have represented the Muses them-selves, uniting the Greek-speaking world in songs written and performed in a multiplicity of regional accents and dialects.

Apollo & Phaethon

As time went on, Apollo, in his role of Phoebus ('The Shining'), god of light from 'clear-seen' Delos, was increasingly identified with the sun-god Helios until the two became almost indistinguishable. In his *Metamorphoses*, the Roman Ovid conflated the two, making Phoebus the father of doomed Phaethon ('Fiery'), the young man who begged to drive the chariot of the sun. Taking the reins, Phaethon could not control his horses, which plunged dangerously low to earth, scorching much of Africa so that it became desert, turning the skin of Ethiopians black and threatening to evaporate the seas until Zeus (Jupiter in Ovid's poem) struck the chariot with a thunderbolt. Phaethon fell into the River Eridanus (identified by Romans with the Po), where his sisters, the Heliades, transformed into black poplars, wept tears of amber in sorrow.

Delos in History & Today

As the site of Apollo's birth (Artemis' birthplace was sometimes debated), Delos possessed tremendous sanctity. In the late seventh century BC, the Ionian islanders of Naxos dedicated a sculptural group of between nine and twelve marble lions (perhaps inspired by Egyptian avenues of sphinxes, such as those linking Luxor and Karnak) on a terrace overlooking the sacred lake.

Six or seven decades later, Peisistratus, bolstering Athens' claim to lead the Ionian Greeks, purified the area around the sacred lake, disinterring remains from a nearby graveyard and reburying them on the far side of Delos. He also began building a temple to Apollo, facing the Sacred Harbour, its inner sanctuary dominated by a massive statue of the god. Meanwhile Polycrates, the *tyrannos* of Samos, dedicated the nearby (and much larger) island of Rhenea to Apollo, linking it to Delos with a chain, through which divine 'energy' could flow.

During the Persian invasion of 490 BC, Hippias (Peisistratus' son, now a Persian collaborator) made lavish sacrifices at Delos to win Apollo's favour for his traitorous cause. He failed. After Persia's defeat, Delos became the site of the assembly and treasury of the Greek – or Delian – League (478 BC). In a solemn ceremony at the Sacred Harbour, Ionian ambassadors swore allegiance to Athens, dropping red-hot iron bars into the sea to seal their pledge.

A colonnaded temple to Apollo was begun just south of that built by Peisistratus, facing a colossal statue of the god (9 m/30 ft tall) dedicated by the Naxians in the seventh century BC. It was not completed until the end of the fourth century BC. When the League's headquarters were transferred to Athens in 454 BC, Athens continued to stake a claim to Delos. In 426/425 BC, during the Peloponnesian War, it removed all graves from the island to Rhenea, proclaiming that henceforth no one might give birth, die or keep a dog on Delos. Athenians also built a third temple to Apollo between the existing two.

In the early Roman era, Delos, now a bustling free port and sizeable community with over twenty thousand inhabitants, hosted a thriving slave market and attracted worshippers of many other gods. Temples were built to Isis and Ba'al, as well as the oldest surviving Jewish synagogue. But Delos' isolation left it vulnerable to attack. By the end of the first century BC its fortunes were already in decline. In time, thanks to its lack of agricultural land, it was abandoned.

Serene yet implacable, Apollo orders an end to fighting on the west pediment of the fifth-century BC Temple of Zeus at Olympia.

Today Delos' only permanent inhabitants are lizards, insects – and quails, which bustle busily about the marble ruins. Although the foundations of its Classical temples and some columns still survive, together with remains of its fine Hellenistic theatre, Roman and Egyptian shrines and Roman houses (some still with wall paintings and mosaics), much of the ancient splendour of the island must be imagined. The sacred lake has now been drained – mosquitoes once danced low over its waters, like Apollo's arrows the bringers of disease – though a solitary palm tree still stands near its parched and fissured shore, while replicas of five Naxian lions keep watch above it. And above them all, Apollo, god of light, stares down unblinkingly.

SOME IMPORTANT DATES & REMAINS

pre-1200 BC	Delos is a centre of Bronze Age worship.
C7th BC	Delos becomes an Ionian cult centre; Naxians dedicate lion terrace and colossal statue of Apollo.
post-546 BC	Peisistratus purifies Delos and builds first temple.
? *c.* 530 BC	Polycrates links Delos to Rhenea with chain.
490 BC	Persians spare Delos.
478 BC	Delian League formed; Athenians begin second temple.
426/5 BC	Athenians again purify Delos and begin third temple.
166 BC	Delos becomes a Roman 'free port'.
late C2nd BC	Delos is a major commercial and slave-trading centre.
88 BC	Delos attacked by Mithridates of Pontus and 20,000 inhabitants killed.
69 BC	Further piratical attacks.
late C1st BC	Delos, depopulated, experiences irreversible decline.

Delos is a popular cruise destination, but independent travellers may take one of the frequent ferries (30 minutes) from nearby Mykonos. All must be prepared for the merciless sun and the lack of any real shade on the island.

Facing the **Sacred Harbour** (separated by a narrow spit from the ancient **Commercial Harbour,** where most now disembark) is the site occupied by three sixth- and fifth-century BC **temples to Apollo,** their unusual west-facing entrances aligned to an earlier Bronze Age shrine. A path (left) leads towards the **Temple of Leto,** the **Avenue of Lions** and the (now drained) **Sacred Lake.** Enthusiastic walkers can proceed to the **Stadium** and **Synagogue** on the far side of the island. Other paths lead off (right) towards the fine **theatre,** above which remains of large houses contain well-preserved mosaics and wall-paintings. In this area, too, are the **sanctuaries of Syrian and Egyptian gods.** A paved pathway leads the top of **Mount Cynthus** with panoramic views of the Cyclades.

The small **Museum** (which also sells refreshments) contains finds from Delos, including the originals of the **Naxian lions,** a **Mycenaean ivory plaque** showing a warrior in a boar's-tusk helmet, **an archaic statue of a young woman,** an impressive **bronze mask of Dionysus** and a second-century BC **statue of Apollo.** There is also a good collection of **pottery** and a stunning (if hastily drawn) **fresco** showing Heracles, two boxers and a musician.

5

Delphi: Seat of Apollo's Oracle, Haunt of Dionysus

Swift over mountain peaks Apollo swooped – to Delphi, poised
on an outcrop facing west beneath the snows of Mount Parnassus.
A cliff towers over it, while far below unfolds a rocky valley bristling
with trees. Here the Lord, Phoebus Apollo, ordained his dazzling
temple, saying: 'This is the place that I have chosen for my radiant
shrine, an oracle for all mankind, who for all time will bring to
me here perfect sacrifices – all those from the lush Peloponnese,
and all who live in Europe and on wave-lapped islands, when they
come to question me. And in my sumptuous temple I will give to
all of them my guidance, and it shall not fail.'

Homeric Hymn to Pythian Apollo, 281–93

Delphi seems suspended between earth and sky. At daybreak, when the sun's rays flood across the crags of Mount Parnassus, washing the cliffs – the 'Shining Rocks' – in dazzling light and bathing terraces of treasuries and temples in a golden radiance, the sanctuary appears to float above the stillness of the valley far below. Later, as shadows shorten and the dry air, hot with the scent of thyme, is thrumming with the rasping of cicadas, eagles can at times be seen soaring effortlessly on the thermals overhead.

They are the birds of Zeus, and legend tells that, wishing to find the centre of the world, the god unleashed two eagles from the opposite and furthest edges of the earth, setting each on an unerring course. They met at Delphi, where in antiquity the location was marked by a cone-shaped altar stone, said to be the very stone that had once been fed to Cronus, the most sacred object in Apollo's temple. It was called the Omphalos, the Navel of the Earth.

First Oracles

As if such a setting were not enough, close to the Omphalos was said to be a chasm, where the rock had split open in an earthquake. From it drifted vapours, which, when inhaled, induced a state of temporary madness and ecstatic (often incoherent) jabbering. The words might be incomprehensible, but their significance was clear: the speaker, possessed, was the mouthpiece of a god. At Delphi, the midpoint between opposites, mankind could commune with the divine.

In the historic period, Apollo reigned supreme at Delphi, but the Greeks traced the origins of his oracle much further back in time. According to mythology, the first to discover it was a goatherd rescuing one of his flock which had fallen into the chasm. Noticing that the beast was shuddering uncontrollably, he climbed down to rescue it. As he did so, he inhaled the vapours and discovered to his wonderment that he could see far into the past and future. In time, the people of the region appointed a girl to serve as priestess, the site became the oracle of Delphi, and goats were offered to the god in ritual sacrifice. It had once been sacred to Poseidon, god of earthquakes, who had torn the cleft apart, but some (perhaps deriving the name Delphi from *delphús*, 'womb') told how in the beginning it had belonged to Gaia, Earth, the mother of all gods:

> First in my prayer, I honour Gaia, first prophet of
> the gods; next, Themis, who (tradition tells) was
> enthroned second on her mother's seat of prophecy;
> third, amicably, not by force, another Titan, Phoebe,
> Gaia's child, succeeded her. She gave it as a birthday
> gift to Phoebus...

So says the priestess of Apollo in Aeschylus' *Eumenides*. But the most common version of how Apollo came to Delphi (and a version ritually re-enacted there well into the Roman period) is also the most violent.

Pythian Apollo

Shortly after his birth on Delos, Apollo set out to destroy the Python that had pursued his pregnant mother Leto. He found the three-headed serpent in the foothills of Parnassus, coiled around the chasm of the oracle of Gaia. It had already ravaged the surrounding countryside, and now for any to come near it, whether man or animal, meant death. But Apollo was the archer god, 'who shoots from afar', and the Python was powerless to approach him. As the serpent reared its heads, snapping its jaws and flickering its tongues, Apollo launched a fusillade of arrows. Each of the hundred arrowheads sank home until, exhausted, and with black slime oozing from its wounds, the Python crashed dead to the earth. As the

Apollo's contest with the Python for the prophetic tripod at Delphi is commemorated on a silver coin (stater) from Croton (south Italy), *c.* 420 BC.

sun rose high, the carcass rotted, and the Python dissolved back into the slime from which it had been born, dripping down into the chasm, until all that remained were bones and the stench of its decay. It was from this decay (*pythesthai* means 'to rot') that the Pythian priestess, through whom Apollo spoke, took her title, and Delphi its alternative name 'Pytho'.

For the Greeks killing must be atoned – even the killing of the Python. So Apollo collected its bones, placed them in a cauldron and consecrated them in the temple which he built above the noxious chasm. Not only that: he inaugurated funeral games, which, in the historical period, were celebrated every four years with contests for music and dance as well as athletics, and were called Pythian in the serpent's honour. The prize was a crown of Apollo's sacred bay leaves.

Yet even this was not enough. Zeus ordained that Apollo must be ritually cleansed from bloodguilt. Local legends told that Zeus chose the Vale of Tempe for the purification; but Apollo preferred either Sicyon or Crete, where the king presided over the rites. Then Apollo returned to Delphi and claimed it as his own. Here, he persuaded Pan, the goaty god of the untamed countryside who sowed sudden panic in both flocks and men, to teach him the arts of prophecy so vital if he were to preside over the oracle. Then, having civilized the local inhabitants, teaching them to plant fruit trees and lead cultured lives, Apollo invited his mother Leto and his sister Artemis to Delphi to celebrate his triumph. But even now the foothills of Parnassus were not entirely safe. As Leto wound her way towards the sanctuary, she was attacked (perhaps at the still jealous Hera's instigation) by the giant Tityos, a son of Gaia. Ripping her veil, he would have raped her, but Apollo and Artemis heard Leto's screams and unleashed a volley of their deadly arrows. As punishment in Hades, the deathless giant lay stretched out, his arms and legs pegged to the ground, two vultures crouching over him, tearing at his liver and delving deep into his bowels.

For the priests of his new temple, Apollo chose Cretan sailors. The Homeric Hymn describes how he spied them far out at sea tacking towards Pylos and, impressed by their nobility, he:

> met them mid-ocean and, taking a dolphin's form, leapt
> on to the deck of their fast ship, where he lay, huge and
> terrifying. No one knew who he was, and they tried to
> heave the dolphin overboard. But he thrashed about
> on the black ship, shaking its timbers, while they sat
> dumbstruck and terrified.

Despite their efforts, the sailors found that they could not control their ship, which glided miraculously into the bay at Crisa below Delphi, where it grounded on the beach. 'And there the lord Apollo, who shoots from afar, leapt up from the ship like a star seen at midday, and lightning flashed around him, and its brightness shot up to the sky; and through an avenue of precious tripods, he strode into his sanctuary.'

At last the sailors recognized Apollo as a god and accepted his will that they should be the guardians of his temple – in this version calling the sanctuary Delphi in remembrance of his appearance as a dolphin (*delphinos*). For many Greeks, who consulted the Delphic oracle for over a millennium, ever alive to the machinations of its priests, ever alert to the ambiguity of its prophecies, it seemed no coincidence that Cretans had an unenviable reputation as liars.

Yet lying (or presumed lying) could provoke Apollo's anger. When he heard from his messenger, a crow, that his pregnant lover Coronis was unfaithful, in disbelief he punished the bird, turning it black (until then all crows had been pure white). Later Apollo discovered the truth, killed Coronis, and made the crow the harbinger of death. Yet even this was not the end. At Delphi, Coronis' father burned down Apollo's temple – for which the god destroyed him.

Dionysus

Although Delphi was predominantly the sanctuary of Apollo, he shared it with another deity. Appropriately for this place of opposites, it was a god as far removed from Apollo's civilizing order as might be imagined: Dionysus. Every year in late October, when the Pleiades can first be seen and snow begins to shroud Parnassus, the dark crags become threatening and wild. Now Apollo was believed to depart from Delphi and spend the winter in the Land of the Hyperboreans (a northern land, identified by one Greek geographer as Britain). For three months at Delphi Dionysus ruled supreme.

Early Greeks envisaged Dionysus bearded, swathed in leopard skins and clutching his talismanic *thyrsus*, a fennel stalk wrapped in ivy (whose evergreen leaves were sacred to the god) and topped with a pine cone. Later, in the fifth century BC, they began to portray him as a beardless, effeminate youth, crowned in a garland of grapes and vine leaves. In truth, he could be anything, for he was above all the god of metamorphosis, who could alter men's perceptions of reality, not least through wine or drama. Fittingly for Delphi, one of his most virtuosic transformations included turning men into dolphins.

The Homeric Hymn to Dionysus tells how pirates captured the young god as he stood 'on a headland which stretched into the barren sea'. Once he was aboard, however, they found that they had more than met their match:

Having transformed its piratical crew into dolphins, Dionysus reclines in his black ship as vines, heavy with grapes, twine round its mast. (Sixth-century BC wine cup.)

Soon miracles began to happen. First wine, sweet-tasting and sweet-smelling, splashed through the black ship, a divine aroma drifted up, and the sailors were amazed. Then, on the highest yardarm, a vine began uncoiling – on both sides – heavy with grapes; and dark ivy twined around the mast, bursting with flowers and thick with berries.... And at the ship's prow the god transformed himself into a lion, terrifying, roaring like thunder.... When the sailors saw it, to escape their evil fate, they all jumped overboard into the sparkling sea, and were transfigured into dolphins.

Only the sympathetic helmsman, who had tried to prevent the pirates' kidnap of the god, survived unscathed. To those who recognized him, Dionysus could be gentle – he was both *Bromios* ('Thunderer') and *Eleutherios* ('Liberator').

It was wise to treat Dionysus' followers with kindness, too. Plutarch (himself a Delphic priest) records that, during the Sacred Wars of 356–346 BC (when neighbouring states fought for control of Delphi), a group of the god's worshippers, maenads from Athens and Phocis, became lost on Mount Parnassus and stumbled in a trance into the market place of hostile Amphissa (7 km or 4 miles from Delphi). Here local women found them at dawn and in silence formed a protective circle round them until the maenads' senses returned. Then they persuaded their husbands to escort the still disorientated worshippers in safety to their frontier.

Meanwhile, Plutarch's contemporary, Pausanias, described how: 'the summit of Parnassus is hard to reach – even for a man in good condition. Its peaks are above the clouds. Only the crazed Thyades [possibly a 'college' of maenads based in Athens] run here in honour of Dionysus and Apollo.' That they honoured both might suggest that this was a special festival, perhaps held to mark one of the two annual transitions of Delphi's 'ownership' from one god to the other.

The Delphians even claimed to possess Dionysus' tomb. Sited near the Omphalos, it was the focus of a cult celebrating the god's death and resurrection. Housed in the Temple of Apollo, on the site of an early temple believed to have been constructed by Apollo himself, it was the setting for several episodes from mythology.

Other Myths at Delphi

Mount Parnassus was where Deucalion's 'ark' came to rest after Zeus destroyed most of mankind in a flood, but Homer mentions Delphi only as the location of the boar hunt which gave Odysseus the scar by which his nurse recognized him on his return to Ithaca.

By the fifth century BC, however, Delphi and its oracle were increasingly important in literature and mythology. Oedipus' misinterpretation of the oracle leads to disaster in Sophocles' *Oedipus the King*, while in Aeschylus' *Eumenides* the matricide Orestes flees to Delphi from Mycenae in the hope of being purified. But it is not to be. The Furies pursue him. In the terrifying prologue, the priestess of Apollo crawls trembling from the temple, horrified and outraged by what she has seen inside: Orestes, drenched in blood, a sword in one hand, an olive branch in the other, sits on the Omphalos as suppliant – while around him the Furies lie sleeping, 'black, abominable, snoring, their breath repugnant, vile gobbets dripping from their eyes'.

Eventually, Orestes is acquitted of his crime in Athens, but he does not embrace a life of piety. In Euripides' *Andromache* he returns to Delphi to engineer the death of Achilles' son Neoptolemus (with whose Spartan wife Hermione, the daughter of Helen and Menelaus, Orestes is in love). A vivid speech describes how Orestes persuaded the Delphians to kill Neoptolemus, who had spent three days admiring the sights, 'going about the temple crypts all crammed with gold, and round the treasuries of men'. (Orestes claimed he was planning a robbery.) As Neoptolemus escaped from the temple:

> The Delphians threw everything they could – arrows, spears, light skewers and sacrificial knives.... They had him trapped; no room to breathe. So he left the altar where men sacrifice, and leapt. The Delphians turned like doves before a hawk, trampling each other, injured, as they jostled for the narrow exits. Then a scream, so terrifying and ghastly, reverberated round the sacred awe-inspiring walls and round the cliffs outside. And in the silence Neoptolemus stood still, his weapons dancing in the light. Then a second cry, blood-curdling and eerie from the inner shrine. It roused the Delphians. They turned to fight. And so Achilles' son was killed there, struck in the lung by a sharp-edged sword. A man from Delphi killed him, one among many more.... They took the body from beside the altar and flung it down outside the sanctuary.

Close to the Temple of Apollo, Pausanias saw a precinct said to contain Neoptolemus' grave.

Another Euripidean tragedy, *Ion*, is set at Delphi. An altogether gentler play, it paints a vivid picture of the sanctuary awakening. Ion, a son of Apollo by Creusa (daughter of Athens' King Erechtheus), who exposed him at birth, has been saved and brought to Delphi to work as a temple attendant. Preparing to sweep out the temple with a broom of myrtle twigs, he describes the morning sun blazing on the crags and addresses his fellow servants:

> The smoke from dry myrrh rises to the temple roof. The Delphic woman sits on her sacred tripod, and sings the words Apollo makes flow through her. So now, Delphic servants of Apollo, go to Castalia's swirling pools, and when you've purified yourselves in their sacred waters, return here to the temple.... I shall perform the tasks I've

been assigned since childhood, purifying the entrance to
Apollo's temple with fresh young laurel shoots and sacred
garlands, sprinkling the ground with droplets of water.
And with my bow, I'll chase away the flocks of birds which
soil the sacred offerings.

Mother and son are later reunited, and Ion returns to Athens to become
the ancestor of the Ionians, many of whom settled in Ionia (in western
Turkey).

All three plays presume some knowledge not only of the myths but
also of the topography and rituals of Delphi, with which they were so
closely linked.

Delphi in History & Today

Although there was an early sanctuary at Delphi, the site gained international importance from the sixth century BC, when the first stone temple
was built. This was burned shortly afterwards, lavishly rebuilt by the
Peisistratid family from Athens, and restored in the fourth century BC.
It is the ruins of this last temple that can be seen today.

Delphi was one of the great meeting places of the Greeks. Some came
to watch or participate in the Pythian Games, whose athletic events took
place in the stadium (built in its present form by the second-century AD
Herodes Atticus), while contests for the Arts were held in the theatre, and
chariot races on the plain at Crisa far below. Others flocked to consult
the oracle, which gave its response on the seventh day of each of the nine
months when Apollo was in residence. Questions ranged widely – from
whether the enquirer would have children to whether and where to found
a colony. Many became famous: in the sixth century BC the Lydian king
Croesus asked whether he should invade his neighbours, the Persians.
The response was that if he crossed the River Halys, the boundary between
them, he would destroy a mighty empire. He did. It was his own. At the
end of the fifth century BC, the oracle announced Socrates as the wisest
man alive (something which the philosopher tried – unsuccessfully – to
disprove by posing questions to self-proclaimed experts, all of whom he
found wanting). It may have reassured Alexander the Great, arriving impe-
riously on a non-consultation day, that he was invincible; and in the
Roman era, the thirty-year-old Nero was relieved to be told to 'beware the
age of seventy-three', believing that this was when he would die. Soon
afterwards he realized his error, committing suicide rather than face
enemies loyal to his seventy-three-year-old general, Galba.

The process of consulting the oracle remains unclear, but petition-
ers, having first sacrificed and purified themselves in the Castalian Spring,
probably put their questions through the priests to the priestess seated

on her tripod above the vaporous chasm, while she moaned in her ecstatic trance. The priests then interpreted what she said, presenting an answer neatly composed in hexameters and almost always so equivocal that they could not be blamed if the advice proved unsatisfactory – one of Apollo's many epithets was *Loxias* ('Ambiguous').

For much of antiquity Delphi was indeed the centre of the Greek world, one of the richest of all sanctuaries. Offerings included gold-and-ivory statues of Apollo from Ionia; a sphinx from Naxos, crouching on a high column; a gold- and silver-plated bull; a bronze column, 8 m (26 ft) tall (dedicated after the Greek victory over Persia at Plataea in 479 BC) in the form of a twisted three-headed Python, which (tripod-like) supported a gold cauldron; as well as countless statues of Apollo, other gods and the great and good of Greece. Here cities and families conspicuously flaunted their wealth, storing it in treasuries or using it to construct or enhance altars and temples. In time almost every god was honoured with a shrine at Delphi, and the sanctuary of Athene Pronaia ('In Front of the Temple'), home to the well-known tholos (round temple), became particularly prominent.

With temples, treasuries and statues, some of solid gold, many set on ever-higher pillars, Delphi was a magnet for would-be plunderers. Twice Apollo is said to have sent rocks crashing down on invading armies: the Persians in 480 BC, and the Gauls in 279 BC. In the end, Gaia herself intervened, or perhaps it was Poseidon. When an earthquake closed the chasm's mouth, the oracle spoke no longer.

Other explanations for the oracle's demise gained legendary status. Christian writers (wrongly) told how, shortly before AD 15, it gave its final utterance: 'a Hebrew boy, a god who rules the blessed, commands I leave this house for ever and return to Hades. In silence leave my altar.' Another account tells how a question from Rome's last pagan emperor, the fourth-century AD Julian the Apostate, was met with the response: 'Tell this to the emperor: the well-wrought hall has fallen to the ground. No longer does Apollo keep his shrine, his prophesying laurel or his murmuring spring. Even the waters of his spring are dry.'

Today, the massive base and five more-or-less resurrected columns are all that remain of Apollo's glittering fourth-century BC temple. Gone are the maxims the god is said to have had inscribed high on its walls ('Know Yourself'; 'Nothing in Excess'; 'Certainty Brings Disaster'), though their wisdom is timeless. The temple pediments which so neatly encapsulated Delphi's duality exist only in fragments – those on the east side showing Apollo (seated on his tripod) with Leto, Artemis and the Muses, a study in poise and harmony, those on the west showing Dionysus and his maenads. Perfection, the Greeks knew, lay in the reconciliation of two opposites. At Delphi, it came close to being achieved.

SOME IMPORTANT DATES & REMAINS

C7th BC	Delphic oracle begins to assume international importance.
582 BC	Pythian Games inaugurated.
late C6th BC	Sanctuary enlarged and colonnaded Temple of Apollo built.
373 BC	Temple of Apollo destroyed by earthquake and subsequently rebuilt.
C1st BC	Oracle in decline.
C1st–3rd AD	Reflowering of Delphi, partly as a tourist destination.
AD 391	Christian Roman emperor Theodosius bans pagan religions, including the Delphic oracle.
? AD 424	Last Pythian Games.

There are several parts to the site today. Half a mile east of the modern village, on the left of the main road, the **Sacred Way** ascends between the remains of once lavish treasuries (including the reconstructed **Treasury of the Athenians**) on a path formerly flanked by statues. This leads to the partially reconstructed **Temple of Apollo** with its fine **altar**, near which a reconstruction of the serpent column is planned. (The remains of the original can be seen in the Hippodrome in Istanbul.) Above is the well-preserved **theatre**. Still further up is the impressive **stadium** (no access), rebuilt in stone in the second century AD.

To the left of the main road, visitors pass first the shady **Castalian Spring** (no access). Further on to the right, a track leads down to the **precinct of Athene Pronaia** containing the foundations of a number of temples, including the evocative reconstucted **tholos**. Close by is the **gymnasium**.

Delphi's rich **Archaeological Museum** contains a fourth-century BC copy of the **Omphalos** and **sculptures** from different phases of the Temple of Apollo (including its fourth-century **pediments**) and the Siphnian Treasury, as well as many offerings made at the site from throughout the Classical world. These include two *kouroi* (statues of male youths; *c.* 580 BC) – identified as Cleobis and Biton – from Argos; the Naxian **Sphinx** (*c.* 560 BC); remains of sixth-century BC Ionian gold-and-ivory **statues of Apollo, Artemis and Leto**; a life-sized **silver and gold bull** from the same period; and the exquisite bronze **charioteer**, traditionally believed to have been dedicated by Polyzelus of Gela in Sicily in around 478 BC following his victory at the Pythian Games. There is also a *kylix* (cup) showing Apollo with his lyre seated opposite a black crow.

6

Ephesus: Artemis & the Cult of the Mother Goddess

I sing of Artemis, goddess of the golden shafts, the hallowed
virgin whose hunting call resounds, who brings down stags,
who pours out arrows, blood-sister to Apollo of the golden sword.
She curves her golden bow across mountains deep in shadow, across
windswept peaks, delighting in the chase, unleashing agonizing
arrows. The summits of high mountains tremble and the matted
undergrowth of woods resounds to wild beasts' bellowing. The
earth shakes and the fish-infested sea. Boldly she advances far
and wide to destroy generations of wild creatures.

Homeric Hymn to Artemis, 1–11

Basking in her nest atop the tall – if somewhat crooked – column, a white stork spreads her wings and gazes languidly around. Hers is an enviable vantage point. Close by to the east is the dusty modern town of Selçuk, its low hill crowned by the towering walls of Ayasuluk Castle. Here too are the sun-washed ruins of St John's Basilica, whose pure-white columns gleam in the early evening light, while, below, crows roost in the ruined minaret of the Isa Bey mosque. Stretching her neck, the stork looks south to where a ridge of mountains rises from flat farmland, with rich fields of cotton, vineyards, olive groves and orchards ripening with oranges and lemons. But her attention is focused closer and below. For in the low-lying hollow, strewn with tumbled masonry and flanked to the west by tall dark trees, is a reedy swamp, alive with frogs, the easiest of pickings for a lazy stork.

For most who come here, though, the site with its one reconstructed column, its submerged foundations and stray marble fragments has a quite different significance. For this was once the Temple of Ephesian Artemis, one of the seven wonders of the ancient world, a place of awe and majesty, the echoing, glittering, incense-laden sanctuary of one of antiquity's most powerful deities. Now it may be little more than a mosquito-haunted swamp, yet in a real sense Artemis is present still. The goddess of nature, the mistress of wild things, the unfettered force of newborn life, she has reclaimed her sanctuary to live on in the teeming reeds and marshland.

The Virgin Artemis

Artemis was one of the most complex and compelling of Greek divinities. Like her twin brother Apollo she was the embodiment of opposites. The protectress of young animals, she delighted in the hunt. An enthusiast for mountain peaks (Homer envisages her 'with her bow, roaming the high ridges of Tagetus'), she was associated with marshy lowlands (Euripides tells how 'she wanders the swamps and sand-bars of the sea, and the foaming eddies of the surf'). And despite being an avowed virgin, she was the goddess whose help women most often evoked when in labour. As the elder sibling, Artemis acted as midwife when their mother Leto bore Apollo on Delos – an experience that both qualified her to preside over childbirth (helped by minor deities such as Eileithyia) and ensured she had no wish to endure the process herself.

In his *Hymn to Artemis*, Callimachus describes how, a precocious toddler, the goddess sat on her father Zeus' knee and demanded:

> Father, let me guard my virginity forever, and give me
> many titles so that Apollo can't outdo me. Give me arrows
> and a bow – wait, father! I'm not asking *you* for a quiver

and mighty bow. Right now the Cyclopes will make me arrows and a supple bowstring! No, but let me be Bringer of Light and wear a belted tunic – knee-length, with an embroidered border – so I can kill wild beasts! And give me sixty daughters of Ocean to dance with me, all nine years old, still children, still wearing young girls' dresses, and twenty nymphs from the [Cretan River] Amnisus to be my handmaidens, to look after my boots when I've finished hunting lynx or stags, and to tend to my hunting dogs. And give me every mountain, but whatever city you see fit – for Artemis goes rarely down into the city!

Enchanted, Zeus agreed, giving her thirty cities and appointing her the guardian of streets and harbours. (*Episkopos*, which Callimachus uses for 'guardian', later meant 'bishop'.)

Callimachus describes how, having visited Sicily, where the Cyclopes presented her with a Cretan-style bow, quiver and arrows, then Arcadia, where Pan furnished her with hunting hounds, Artemis discovered five hefty hinds with golden horns grazing in a meadow. Resisting her instinct to shoot them, she rounded them up, tamed them and yoked them to her chariot – all bar one, which escaped and later caused Heracles much grief when he was sent from Tiryns to capture it. Artemis then perfected her archery, firing at an elm, an oak and a boar before turning her arrows on 'a city of unjust men', whose cattle died and crops withered as old men mourned their sons and women died in childbirth. They were by no means the last to experience her wrath.

The Wrath of Artemis

In her state of perpetual adolescence, Artemis quickly took offence at perceived slights – as one of her attendants, the nymph Callisto, discovered. Like all Artemis' coterie, she had taken an oath of virginity. But this meant nothing to Zeus, who disguised himself as Artemis and seduced her. Later, while they were bathing, Artemis recognized the signs of Callisto's pregnancy. Outraged, she showed no mercy. An early poem attributed to Hesiod tells how she changed Callisto into a bear. Others maintained that it was Zeus or Hera who performed the transformation and that Artemis shot her pregnant acolyte with an arrow. Happily, Zeus saved Callisto's son, Arcas, smuggling him to safety, and turned Callisto into a constellation – the Great Bear. In Classical times bears played a role in worshipping Artemis: girls on the cusp of adolescence serving at Artemis' sanctuary at marshy Brauron near Athens (where Iphigenia, sacrificed to appease her, was honoured with a hero-shrine) were known as 'she-bears'.

Artemis watches while Actaeon is torn apart by his own hounds on a metope from Temple 'E' at Selinunte, Sicily.

Actaeon, too, provoked Artemis' anger. A prince of Thebes, he was hunting with his comrades when, straying from the path, he came across a pool in which the goddess and her nymphs were bathing naked. Some say that he tried to rape her; others that when Artemis caught sight of him, she was flustered. She knew that, young as he was, Actaeon would soon be boasting to his comrades, describing her naked body in excruciating detail. So she transformed him into a stag. Bewildered, Actaeon bounded off; his hounds gave chase; the stag was felled; and Actaeon was torn to pieces by his dogs. Pausanias writes that his ghost then terrified the countryside, being placated only when his remains were buried and a bronze statue of him was riveted with iron to a rock.

Artemis of Ephesus & the Amazons

Throughout the rest of Greek world Artemis was imagined as a virgin huntress. But not at Ephesus. Here her cult statue was unique, as surviving copies show. Each is subtly different, but she typically wears a tall crown adorned with winged beasts and topped by a model of the city or its temple, a garland of fruits draped round her neck. On her short cape appear signs of the zodiac, and from her long tight dress rows of animals stand out in sharp relief: lions and griffins, leopards and goats, bulls and bees. But most eye-catching is the profusion of egg-like spheres which cover her from chest to waist. It is unclear what they symbolize. Some say (nipple-less) breasts, others gourds, still others bulls' testicles. Whatever they are, they clearly proclaim Ephesian Artemis as the essence of fertility.

Why such a difference? When most ancient civilizations met, they delighted in finding similarities between each others' gods and, where possible, merging them in a process known as syncretism. Usually the resulting deity was recognizable to both cultures. Not so at Ephesus. Here, migrating Greeks apparently discovered an ancient Asiatic goddess of wild animals (perhaps the Great Mother Goddess, Cybele), in whose essence but not appearance they saw similarities with their own goddess of wild nature. A venerated cult statue of this native goddess – which some said had fallen from the skies, a gift from Zeus – was probably already in existence at Ephesus. So the Greek settlers retained her physical attributes, but gave her the familiar name of Artemis.

They also gave her a distinct form of worship, again probably adopted from earlier cult practices. In an exception to the Greek norm, virgin priestesses were augmented by 'Megabyzi', eunuch priests like those who served Cybele. Curiously, sources disagree about whether laywomen were allowed into her precinct. The aptly named Artemidorus ('Gift of Artemis'), a second-century AD writer on dreams and a native Ephesian, wrote that women were forbidden entry on punishment of death.

Ephesian Artemis had her own mythology, too. Local legends told that she was born not on Delos, but at Ephesus itself. As for her cult and statue, Callimachus recognizes their 'barbarian' origins:

> The Amazons, whose hearts are set on battle, set up
> a wooden image to you [Artemis] beside the sea at
> Ephesus beneath an oak tree, and Hippo [their queen]
> performed the sacrament. The Amazons danced a war-
> dance round the statue, first with shields and armour,
> then in a circle with the dancers widely spaced. And
> pipes played loud, a shrill accompaniment.... Feet
> beat; quivers rattled. And afterwards a great temple
> was erected round the wooden statue, richer and more
> sacred than any other which the dawn might see. It
> easily surpasses Delphi.

The Amazons' association with Artemis' temple at Ephesus was entirely logical. Like the goddess, this legendary tribe of fierce warrior women rejected sex, except when absolutely necessary to increase their numbers. And like Cybele, they were non-Greek, coming from beyond the fringes of the civilized (Greek) world. Fifth-century BC Greeks believed that their home was in Scythia (modern Crimea).

The name 'Amazon' was thought to derive from the Greek *a-mazos*, 'without a breast'. As the Roman historian Justin explained: 'These maidens used to exercise with weapons, on horseback and in the hunt. They burned off the right breasts of their young girls so that they would not impede them as they fired their arrows. For this reason they are called Amazons.' However, Greek sculptors and artists never show this mutilation, and it is more likely that their name derives from the Indo-European *hamazan* ('warriors').

Encounters with Amazons often resulted in a heady mixture of romance and death. When Heracles was sent to steal the battle belt of Hippolyta, the Amazonian queen, his confederate Theseus fell in love with and abducted her sister Antiope, by whom he had a son, Hippolytus (himself an ardent follower of Artemis). In retaliation the Amazons invaded Attica, almost capturing Athens, and their defeat was a popular subject for artists. Pindar writes that it was during this expedition that they founded the temple at Ephesus, establishing its sanctuary as a place of asylum.

At other times Amazons attacked Asia Minor – both Lycia (south of Ephesus), where they were defeated by Bellerophon, and Phrygia, where they fought against Priam, later the king of Troy. In the Trojan War, however, the Amazons took the Trojans' side against the Greeks, fighting (as Homer admiringly records) 'like men'. Here, their queen Penthesilea was mortally wounded by Achilles, but as she died Achilles fell in love with her. The late sixth-century BC vase-painter Exekias captured the scene, while the fourth-century AD epic poet Quintus from nearby Smyrna imagined Achilles standing over Penthesilea's body, gazing on her:

> in her armour, like Artemis, the huntress, child of
> Zeus, when she lies sleeping, tired from the pursuit
> of lions with arrows over all the rolling hills. In death
> Aphrodite of the shining crown, the bride of Ares, made
> her beautiful, so that Achilles might be wounded by the
> bitter arrow of remorseful love.... His heart was broken
> with regret that he had killed so sweet a creature, whom
> he might have taken home to Phthia, rich in chariots,
> his queen, his bride. A daughter of the gods, she was so
> perfect, so divinely tall and so divinely beautiful.

Achilles stabs the Amazon queen
Penthesilea, as imagined by the
sixth-century BC vase-painter Exekias.

So closely connected were the Amazons with the Artemision (or Temple
of Artemis) at Ephesus that many statues of them were dedicated there,
including examples by the great sculptors Polycleitus and Pheidias.

Great is Diana of the Ephesians

In Roman times the Artemision grew in importance, while Ephesus
became the busiest commercial hub in Asia Minor. Its powerful Jewish
community attracted the radical Christian preacher Paul on his evangeliz-
ing tour of the Greco-Roman world. His impassioned sermons (AD 54–57)
led to the burning of books (worth 'fifty thousand pieces of silver') and
brought him into direct conflict with Ephesian silversmiths, who turned
out souvenir replicas of the Artemision and its statue. Acts of the Apostles
(the King James translation of which calls Artemis by her Roman name,
Diana) describes how:

> A certain man named Demetrius, a silversmith, which
> made silver shrines for Diana, brought no small gain
> unto the craftsmen; Whom he called together with the
> workmen of like occupation, and said, 'Sirs, ye know that

by this craft we have our wealth. Moreover ye see and hear, that not alone at Ephesus, but almost throughout all Asia, this Paul hath persuaded and turned away much people, saying that they be no gods, which are made with hands: So that not only this our craft is in danger to be set at nought; but also that the temple of the great goddess Diana should be despised, and her magnificence should be destroyed, whom all Asia and the world worshippeth.' And the whole city was filled with confusion.

When the rioters caught two of Paul's companions and dragged them into the theatre, one of the Jewish community called for calm and tried to address the crowd. 'But when they knew that he was a Jew, all with one voice about the space of two hours cried out, Great is Diana of the Ephesians. And when the townclerk had appeased the people, he said, "Ye men of Ephesus, what man is there that knoweth not how that the city of the Ephesians is a worshipper of the great goddess Diana, and of the image which fell down from Jupiter?"'

Although the townclerk eventually managed to disperse the crowd, Paul, who had kept – or been kept – well away, prudently left Ephesus as soon as possible.

The Coming of the Virgin Mary

The silversmiths' fears were well grounded. Just as Artemis may have supplanted the Asiatic mother goddess Cybele, so she in turn was superseded at Ephesus by the Christian virgin mother, Mary. At Ephesus in AD 431 the Third Ecumenical Council of bishops granted Mary the title 'Mother of God', adopting the tradition that the apostle John (to whose care Christ had entrusted her) brought Mary to Ephesus and arranged for her to live in a house on the slopes of Mount Coressus (now called Bülbüldağı, 'Nightingale'). Today John's tomb lies in the ruined basilica on Selçuk's Ayasuluk Hill.

Belief in Mary's connection to Ephesus was strengthened in the early nineteenth century AD when a bed-ridden German nun, Sister Anne Catherine Emmerich, claimed to experience a number of visions. In them Mary described the crucifixion and her subsequent life in Ephesus, as well as the house in which she lived there. The accounts were published and in 1881 a French priest, Abbé Julien Gouyet, used them to try to locate the house. He found a remote ruin, revered by local Christians, which fitted perfectly with the vision. Ten years later another search led two Smyrnan priests to the same place, since when Meryem Ana or 'Mary's House' has become a place of pilgrimage. Whatever the visitor's beliefs, the setting of the small house, which now serves as a chapel, is sublime.

Eight Sleepers

Ephesus is the site of another Christian legend, that of the Seven Sleepers. During persecutions under Rome's emperor Decius in the mid-third century AD, seven young Christian zealots were walled up in a cave. After praying, they fell asleep, and awoke only when they heard the stones being removed from the cave-mouth. Emerging into the daylight, they sent one of their number with money into Ephesus to buy food, warning him to take care not to be arrested. He returned with amazing news. Not only were buildings blatantly displaying the sign of the cross, but shop-keepers had asked why he was trying to use obsolete coinage. The young men then discovered the dramatic truth: a Christian emperor was on the throne; Christianity was the official religion of the Greco-Roman world; and they had slept for nearly two hundred years. Still bewildered, they were led into the presence of the bishop, where, after recounting their experiences, they died.

The story has parallels in earlier myth. In a cave on Mount Latmus, south of Ephesus, Classical Greeks believed another hero slept. He was the beautiful Endymion, the shepherd who first tracked the phases of the moon. As he gazed into the skies, the moon-goddess Selene fell in love with him. She begged Zeus to give Endymion to her, and make him both immortal and forever young. So Zeus caused the shepherd to stretch out in a cave and lulled him into everlasting sleep; each night Selene lay with him in love until (unwittingly) he fathered fifty daughters. Since Selene is another aspect of Artemis (both are moon-goddesses), it is tempting to find in this story a memory of the all-fertile mother goddess, whose statue adorned the Artemision at Ephesus.

Ephesus & the Artemision in History & Today

Originally on the coast, the hill of Ayasuluk was inhabited in Neolithic times and further settled in the Bronze Age. Some Classical writers claimed that both city and Artemision were founded by a local man, Coressus, and the eponymous Ephesus, son of Caystus, the local river-god; others said that the sanctuary, which offered asylum to fugitives and criminals, was established by the Amazons; still others told of tenth-century BC Athenians and an exiled prince, Androclus. The Delphic oracle advised him to settle where he saw a leaping fish and running boar. As his men were cooking fish, their pan fell over and the fish fell out; the oil ignited; the undergrowth caught fire; and a boar, which was asleep nearby, burst out. Androclus slew the animal and founded his city, gleefully reminding his followers that the oracle had promised it would have a splendid future. It did.

Ephesus grew in importance, thanks partly to the Artemision close to the sea on the marshy plain. While most Greek temples faced east, some temples of Artemis faced west. The Artemision was one of them. Although the first temple was destroyed by migrating Cimmerians from beyond the Black Sea around 650 BC it was soon rebuilt. Then a century later Croesus, king of Lydia, besieged the city. Herodotus writes that to harness the Artemision's divine power: 'The Ephesians dedicated the city to Artemis and stretched a rope from the temple to the city walls.' Nonetheless, Ephesus was captured, but wealthy Croesus was benign. Thanks to his patronage, the Artemision became one of the finest temples in the Greek world, with a double colonnade and carved column drums showing a procession of worshippers.

Despite the Ephesians' participation in the Ionian Revolt against the Persians (499–493 BC) – the first battle on Ionian soil was fought at Ephesus – the city and temple were spared by Persia's Great King. Nonetheless, there was rejoicing when Ionia was liberated in 478 BC. In 411 BC a deal between Sparta and Persia, ratified by the rest of Greece in 386 BC, saw Ephesus again pass into Persian hands. Thirty years later, desiring celebrity, a deluded arsonist, Herostratus, burned down the Artemision. Strabo records that, undaunted, the Ephesians 'collected their womenfolk's jewelry and their own belongings, and sold the columns of the former temple' to pay for the rebuilding. Work was incomplete when Alexander the Great 'liberated' Ephesus in 334 BC, but the citizens refused his help to finish it, suggesting that it would be wrong for one god to dedicate offerings to another.

With its forest of 127 columns, many carved in high relief, the new Artemision was one of the seven wonders of the ancient world. The second-century BC poet Antipater of Sidon enthusiastically wrote:

> I have gazed on the high walls of Babylon, atop which
> chariots can drive, and on Zeus' statue at Olympia. I have
> seen the hanging gardens, Rhodes' colossus of the sun,
> the great works of the mighty pyramids and the towering
> Mausoleum; but when I looked at Artemis' temple
> rising to the clouds those other wonders faded and I
> said: 'Except for Mount Olympus, there is no other sight
> beneath the sun which can compare.'

In the first century AD, Pliny the Elder considered the temple to be the most magnificent in the Greek world, writing that it was deliberately built on a marshy site to protect it against earthquakes and that in order to provide stability, layers of charcoal were trodden into the marsh, with fleeces placed on top of them. This technique, known as 'seismic isolation', mirrors the practice of modern structural engineers in earthquake zones.

By the early fourth century BC, sediment from the River Cayster rendered Ephesus' harbour unusable, so around 290 BC one of Alexander's successors, Lysimachus, relocated the city nearby to the west. When the Ephesians refused to leave their homes, he blocked the sewers during a heavy rainstorm. They soon complied. The new city thrived, until in 133 BC it was bequeathed to Rome by the Pergamene king Attalus III. A century of depredation followed, with high taxes, an ill-judged alliance with the bloodthirsty Mithridates, king of Pontus, who murdered Ephesus' Roman citizens and sympathizers, and consequent reprisals at the hands of the Roman general Sulla.

In the first century BC, Ephesus' citizens lionized Mark Antony (who arranged for Cleopatra's sister Arsinoë, a priestess of Artemis, to be assassinated on the temple's steps in 41 BC). Even so, when Augustus became Rome's emperor in 27 BC he made Ephesus the capital of the province of Asia. According to Strabo, its wealth and population grew by the day, and many of its most visited remains, including the theatre and the Library of Celsus, date from this period in its history.

In AD 263 the Goths sacked both city and temple, but Ephesus' importance remained constant. Nature dealt the final blow. By the seventh century AD, the Cayster's silt made even the Hellenistic port unusable. Earthquakes, raids and massacres by Arabs and Turks led to massive depopulation. When Ayasuluk was resettled under the Seljuks, many Classical buildings were plundered for stone, and the marble from the Artemision ground down for lime. Today Ephesus lies 5 km (3 miles) from the sea, and the bay on which the city stood is fertile farmland.

Rediscovering the Artemision

The nineteenth-century AD British engineer John Turtle Wood was determined to locate the site of the lost Artemision. In 1866 he discovered inscriptions describing the route of a procession between the temple and the theatre to celebrate Artemis' birthday. Reasoning that if he found the landmarks which it listed, he would find the temple, Wood set to work.

The trail led from the theatre to the Magnesian Gate, where the procession entered the city. From here Wood continued northeast past the hero-shrine of Androclus to the Stoa of Damianus, which he knew was built to shelter those walking to the Artemision. When he uncovered inscriptions marking the sanctuary's boundaries, Wood realized he was near his goal, and on 31 December 1869, nearly 6 m (20 ft) below ground level, he discovered the Artemision's marble pavement, in his words, 'so long lost, so long sought for, and so long almost despaired of'. Wood pumped out the marshy water and completed his excavations, and in time, using drums from the jumble of broken masonry, restorers raised one column, on the top of which a stork lands every year to build its nest.

SOME IMPORTANT DATES & REMAINS

c. 6000 BC Ayasuluk Hill and surrounding areas inhabited.

1500 BC Mycenaean settlement and tombs on Ayasuluk Hill.

C10th BC Traditional date of Athenian foundation of Ephesus.

c. 650 BC Cimmerian attack destroys first temple.

c. 560 BC Croesus defeats Ephesus and finances building of archaic temple.

499–493 BC Ionian Revolt.

478 BC Ephesus liberated from Persians.

411 BC Sparta acknowledges Persia's claims to Ephesus.

386 BC Mainland Greece accepts Persia's rights over Ephesus.

356 BC Herostratus burns archaic temple.

334 BC Alexander the Great 'liberates' Ephesus and offers to fund new temple.

c. 290 BC Lysimachus relocates Ephesus.

133 BC Ephesus bequeathed to Rome.

88 BC Ephesus sides with Mithridates of Pontus against Rome.

86 BC Ephesus reclaimed by Sulla.

27 BC Ephesus becomes capital of the province of Asia.

AD 54–57 Paul's visit provokes a riot.

AD *c.* 100 John, who perhaps brought Mary to Ephesus, dies.

AD 263 Gothic tribes destroy the city and Artemision.

AD 431 At Ephesus, Third Ecumenical Council proclaims Mary 'Mother of God'.

AD 654 Arabs sack Ephesus.

AD 1819–24 Sister Anne Catherine Emmerich's visions.

AD 1869 John Turtle Wood locates Artemision.

AD 1881/1891 Two expeditions locate Mary's house.

The **Artemision** lies in an unprepossessing hollow west of Selçuk. Other than one reconstructed column, only scattered stones and part of the pavement can be seen and often these are below water since the site is marshy and overgrown. However, visitors with a good imagination and site plan will find their visit deeply rewarding.

Continuing out of Selçuk, a road leads (left) to the Hellenistic and Roman city. Souvenir stalls crowd the entrance. A path leads south to meet the colonnaded '**Harbour Street**', once the road from the port to the magnificent **theatre** (capacity 24,500). From here '**Marble Street**' leads south past the **Lower Agora** to the much-restored second-century AD **Library of Celsus** (capacity 12,000 manuscript rolls). The 'Street of the Curetes' runs uphill. Right, under a hangar, are **Roman houses** with breathtaking **wall-paintings**. Left are **latrines**. Past a **temple of Hadrian** and **fountain of Trajan** are the **Odeon, Upper Agora** and **Magnesian Gate**. From the carpark, another track veers off (right) to the **Coressian Gate**, the **stadium** and the **Cave of the Seven Sleepers**.

Ephesus is one of Turkey's most popular tourist destinations. In peak season it is hot and packed with slow-moving throngs, whose polyglot presence gives some idea of what Ephesus' bustling streets must have been like at the city's commercial height. Those wishing to experience the site's romance should plan an off-peak visit in the early morning or late afternoon.

To reach **Meryem Ana**, the House of the Virgin Mary, take the turn-off (right) from the D550 south of Selçuk, which skirts the archaeological site by the Magnesian Gate, and continue several miles up the winding road towards the summit of Mount Coressus. The reward is a spiritually uplifting place amid tall trees with a spring nearby, clean air and a tranquillity so often lacking at the site below.

Selçuk's recently renovated **archaeological museum** contains Roman **statues of Ephesian Artemis** found in the Upper Agora, **architectural details** from the Artemision and models of the temple. Among many exhibits are an **ivory frieze** commemorating Trajan's Parthian wars and fine sculptures, including one of **Androclus**. Others, once part of a group associated with a fountain house, represent **Odysseus and his companions in Polyphemus' cave**.

7

Paphos: Garden of Aphrodite

My song shall be of Aphrodite, queenly, golden-crowned and beautiful. Hers are the strong-walled towns of sea-washed Cyprus, where the West Wind, moist and warm, once carried her in downy foam across the rolling, moaning sea. Gladly the golden-ribboned Seasons welcomed her and clothed her in a heavenly dress. On her immortal head they set a golden crown, well-wrought and beautiful; in her pierced ears they placed jewelry of gold and mountain-copper; and at her soft throat and her radiant breasts they hung gold necklaces, such as the golden-ribboned Seasons themselves wear when they go to their father's house to dance the sensuous dances of the gods. When they had finished dressing her, they led her to the gods. They were enchanted at the sight, each stretching out his hands to her, each praying that he might take her home to be his wedded bride, breathless in his wonder at her beauty.

Homeric Hymn to Aphrodite, 1–18

On the west coast of Cyprus, the low headland at Paphos shimmers like a mirage in the baking sun. Nothing moves. And yet the air pulsates. It pulsates to the rhythm of dry cicadas' screams as they drill their parched crescendo with increasing fervour through the searing heat in desperation to attract a mate. It pulsates in the rock-cut tombs, and in the theatre's dusty bowl; it pulsates on the empty ancient streets, the crumbling cairns, the heavy palm trees. It pulsates in the rustling vibration of scorched grasses.

It is too hot, too merciless to stay here. Rather, we should drive south, out of modern Paphos with its garish bars and noisy nightclubs, down through the concrete cubes of Yeroskipou until, a little way past Kouklia, we reach the sea. Here, we shall scramble down the sandy dunes to the white-pebbled beach. The sea is turquoise. A lazy swell rolls slowly from the far horizon, curving closer, arcing until – with the softest sigh – its ripples stroke the shore. Only where the stack of rock thrusts unyielding from the waves does the sea foam, frothing and fermenting round the jagged base. It is a hypnotic place, a place of magic. For it was here from this white spume that many Greeks believed the goddess Aphrodite first rose dripping from the waves.

The Birth of Aphrodite
Aphrodite ('Foam-Born'), goddess of desire and sex, was conceived when Cronus castrated Ouranus, his father. The severed genitals fell into the

sea, froth effervesced around them, and Aphrodite first rose, naked and magnificent, standing on a scallop shell. Some said the shell conveyed her first to Cythera off southwest Greece, but, finding the island too insignificant, she continued on to Cyprus. Here she came ashore at the beach now called Petra tou Romiou ('The Greeks' Rocks') near Palaepaphos, a few miles south of modern Paphos. The sixth-century BC poet Anacreon imagined Aphrodite returning here to swim:

> Like a lily in a garland of violets, she shimmered on
> the glassy sea, while on dolphin-back the wily Eros and
> care-free Desire rode the metallic waves, and troupes of
> fish arced, sinuous, beneath the waters, playing with the
> Paphian goddess as she swam.

But Homer knew another account. For him, Aphrodite was born at Dodona in Epirus, the daughter of Zeus and Dione, a local goddess, whose name is simply a form of Zeus' own. During fighting in the *Iliad*, when Aphrodite, her wrist injured, runs to her mother, Dione, for comfort, Zeus advises her: 'War is not your vocation, child! Look to love and marriage, and leave fighting to swift Ares and Athene!'

Two Aphrodites, Two Erotes?
Some Greeks argued that there were in fact two Aphrodites, a notion explored in Plato's *Symposium*, where a lawyer called Pausanias argues that there is a 'Heavenly' Aphrodite, born from the waves, and a 'Common' (or 'Pandemic') Aphrodite, born from Zeus and Dione. 'Heavenly' Aphrodite, born from Cronus' genitals without a mother, inspired pure love and was

The birth of Aphrodite: the goddess
reclines on her scallop shell while
Erotes gambol around her, on a fresco
from Pompeii's 'Casa di Venus'.

Paphos: Garden of Aphrodite

manifested in homosexual desire. 'Common' Aphrodite, being the product of both male and female parents, was responsibile for heterosexual love – and, because this goddess was younger and more immature, Pausanias argued that her form of love was arbitrary and superficial.

A similar duality affected Eros (plural, Erotes), Aphrodite's male companion god of lust. For Hesiod, he was the oldest of all gods, born at the dawn of time, and in mystic Orphism he was the son of Night and Erebus (Darkness). More commonly, however, Eros, with his bow and arrows ready to pierce his victims' hearts with love, was said to be the son of Aphrodite, a young winged cupid, smiling and amoral, the product of his mother's adultery with Ares, god of war.

Aphrodite's Love-Affairs with Gods

Aphrodite was the embodiment of desire. In literature and art she was pictured riding in a golden chariot drawn by sparrows, doves or swans, naked and possessed of powerful eroticism. Only a very few could resist her charms. The fifth-century AD epic poet Nonnus described how Zeus tried to rape her immediately she landed at Paphos. A tenth-century AD Byzantine dictionary maintains that they did sleep together and that their son was the prodigiously endowed fertility god, Priapus. (Still others said that Priapus was the son of Aphrodite and Dionysus.)

To prevent the male gods fighting over Aphrodite, Zeus (or Hera) hastily arranged her marriage to Hephaestus, the lame blacksmith. While he devotedly showered her with gifts of his own making, including a sash which made its wearer (even more) irresistible, Aphrodite embarked on numerous affairs. Among her conquests were Hermes (their child was Hermaphroditus, in whom male and female attributes were combined) and Poseidon. But her most notorious liaison was with Ares, in the *Odyssey* the subject of one of the bard Demodocus' poems.

Seeing Aphrodite and Ares making love, Helios immediately informs Hephaestus. Indignant, Hephaestus sets a trap, an unbreakable net, as thin as gossamer, 'invisible even to the gods', which he drapes around his marriage bed. Then he announces his departure for a lengthy stay in Lemnos (one of his cult centres). Seizing his chance, Ares sneaks into Hephaestus' house, where he takes Aphrodite to bed. But the web closes, holding them fast. Hephaestus returns and bawls in anger. While the goddesses remain at home 'out of shame', the gods are soon jostling and laughing as they watch the two adulterers caught *in flagrante*. Only when Poseidon stands bail for Ares, guaranteeing an end to the affair, does Hephaestus release them – at which Ares immediately retreats to the savage north and 'laughter-loving Aphrodite fled to Paphos'. Some say that Hephaestus soon divorced Aphrodite, enabling her to have two children by Ares: Eros and Harmonia (Harmony).

Others found the story less amusing. Plato uses it to argue that much so-called great literature is immoral, a pernicious influence on impressionable minds. In his ideal state such passages would be censored or, better still, poets banned altogether. After all, the entire *Iliad*, arguably the greatest epic poem, was predicated upon Aphrodite's wantonness: it was thanks to her that Helen left her husband to elope with Paris to Troy.

Aphrodite's Love-Affair with Anchises

Aphrodite had long taken a close interest in Troy – and especially in one of its princes, Anchises, the son of Troy's founder, Ilus. A Homeric Hymn tells how Zeus made her fall in love with Anchises when she saw him herding cattle on Mount Ida:

> As soon as she saw him, laughter-loving Aphrodite felt
> desire for him, and lust took hold of her. So she went
> to her sanctuary at Paphos in Cyprus, its altar sweet
> with incense, and she entered her sweet-perfumed
> temple, pulling the glittering doors fast shut behind
> her. And there the Graces bathed her and anointed her
> with heavenly oil, with which gods cover their immortal
> bodies, sweet heavenly oil, and the air was filled with
> perfume. And laughter-loving Aphrodite dressed in
> her sumptuous clothing and hung herself in gold, and
> hurried off to Troy, leaving Cyprus so fragrant, running
> lightly on the high path of the clouds.

Disguised as a mortal girl, she bewitched Anchises:

> Her dress was brighter than any fire – golden, beautiful
> and intricately woven. It shone at her soft breasts like
> the moon, so wondrous to see! And she wore twisted
> bracelets and glinting earrings shaped like flowers,
> and around her soft throat were exquisite necklaces.

Anchises could not resist. Believing her to be a mortal, he took her to a cave, undressed her and lay with her on the pelts of bears and lions. Only afterwards did Aphrodite admit her true identity, prophesying that she would bear Anchises a son, Aeneas. In the *Iliad*, Aeneas is one of Troy's greatest warriors, and later he became the hero of the Latin epic, Vergil's *Aeneid*, which traced his journey from Trojan refugee to founder of Rome.

Aphrodite warned Anchises that if he revealed what had happened, Zeus would smite him with a thunderbolt. But a Roman mythographer tells that, when drunk, he forgot her warning, boasted of his conquest and was blasted by Zeus – not fatally, but enough to cripple him. Anchises was not Aphrodite's only mortal lover. More famous was Adonis, who (some said) was also born in Paphos.

Aphrodite & Adonis

Myrrha (also known as Smyrna) tricked her own father, Cinyras, king of Paphos, into sleeping with her. When Cinyras discovered what he had done he tried to kill his daughter, but the gods transformed her into a tree, which still weeps drops of myrrh. In time, the tree split open and gave birth to a boy, Adonis. When Aphrodite found him, his beauty overcame her. To hide him from the other gods she placed him in a chest, which she gave for safe-keeping to Persephone. But when Persephone opened it and saw what lay inside, she too became enamoured of Adonis and refused to return him to Aphrodite. The goddesses asked Zeus to arbitrate. He ruled that Adonis should live with each for a third of the year and spend the remaining third with whichever goddess he chose. Adonis chose Aphrodite.

Obsessed with Adonis' aching beauty, Aphrodite even accompanied him on hunting expeditions in the mountains, desperately anxious lest an animal attack and kill him. Repeatedly she begged him to take care. But one day, when he was alone, his hounds surprised a sleeping boar. Triumphantly Adonis tried to skewer it with his javelin, but he only struck a glancing blow. Maddened by pain, the boar sliced Adonis' groin.

As Adonis lay dying, Aphrodite passed overhead in her chariot drawn by swans. Unable to save him, she transformed his blood into a sea of anemones, whose life is short and whose petals fall at the slightest breath of wind. Then, tearing her hair, she laid out his body on a bed of lettuce leaves and mourned him:

> Tender Adonis is dying, my Aphrodite. What are we to
> do? Beat your breasts, and rip your tunics! Weep for him!

When Sappho wrote these lines around the turn of the sixth century BC, Adonis' cult was widespread across the Aegean. Indeed, despite his close association with Paphos, Adonis was probably originally a Near Eastern god of vegetation, perhaps travelling to Greece from Ugarit (in modern Syria), where his name 'Adon' or 'Adonai' meant 'Lord'. In early summer festivals Greek women mourned his death, tending special gardens of fast-growing, fast-dying plants such as lettuce and fennel sown in shallow earthenware pots and left on roof tops to wither in the sun. The emphasis was on death not resurrection, but his cult contained the seeds of hope: just as the infant Adonis stayed with Persephone in Hades for only

As Eros flutters by, a relatively demure Aphrodite
places her hands on the shoulders of her
reclining lover Adonis. (Attic red figure water jar,
c. 450–400 BC.)

a third of the year, so his spirit would return each year to lend his life-giving vitality to nature for the remaining two thirds.

Gardens played an important role in Aphrodite's worship, too. A garden was dedicated to her on the Athenian Acropolis, while just outside Paphos modern Yeroskipou takes its name from the 'Hieros Kēpos' ('Sacred Garden'), which Ovid says contained a tree with 'gold leaves on gold branches'. It was an important staging post in the annual procession from Paphos to Aphrodite's temple at Palaepaphos (modern Kouklia), which culminated in a festival of athletics and the Arts.

Pygmalion, King of Paphos

Adonis' grandfather was Pygmalion, king of Paphos. The Church Father Clement of Alexandria tells how Pygmalion 'fell in love with an ivory statue of Aphrodite', adding disapprovingly, 'which was naked'. Ovid was more expansive: Pygmalion rejected women when the daughers of another king embraced prostitution. Instead, a sculptor, he created a jointed ivory statue of a beautiful young girl and fell in love with it, bringing gifts and caressing it adoringly as if it were alive. At the Festival of Aphrodite, Pygmalion stood at the altar, heady with frankincense, and coyly prayed that he might find a wife as beautiful as his statue.

Aphrodite knew that he really wished to marry the statue itself, and granted his secret desire. When Pygmalion returned home, he threw his arms around his statue and kissed it passionately – and the statue came to life. Blood flowed through its veins; its pale cheeks blushed; and its eyes opened to meet his. After nine crescent moons had swollen to fullness, as Ovid delicately puts it, Pygmalion's new wife bore a son. His name was Paphos, and from him the city took its name.

Paphos in History & Today

A fertility goddess was worshipped on the flat limestone hill at Palaepaphos from the early third millennium BC. Around 1200 BC a temple precinct was constructed with a megalithic sanctuary wall adorned with horns of consecration and containing a pillared hall and altar. In the *Odyssey*, after her encounter with Ares, Aphrodite flees to this 'sweet-scented altar', where the Graces bathe her, 'anointing her with that immortal oil which glistens on the deathless gods, and clothing her in a beautiful dress'.

Other temples of Aphrodite contained seductive statues of the goddess as a beautiful naked woman, but at Palaepaphos she was worshipped in the form of a conical white stone. (Curiously, the corresponding stone in the local museum is black.) In the first century AD after earthquake damage the sanctuary was rebuilt on a larger scale, incorporating the Bronze Age complex, but now with banqueting rooms with lavish mosaics.

Aphrodite's worship involved sex. Sacred prostitutes served at her shrine and Herodotus even hints that it was a rite of passage for every freeborn woman to prostitute herself at her temple. Describing 'the most sordid of Babylonian customs', he writes how, wearing rope headbands, the women sat in the sanctuary in rows, while men walked up and down to make their choice. No woman could leave until she had 'discharged her duty to the goddess', so, while 'those who are tall and beautiful soon leave, the less attractive ... sometimes have to stay for three or four years. There is a similar custom in some parts of Cyprus.' He probably means at Paphos.

In 498 BC the Persians and Greeks fought for control of Cyprus and Palaepaphos was besieged. Archaeology confirms the scale of operations. Huge earthworks were thrown up against the two-hundred-year-old city walls; siege engines were deployed; and although the Palaepaphians dug tunnels underneath the Persians' positions with the aim of toppling their towers, they could not save their city. The Persian siege ramp was so massive that, when new walls were built more than a century later, it was incorporated into them.

Palaepaphos remained an important cult centre, but the city that sprang up around it was eclipsed by a new settlement (modern Paphos) on the coast 12 km (8 miles) to the north, probably founded by Ptolemy I of Egypt in 294 BC. Pausanias placed its first foundation earlier, when ships of the Arcadian king Agapenor were blown off course after the Trojan War. In an enviable position, it had a fine harbour and well-protected acropolis. A rich necropolis dating from the third century BC to the fourth century AD (wrongly named the 'Tombs of the Kings') attests to its wealth: underground tombs are arranged like rooms of the living around central courtyards, their porticos supported by fine Doric columns.

In 58 BC Cyprus passed to Rome. It was a time of great prosperity. Now the island's capital, Paphos basked in its wealth, and many fine mosaics were laid down. As a seat of both temporal power and pagan religion, Paphos attracted the Christian preacher Paul. His visit in AD 45 included an audience with the Roman governor, Sergius Paulus, and a contretemps with a local priest. Acts of the Apostles records how Paul dealt with both, beginning with the priest (or sorcerer in the King James version):

> Then Saul, who is also called Paul, filled with the Holy Ghost, set his eyes on him. And said, O full of all subtlety and all mischief, thou child of the devil, thou enemy of all righteousness, wilt thou not cease to pervert the right ways of the Lord? And now, behold, the hand of the Lord is upon thee, and thou shalt be blind, not seeing the sun for a season. And immediately there fell on him a mist and a darkness; and he went about seeking some to lead him by the hand. Then the deputy, when he saw what was done, believed, being astonished at the doctrine of the Lord.

Local tradition suggests that Paul's success in converting the Roman governor (or 'deputy') came at a price. In the grounds of the twelfth-century church of Agia Kyriaki in Paphos is a pillar, tied to which (it is said) Paul received thirty-nine lashes of the whip in punishment for his aggressive proselytizing.

Paphos thrived until the fourth century AD, when severe earthquake damage and the banning of pagan religions by the Roman emperor Theodosius curtailed much of its economic and religious power. A Saracen raid in 653 dealt the final blow. The town remained a quiet haven until 1983, when the opening of Paphos International Airport precipitated a surge in tourism. Now, in part because many Cypriotes have family in north London, it is as common to hear English spoken as it is Greek.

SOME IMPORTANT DATES & REMAINS

c. 2800 BC	First signs of worship at Palaepaphos.
c. 1200 BC	First temple precinct at Palaepaphos.
498 BC	Persian siege of Palaepaphos.
c. 340 BC	New city walls built at Palaepaphos.
? 294 BC	Ptolemy I Soter of Egypt relocates city to Paphos?
58 BC	Rome takes possession of Cyprus.
AD 45	Paul visits Paphos.
AD 653	Saracens raid Paphos.
AD 1983	Opening of Paphos International Airport.

Paphos is a UNESCO World Cultural Heritage Site. The Archaeological Park embraces not only the evocatively melancholic **Tombs of the Kings** but also a large swathe of the Hellenistic and Roman town including its **Agora** and a fine **Odeon** nestling beneath the modern lighthouse.

The chief delights are the fine third- to fifth-century AD **Roman mosaics**, displayed *in situ* in villas. Many show scenes from mythology, including such legendary lovers as Zeus and Ganymede, Phaedra and Hippolytus, Peleus and Thetis – and Narcissus. Paphos' **Archaeological Museum** houses finds from the Neolithic, Classical and Byzantine periods, including **tombstones, sarcophagi** and a marble **bust of Aphrodite.**

Palaepaphos, 12 km (8 miles) south of Paphos in Kouklia, is easily accessible by road. Little remains of the **Sanctuary of Aphrodite,** save a replica of a **mosaic** showing **Leda and the Swan.** Kouklia Museum in a restored Crusader manor house contains a black **aniconic stone,** perhaps worshipped as Aphrodite. Beside the road out of Kouklia are the impressive remains of the Persians' earthworks and Paphian tunnels from the siege of 498 BC. A few miles further on, Petra tou Romiou has a pebble beach, impressive rock formations and refreshment facilities. Although it may be tempting to rise like Aphrodite from the waves, beware of strong currents.

Travellers wishing to experience more archaeology should continue east to Curium with its impressive **theatre** and **Temple of Apollo.** Two less historically sound, yet nonetheless evocative sites lie north of Paphos. In Kili the so-called **Baths of Adonis,** complete with waterfall and pool, boast a statue of Aphrodite and Adonis and promise fertility to women who touch Adonis' phallus. At the **Baths of Aphrodite** further north near the coast at Latchi a sign proclaims: 'Aphrodite, goddess of love and beauty, used to bathe in the small pool of this natural grotto ... Please do not swim.'

Pylos: Where Nestor Ruled & Hermes Hid the Cattle of Apollo

Helios the sun-god left his limpid pool and rose into the brazen
sky to bring daylight to gods and mortal men across the fertile
plough-lands. And so they came to Pylos, the well-built citadel of
Neleus. Here on the beach the people were all making sacrifice,
slaughtering black bulls to Poseidon, the dark-haired shaker of the
earth. They were seated in nine companies, five hundred men
in each, and each company had nine bulls. When the men of Pylos
had tasted the entrails and were burning the thigh pieces for the god,
the others quickly put in to shore, hauled up and furled their fine
ship's sail, let down the anchor-stone and disembarked. Telemachus,
too, disembarked, and with him went Athene.

Homer, *Odyssey*, 3.1–12

Noontide, and the molten sun hangs in a cloudless sky. Insects murmur drowsily in dry air, aromatic with the woody scent of shrubs and arid grasses. Their high-pitched voices throb in counterpoint to the rhythm of the waves as they lap and fizzle far below. Beyond the lagoon with its scrubby sandbars, haze shimmers on the sheltered bay of Navarino, its mouth almost enclosed by the rocky spine of the waterless, long, narrow island of Sphacteria. In the distance modern Pylos is an exuberance of pretty houses, its town square bounded on one side by a sheltered harbour – café chairs and tables in the shade of leafy trees; yellow nets laid out to dry; lolling boats; and shoals of tiny fishes gliding in clear glassy water.

Despite the breadth of the horizon, with its pale blue mountains, patchwork farmland and the coastline stretching north beside the gentle swelling sea, a nearer bay demands the eye. Its narrow entrance flanked by steep-curved hills, it is a perfect horseshoe of turquoise water, soft white sand, and lilies flowering in the sand dunes. It is perhaps the most idyllic beach in all of Greece. On its western headland, Coryphasion, below the crumbling grey walls and squat square towers of a Venetian castle, is a portal to an ancient past – a cave where stalactites hang like red and rusty oxhides from the high roof. For it was here (so legend tells) above the cove (where Nestor's men of Pylos once made sacrifice and which today the Greeks call Voidhokiliá, Ox-belly Bay), that the newborn Hermes hid the stolen cattle of Apollo.

The Birth & Babyhood of Hermes

The Homeric Hymn to Hermes tells how, like so many other gods and heroes, Hermes was the result of one of Zeus' extramarital liaisons. Smitten by dark-eyed Maia, a nymph with magnificent hair, who lived in a cave on Mount Cyllene on the borders of Arcadia, Zeus 'joined with her in the dark of night, while pale-armed Hera slept'. The Hymn catalogues some of Hermes' many attributes:

> shifty, wily, thieving, a cattle driver, a dream-bringer, a watcher in the night, a thief beside the doors, he would soon show his famous deeds to the undying gods. Born at the dawn, by noon he was master of the lyre, and in the evening he stole the cattle of Apollo, who shoots from afar.

Within hours of being born Hermes had already leapt from his cradle, discovered a tortoise munching outside by the cave mouth, killed it (the description in the Hymn is gruesome) and used its shell as the basis of an instrument of his own invention – the lyre – to the accompaniment of which he sang of his own conception and birth. However, such entertainment was insufficient for the hours-old trickster god. His exertions had brought on an appetite. To assuage it Hermes turned cattle-rustler.

Pylos & the Cattle of Apollo

He headed to Pieria, where the gods pastured their cattle. Picking fifty of the finest beasts, he drove them swiftly south, making them walk backwards so that their tracks led not from but towards Pieria. But before he did so he contrived a plan to baffle any searchers even more: to mask his footprints, he made the first pair of sandals by plaiting together sprigs of tamarisk and myrtle.

'Across dark mountains, through valleys loud with gusting winds and over flowering meadows' Hermes drove the cattle until near dawn he reached Pylos. But the location of this Pylos was the subject of debate. The Hymn places it by the River Alpheus near Olympia – where there was once a coastal settlement called Pylos. But the same Hymn tells how, having slaughtered and cooked two of the cattle (with the help of his newly invented fire-stick), Hermes: 'spread their hides across the adamantine rock, where they still remain so many ages later'. Many saw this as a reference to the hide-like stalactites in the cave at Voidhokiliá, and in later tradition this Pylos won out.

Replete, Hermes returned to his cradle on Cyllene, 'slipping sideways through the closed door like late-summer mist'. But it was not long before the clear-seeing Apollo discovered his cattle hidden in the cave and tracked down Hermes. Despite the infant's protestations, Apollo commanded Hermes and Maia to accompany him to Mount Olympus, where both parties put their case before the gods. Naturally, Zeus could not be deceived and he ordered Hermes to return the cattle to Apollo.

Together the two adversaries returned to Pylos, where Apollo first liberated his cattle then tried to tether Hermes with withies. Hermes had other ideas. He caused the withies to take root, sprout and encircle the cattle; then, strumming his lyre, he sang a long bewitching song about the birth of the gods and the creation of the earth. Apollo was enchanted and proposed a settlement: if Hermes gave him the lyre and taught him to play it, Apollo would overlook the theft and champion the newborn god, making him master over flocks, herds and pasturelands. He would also give Hermes the *kerykeion* (or herald's staff, also known by its Latin name, *caduceus*). The Hymn describes it as a 'three-branched' magic golden wand, but it is usually depicted as a rod around which two snakes intertwine, and occasionally tipped with outstretched wings. Hermes could not refuse. So at Pylos the two gods were reconciled and forged a tight-bound friendship.

Hermes' Other Attributes

As well as being associated with the countryside (where he could be heard playing another of his inventions, shepherds' pipes), as the archetypal thief and liar Hermes was also linked with trade and commerce, where his trickery and cunning served him well. Counter-intuitively (given his contempt for the truth) but unavoidably (given his possession of the *kerykeion*), Hermes also became Zeus' trusted messenger. In the course of his duties, he helped invent that great aid to communication: writing. As Zeus' messenger he was the patron of mortal heralds, too, identified in art by his broad-brimmed sun hat and winged sandals. And because his duties involved so many journeys, Hermes was the god of travellers.

The journeys over which Hermes presided were not only physical. As Psychopompus (Conductor of Souls) Hermes accompanied the spirits of the dead to Hades, while as Oneiropompus (Conductor of Dreams) he sowed true or lying visions in the minds of those whom he lulled to sleep with his staff. Hence Hermes, god of ghosts, became associated with magic and necromancy. Especially in Hellenistic Egypt, the long-lasting cult of Hermes Trismegistus became popular with mystics.

Many Greek gods embodied opposites. Thus Hermes was god of both theft and security. Guard dogs were under his protection, and throughout antiquity statues of Hermes known as *hermai* (herms) stood at house doors to ward off evildoers. These were simple four-square pillars sometimes topped by the god's bearded head but always adorned with his erect phallus. When almost all Athens' *hermai* were smashed on the eve of an expedition against Sicily in 415 BC, it was interpreted (correctly) as a bad omen. Since a safe house is a happy house, Hermes presided, too, over banquets such as Nestor's on the beach at Voidhokiliá. In fact, whenever a sudden silence fell over a roomful of banqueters, it was commonplace for someone to observe: 'Hermes has entered the room'.

Nestor, King of Pylos

In Homeric epic Pylos is ruled by the wise (if garrulous) old Nestor. In the *Iliad* he is:

> the sweet-voiced, clear-tongued speaker of the Pylians,
> whose voice, when he spoke, was sweeter than honey.
> Already two generations of men, born and raised with
> him in sacred Pylos, had withered in his lifetime and now
> he ruled over a third.

As a youth, Nestor had taken part in many adventures, joining both the boar hunt at Calydon and the voyage of the *Argo* from Iolcus, his father Neleus' childhood home. After quarrelling with his brother Pelias, Neleus left Iolcus and settled as king in Pylos, where he fathered twelve sons. However, he took the wrong side in a war between Heracles and Elis (near Olympia). In retribution, Heracles sacked Pylos and killed Neleus' sons – all except Nestor, who was living in nearby Gerania (hence his Homeric epithet 'Geranian'). When the dust settled, Heracles befriended Nestor and made him king of Messene.

Weakened but unbowed, Neleus continued to rule Pylos. Responding to the theft of a chariot, which he had sent to the Olympic Games, he requested Nestor to conduct a cattle-raid across the border into Elis. In the *Iliad*, Nestor describes how he and his men drove off

> fifty herds of cattle, the same number of sheep, the same
> of pigs, the same of roaming goats, and a hundred and
> fifty chestnut horses, each one of them a mare, and many
> with a foal beneath her, suckling. At night we drove them
> inside Neleus' city, Pylos.

The Elians responded by crossing the River Alpheus into Neleus' territory. Nestor led his army out to meet them. First blood was his. He leapt into his victim's chariot:

> and took my place in the front rank.... Then, like a black
> storm cloud, I charged. I brought down fifty chariots,
> and for each chariot two men bit the dust, felled by my
> spear.... Into the hands of Pylian men Zeus put great
> strength. Across the vast plain we pursued them, killing
> them and stripping their bodies of their armour.... And
> all praised Zeus among the gods; but among men they
> praised Nestor.

Nestor was not just a fine warrior. He was an athlete, too. On another occasion he describes how he took part in funeral games, winning contests in boxing, wrestling, racing and javelin. Only in the chariot race was he defeated. 'Thus I was once. But now younger men must face such challenges and I must yield to harsh old age, though once I ranked among the greatest of the heroes.'

Succeeding Neleus as king of Pylos, Nestor took part in the Trojan War, where he enjoyed his role as elder statesman. Despite his old age he was still keen to fight – Pindar describes how, when one of his horses was shot down, Nestor was marooned in his chariot; as Troy's Ethiopian ally Memnon bore down on him, Nestor's son Antilochus stepped between them, sacrificing his life for his father. However, it was for his counsel (usually given at some length and not always the best) that Nestor was

A fresco from the palace at Pylos dating from the
thirteenth century BC shows a battle raging across a river
between helmeted warriors and light-armed soldiers.

held in highest esteem. Agamemnon declared that with ten such advisors Troy would 'soon fall to our hands, taken and destroyed'. Nestor was one of the few Greek commanders to return safely home from Troy and enjoy prosperity.

Telemachus at Pylos

Not so Odysseus of Ithaca. When he was still missing ten years after the war ended, his son Telemachus sought news of him from his surviving comrades. His first port of call was Pylos, where he found Nestor and his followers feasting on the beach. Once Nestor learned Telemachus' identity, he unleashed a stream of reminiscences of the Trojan War and the murder of Agamemnon at Mycenae, and of his own homecoming ('the wind did not fail us once, but a god caused it to blow'). Then he invited Telemachus to his palace:

> The Geranian horseman Nestor led his sons and his
> sons-in-law back to his beautiful palace. When they
> reached the shining royal palace, they sat down in
> order on couches and thrones. As they came, the old
> man mixed wine in a mixing bowl, ten years old and
> sweet to taste, which the housekeeper had opened, and
> undone the fastening.... When they had drunk to their
> satisfaction, each man went home to sleep, but the
> Geranian horseman Nestor told godlike Odysseus' dear
> son Telemachus to sleep on a corded bedstead beneath
> the echoing portico.

Next day, Nestor arranged for his youngest daughter to bathe Telemachus and anoint him with oils before providing him with a chariot and charioteer (his own son, Peisistratus) and sending him off on the next leg of his quest to Sparta and the court of Menelaus.

These descriptions are particularly evocative in the light of the discovery of a Bronze Age palace inland from Voidhokiliá near modern Chora. Excavations begun by Carl Blegen in 1939 revealed an unprecedentedly large cache of Linear B tablets, which confirmed that its Bronze Age name was Pylos. They also brought to light a well-appointed megaron (central hall), its walls adorned by fine frescoes – and a painted bath (which the romantically inclined believe to be the very bath in which Telemachus was bathed).

Pylos in History & Today

In antiquity at least two other sites (further north on the west coast of the Peloponnese) were associated with Nestor's palace. One, close to the

River Alpheus and Elis, accords well with geographical references in the *Iliad* and the Homeric Hymn to Hermes, mentioned above. However, since Blegen's discovery of the palace at Chora, with Linear B tablets identifying it as Pylos, this is now accepted as the site. Today it is sign-posted: 'Nestor's Palace'.

Occupied from around 1700 BC, the palace formed the nucleus of a walled city, itself the centre of a much wider community (with over 50,000 inhabitants). Linear B tablets reveal a highly regulated state administered by civil servants, who kept close watch on details such as the size of sheep flocks, the quantity of vines and fig trees on royal estates (there were a thousand of each) and the number of broken wheels awaiting repair. Industry, including perfume manufacture, was conducted close to the palace. Meanwhile, frescoes from the palace show scenes from nature, both real and imagined (including deer, dogs, lions and griffins), as well as two whose subject matter reflects myths associated with Pylos: on one a young man plays a lyre; on another a battle rages across a river.

The tablets also provide tantalizing glimpses of Pylos' religious life. Although no religious texts survive (probably none existed), there are apparent references to offerings made to Potnia (the mother goddess), Zeus, Hera, Poseidon – and Hermes. In addition, royal tholos tombs were found both near the palace (containing a staggering amount of gold and gold leaf) and at Voidhokiliá. Pottery sherds from the cave at Voidhokiliá suggest it was a Bronze Age cult centre.

Pylos was overrun around 1200 BC. In Classical times the region of Messene, to which it belonged, was annexed by Sparta and its inhabitants enslaved. In 425 BC, during the Peloponnesian War, the Athenian general Demosthenes occupied and fortified Coryphasion, reasoning that it would provide an excellent base from which to attack Spartan territory and rally disaffected slaves. The Spartans responded, besieging Coryphasion by land and stationing troops on the adjacent (waterless) island of Sphacteria. When the Athenian navy cut them off, the Spartans surrendered for the first time in their history, and 120 elite Spartiates became prisoners-of-war.

In AD 1827 the joint fleet of Great Britain, France and Russia, charged with ensuring the withdrawal of the Ottoman Turks from the Peloponnese, sailed into Navarino Bay. When the Ottoman general Ibrahim Pasha resisted, allied gunboats opened fire. Fifty-three Turkish ships were sunk, many of whose wrecks can still be seen today. Five years later, Greece won her independence.

Pylos

SOME IMPORTANT DATES & REMAINS

c. 5000 BC	Neolithic settlement at Voidhokiliá.
c. 1700 BC	Foundation of 'Nestor's Palace'.
c. 1200 BC	Destruction of 'Nestor's Palace'.
425 BC	Athenians capture Coryphasion and defeat Spartans on Sphacteria.
AD 1204	Crusaders capture Pylos during Fourth Crusade.
AD 1572	Turks capture Pylos and build Neokastro fortress.
AD 1827	Ottoman Turks defeated at Battle of Navarino.
AD 1939	Carl Blegen first excavates 'Nestor's Palace'.

'Nestor's Palace' is 18 km (11 miles) northeast of modern Pylos near the village of Chora. The site is covered by an unattractive roof, and at the time of writing it was closed for renovation. From the site entrance the route passes through a *propylon* (antechamber). Left is the **Archive Room**, where most of the Linear B tablets were discovered. Through the *propylon* is a **courtyard**. This leads through a series of antechambers to the **megaron**, with a central circular **hearth**, 4 m (13 ft) in diameter, and the bases of four columns, which originally supported an upper gallery. Corridors lead from antechambers to **storage rooms** and (right) the **bathroom**, complete with terracotta bath and the jugs with which to fill it. Southwest are the remains of an earlier palace (mostly covered over), while northeast are workshops, wine cellars and a (reconstructed) **tholos** tomb.

Voidhokiliá lies across the Bay of Navarino from Pylos, adjacent to the lagoon of the Voidhokiliá Wetland Reserve. A rough track leads from the Pylos-Kyparissia road. The **cave** is at the far side of the bay on the slopes of Coryphasion. Above (the climb is strenuous) is the Venetian castle of Palaikastro on the site of Demosthenes' fifth-century BC **fortifications**. On the nearer headland (hard to find) is a **tholos** tomb. The white-sanded beach affords good bathing.

There is a small **museum** in Pylos, but most of the finds from 'Nestor's Palace' and the surrounding area that are not in Athens' National Archaeological Museum are in **Chora** museum 4 km (2½ miles) north of the palace. These include **frescoes**, **gold jewelry** and **Linear B tablets**. At the time of writing this museum was closed for renovation.

9

Olympia: Pelops
& the Games

[Pelops] is honoured in glorious offerings of blood at his
tomb by the crossing of the Alpheus, a place of pilgrimage by
the altar where strangers throng past number. The fame of the
Olympic Games – of Pelops' games – blazes over all the
broad-backed earth. Whoever triumphs here wins for his
life a honeyed calm.

Pindar, *Olympian Ode 1*, 90–99

On the Hill of Cronus, trees are washed in golden sunlight. Already the mist, which had blanketed the patchwork fields beside the River Alpheus at dawn, has dissipated, leaving nothing but an incorporeal haze. In the village – a snatch of music blaring from an open window; a barking dog; an engine spluttering to life – metal window grilles are being wound up, shop doors propped open, tables set on narrow pavements, heady coffee brewed.

Along the road, across the bridge, where the lazy River Cladeus glides between rushes, the sanctuary is stirring too. Tall pines resonate with the twittering of sparrows and the cicadas' chirr. On a statue base a gecko, basking in the dry heat, greets the day, while across the aromatic earth, shadows of tall columns roll in elongated ranks across the ground as ancient shrines awaken to the sun – the Temple of Hera, the Temple of Zeus, and other lesser buildings, too: treasuries; gymnasia; a fountain house; a Hellenistic luxury hotel. Through the elegant arched tunnel early autumn cyclamen are flowering, studded jewels of pink and white, on the stadium's embankments. Perhaps more than at any other site in Greece, nature and the work of man seem to exist in harmony here in this most magical of places, named from the greatest god of all, Olympian Zeus: Olympia.

Zeus' Victory at Olympia

Many myths accounted for Olympia's importance, but none agreed. However, for the 'learned antiquaries of Elis' (the city which administered Olympia) it was clear why the site held such significance: this was where Zeus defeated his father Cronus to become the king of heaven. But to the traveller Pausanias' dismay even the Elians crossed swords:

> Some maintain that it was here that Zeus wrestled with
> Cronus for the kingdom; others that Zeus held games
> here in celebration of that victory. They say that the list of
> champions included Apollo, who defeated both Hermes
> at running and Ares at boxing.

Nevertheless their explanations united two key elements which made historical Olympia so important: the worship of Zeus and the Olympic Games. More, the suggestion that the Games celebrated Zeus' defeat of Cronus not in battle but in the (slightly) more civilized sphere of sport allowed the vanquished Cronus to be worshipped at Olympia. Pausanias wrote that every spring equinox, at the Elean new year, so-called King-Priests climbed the wooded slopes above Olympia and sacrificed to Cronus on the summit of the hill which bore his name: the Hill of Cronus.

At Elis, Pausanias heard another foundation myth for the Games with a rather more tenuous link to Zeus. It told how, on Mount Ida in Crete, the young Zeus was entertained by Curetes or Dactyls, young male gods who staged footraces, with olive crowns awarded to the winners. The eldest of the Curetes, whose name (like that of the great hero) was Heracles, subsequently introduced the footrace into mainland Greece, where it formed the basis of the Olympic Games, held – because there were five Curetes – every fifth year (Greeks counted inclusively).

Pelops & the Fatal Chariot Race

For others the Games had more bloody origins. Zeus' grandson Pelops was originally from Lydia. His father Tantalus was so loved by the gods that he regularly dined with them. But this was not enough for Tantalus.

With Hippodameia standing in his chariot, Pelops, his head crowned with the victor's olive wreath, guides his chariot team. (Fifth-century BC Attic red figure vase.)

Begrudging the fact that, while he ate meat, the gods feasted on ambrosia and nectar, he contrived an unpalatable trick. He killed young Pelops, cut him up and served him to the gods in a well-seasoned stew. Only Demeter was deceived. Mourning the abduction of Persephone, she nibbled on a portion of shoulder. The others, furious at Tantalus, condemned him to eternal thirst and hunger. As for Pelops, the gods wiped the sauce from the gobbets of his flesh and reassembled him – all bar the shoulder that Demeter had consumed. This they replaced with an ivory prosthesis. Reanimated, Pelops was so handsome that Poseidon fell in love with him and taught him to be an accomplished charioteer, a skill which soon stood him in good stead.

Word reached Pelops of a beautiful princess, Hippodameia. Terrified by a prophecy that his son-in-law would kill him, her father King Oenomaeus of Elis was challenging any who sought her hand to a chariot race. One by one the suitors were defeated and eighteen grinning heads, impaled on stakes, adorned King Oenomaeus' palace. Pelops was determined not to join them. Poseidon had given him a team of swift winged horses, but still Pelops was reluctant to take chances. So, with Hippodameia's agreement, he bribed her father's chariot-technician Myrtilus, offering to share with him not just the kingdom but also Hippodameia's bed if he replaced Oenomaeus' metal lynchpins with counterfeits made from beeswax. Enthusiastically Myrtilus agreed. As Pelops and Oenomaeus raced ever faster, the heat from the wheels' spinning caused the wax to melt. The wheels flew off, the chariot collapsed, and Oenomaeus' horses dragged him to his death.

Predictably, Pelops refused to honour his side of the bargain. Instead, he threw Myrtilus into the sea. As he fell from the high cliff, Myrtilus cursed Pelops and his family, setting in motion a cycle of misery that would haunt them in later generations. Too late, Pelops recovered Myrtilus' remains and buried them at Olympia, where, to placate Oenomaeus' angry ghost, he held athletic games in the dead king's honour, the forerunner of the Olympics. Meanwhile, Hippodameia gave thanks to Hera (goddess of marriage) by inaugurating the *Heraia*, a women's festival which included a footrace.

The Games of Heracles

Citing another explanation for the Games' origins, Pindar says they were founded by the Greek hero Heracles. King Augeas of Elis refused to pay Heracles his agreed fee for cleaning out his stables. In response Heracles killed the king's nephews Cteatus and Eurytus (often shown in art as conjoined twins). Full-scale war ensued, which ended only when Heracles defeated Augeas, occupied his land, and, to mark his victory inaugurated the Olympic Games in Zeus' honour:

measuring out the sacred grove on behalf of his peerless father. He fixed the boundaries of the Altis [the Olympic sanctuary], separating sacred from profane, and designating all the space around it as an area in which to rest and feast. Besides the twelve ruling gods, he paid honour to the River Alpheus; and he named the hill the 'Hill of Cronus' – before, when Oenomaeus ruled, it had been nameless, thick with snow.

Pindar describes these first games, listing victors in contests such as wrestling, chariot-racing and the discus, while Pausanias records that attendees had another cause for gratitude to Heracles:

According to legend, when he was sacrificing at Olympia, Heracles was plagued by clouds of flies. So, either because the idea came to him himself or because someone else suggested it, he sacrificed to Zeus Apomuios [Zeus Who Banishes Flies], and so the flies were banished to the other side of the Alpheus. They say that, following his example, the Eleans sacrifice to Zeus Apomuios to drive flies away from Olympia.

Olympia in History & Today

The first historical Olympic Games were the earliest event to which Greeks confidently assigned a date – the year equivalent to our 776 BC. Revealing yet another foundation myth, Pausanias writes that at this time the Delphic oracle advised King Iphitus of Elis to put an end to a rash of wars and plagues by renewing the Olympic Games, which had been long abandoned. For the next fifty-two years of their existence the only contest was the '*stade*' footrace (the origin of our word 'stadium'), a dash of approximately two hundred yards. The focus of the first Olympics was on religion, not athletics, and even when they were enlarged to cover five days, ritual dominated the pivotal third day, coinciding with the August full moon. A night-time ceremony at Pelops' grave mound was followed next morning by the sacrifice of a hundred oxen to Zeus, with footraces run that afternoon.

Held every four years at a rural sanctuary far from any city, the early Olympics were essentially a local festival. Records suggest that the first victors came exclusively from Elis. As more events were added, however, and the renown of the Games increased, ever larger numbers of athletes from throughout the Greek world strove to compete, until by the sixth century BC the Olympics were a panhellenic festival, whose participants were protected by a ritual truce. However, participation

Four bearded adults and a youth
sprint naked on an amphora awarded
to the winner of the Panathenaic
stade race, *c.* 530 BC.

was restricted. Competitors and audience had to be Greek-speakers, free from blood-guilt and male. (The *Heraia*, a separate festival, was held for women.)

By the early sixth century BC the programme was enlarged to include boxing, wrestling and the pentathlon, as well as equestrian events: horse- and chariot-racing. The sanctuary, too, was enhanced. The Temple of Hera, first built in wood in 700 BC, was gradually restored in stone, and in the fifth century BC the magnificent Temple of Olympian Zeus was constructed in marble, paid for from the spoils of Elis' victory over its neighbour, Pisa. With sculptures featuring characters from each of Olympia's prehistoric foundation myths (Zeus, Pelops and Heracles), the building housed a seated statue of Zeus 12 m (40 ft) tall and faced in gold and ivory. Constructed by Pheidias, it was one of the seven wonders of the ancient world. As the Roman philosopher Epictetus remarked: 'You journey to Olympia to gaze on the statue of Zeus and every one of you would think it a great misfortune to die never having seen it.'

With vast numbers flocking to the Games, living conditions during the festival could be difficult. Epictetus complained about 'the cacophony, the din, the jostling, the shoving, the crowding', asking: 'Are you not burned by the sun? Are you not squashed by the crowds? Can you get clean? Don't you get drenched by the rains? Don't you have to endure noise and tumult and all the other unpleasantness?' He concluded nonetheless: 'I think that you are happy to put up with all of this when you think of the splendour of the spectacles.'

The festival afforded opportunities not just to athletes. Near the Temple of Hera, a row of treasuries proclaimed the wealth of (primarily) Doric cities. Individuals preened too. Draped in a cloak embroidered in gold letters with his name, the artist Zeuxis advertised his wares; Herodotus read from his *Histories* in the west portico of the Temple of Olympian Zeus; and the philosopher Hippias of Elis, who produced the first victors' lists, paraded his skills in rhetoric and metalwork. Sculptors vied for commissions to create statues of winning athletes and chariot teams, and politicians, too, exploited the Games. In 416 BC the Athenian Alcibiades entered seven chariot teams, coming first, second and fourth (or third in some sources) before entertaining every spectator at a banquet provided at his own expense. After his victory at Chaeronea in 338 BC, Philip II of Macedon erected a round temple in honour of himself and his family; and in AD 67 Nero was crowned victor in the chariot race despite falling from his chariot, being helped back in and still failing to complete the course.

Olympia's wealth made it vulnerable. It was attacked by the Heruli in AD 267 and sacked by Alaric the Goth in 397. By then many of its treasures had already been carried west to Rome. Even the statue of Zeus was gone. An attempt to move it in around AD 40 had failed – workmen were frightened off when it emitted unearthly groans – but in 390 it was dismantled and shipped to Constantinople, where it provided inspiration to Christian icon painters wishing to represent the face of God.

Despite the outlawing of pagan practices in 391, the Games may have continued until 425. Stripped of its festival, Olympia was nothing. In 522 and 551 earthquakes toppled its temples. In the following centuries the River Alpheus changed its course, silting up the site to such an extent that by the eighteenth century its location was unknown. In 1766 the English antiquary Richard Chandler rediscovered it; initial excavations were begun in 1829, and in 1875 the German School of Archaeology began a thorough survey. But it was only in 2008 that the site of the hippodrome was discovered.

In 1896 the Frenchman Baron de Coubertin inaugurated the modern Olympic Games held not at Olympia but in Athens and inspired by the combined ethos of the ancient festival and the English public school. Now staged in venues across the world, the Games are heralded by a ceremony in which characters clad in pseudo-Classical garb light a torch in front of the Temple of Hera at Olympia. Without ancient pedigree, this ritual was invented by the cinematographer Leni Riefenstahl to enhance her film glorifying the 1936 Berlin Olympics under Adolf Hitler.

Olympia

SOME IMPORTANT DATES & REMAINS

C10th BC	Evidence of burnt offerings.
776 BC	Traditional date of first Olympic Games.
700 BC	Temple of Hera built (in wood).
458 BC	Temple of Zeus completed.
430 BC	Statue of Zeus completed.
416 BC	Alcibiades enters seven chariots.
c. **338 BC**	Philippeion built.
AD 67	Games postponed from AD 65 to allow Nero to compete (and win).
AD 267	Heruli attack Olympia.
AD 397	Goths attack Olympia.
AD 425 ?	Last Olympic Games
AD 1766	Richard Chandler rediscovers Olympia
AD 1896	Baron de Coubertin launches modern Olympic Games (in Athens).

Being flat, leafy and large enough to absorb crowds, Olympia affords a pleasant visit. From the entrance, a path leading to the Altis (sanctuary) passes the **palaestra** (gymnasium) (right) and the **prytaneum** (administration building) (left) before reaching the partially restored **Philippeion**. From here it is best to take a clockwise route past (left) the **Temple of Hera** and the **exedra** (fountain) **of Herodes Atticus**, and (right) the sites of **Pelops' grave mound** and the **Altar of Zeus**. Next are the **treasuries** (left on the rise) and vaulted passage into the **stadium**. Continuing clockwise the **Stoa of Echoes** (where trumpeting competitions were held from Hellenistic times) is on the left. Further on are the remains of **Nero's villa** near the **bouleuterion** (Council Chamber, where athletes swore an oath to compete fairly). Close by, too, are the remains of the **Temple of Olympian Zeus** and a pillar once surmounted by a statue of Victory by Paionios. Further on is (left) the **Leonidaeum** (a late fourth-century BC hotel) and (right) the **workshop of Pheidias**, whose dimensions exactly replicate those of the *cella* of the Temple of Zeus and where the sculptor and his team worked on the statue. Later converted into a church, when excavated it yielded a cup inscribed, 'I belong to Pheidias'.

Highlights of Olympia's **Archaeological Museum** include **sculptures from the Temple of Zeus** (pediments showing Pelops, Zeus and Apollo; metopes showing the Labours of Heracles); the **Victory of Paionios**; a fifth-century BC terracotta of **Zeus and Ganymede**; the **helmet of Miltiades** dedicated after the Battle of Marathon in 490 BC; and a Roman marble copy of a bronze statue of **Hermes** by Praxiteles.

Thebes: City of Dionysus, Oedipus & Heracles

Shafts of bright sunrise, more beautiful than any which bathed seven-
gated Thebes before! Gold daybreak, dawning, blazing over Dirce's
streams – you watched the Argive army turn and flee, their white
shields, armour, bridles glittering! ... Victory has smiled on Thebes
and her war-chariots, rejoicing with us in our victory, now we have
put an end to fighting, put it all behind us! Let's visit all the temples,
singing, dancing, all night long! And, as he pounds the Theban soil in
his ecstatic dance, may Dionysus be our leader!

Sophocles, *Antigone*, 100–09, 147–54

Visit Thebes with low expectations and you may yet be disappointed. Little remains of the once-powerful ancient city. Instead, a provincial agricultural town leaches unappealingly across steep ridges where palaces once stood, as peeling whitewashed houses with dusty orange roof-tiles spill down the gulleys in a grid of urban sprawl, a merciless confusion of narrow one-way streets.

Occasionally, though, you stumble blissfully across a pocket of history hidden in an unexpected corner – the overgrown foundations of an ancient gate; the traces of a Bronze Age palace; or here, on a wooded rise above the huddled houses, the remains of the temple of Apollo Ismenus. Climb the hill and stand among the pine trees as the warm sun filters through their branches, breathe in their resinous scent, and you are still struck by the spirit of the place, an ancient quiet amid the bustle of the present.

The Birth of Dionysus

Myth-rich Thebes was first and foremost the city of Dionysus, for it was here that the god was conceived. Yet his gestation and delivery were hard. When Princess Semele was bathing naked in the River Asopos, cleansing herself from the spattered blood of a sacrificial bull, Zeus spied her radiant beauty and felt lust's stirrings. Intent on seduction, he disguised himself as a handsome young man, and soon he was a regular yet furtive visitor to Semele's bedchamber. But Hera, Zeus' wife, found out and wreaked her vengeance.

Hera, too, was a mistress of disguise, and dressed as an old woman she won Semele's trust. When the girl discussed her lover, Hera professed disbelief. Did Semele know who the young man was? Had he told her anything about himself? Surely it was time to learn all she could about him – especially as Semele was pregnant. So that night Semele badgered her ardent admirer to promise to do anything she asked. Innocently, he agreed – but when Semele demanded he reveal his true identity, Zeus was horrified. For Zeus' true identity was the white heat of the lightning blast, which no human could experience and still live. Yet, he had sworn an oath.

Allowing himself a last look at Semele's unparalleled loveliness, Zeus exploded in a blaze of sulphur, engulfing the room in sudden fire. But in the moment before Semele was vaporized, Zeus plunged his hand into her womb and rescued the child that she was carrying. Then he sliced open his thigh, inserted the foetus and carried it until it was old enough to be delivered. The son he bore was Dionysus. (Subsequently Dionysus rescued Semele from Hades and elevated her to Mount Olympus.) When Pausanias visited Thebes, he was shown the house in which Semele lived. It was so sacred that no one might enter it.

A goddess (perhaps Hera) prepares to snatch the ivy-crowned baby Dionysus as he is born from Zeus' thigh. (Late fifth- to early fourth-century BC Athenian red figure wine cup.)

Dionysus in Exile from Thebes

While Dionysus was being brought up by the Curetes in Crete (where he was known as Zagreus), Hera commanded the Titans to distract Zeus' love-child with toys and rattles, tear him limb from limb, boil him in a cauldron and eat him. Mercilessly they obeyed, but somehow the still-beating heart survived. While Zeus retaliated, destroying the Titans in a salvo of thunderbolts, Athene salvaged the heart and set it inside a gypsum doll, from which Dionysus was coaxed back to life, earning him the title 'Twice-Born'. (Others said that Zagreus was an older god, similarly torn apart, whose surviving heart Zeus placed into the embryonic Dionysus shortly after Semele conceived him.) Dionysus was then raised by nymphs on the craggy slopes of Nysa, an elusive mountain claimed by Africans and Asiatics alike and which together with the prefix Dios (meaning 'of Zeus') may have inspired his name.

Like Apollo, Dionysus was able to possess and prophesy, but his nature was darker and more earthy. His power lay in the untamed burgeoning of nature and, through wine, drugs or drama, he could skew perceptions, causing his devotees (and enemies) to behave in ways they otherwise would never have imagined. To him belonged the vine and wine; and early in his divine career (perhaps goaded to madness by Hera), Dionysus wandered east as far as India, planting vineyards and teaching mankind the art of viticulture. Almost always he was accompanied by his *thiasos*, a throng of revellers: satyrs (half-men, half-goat) and silenoi (half-men, half-horse), and nymphs and maenads, women, who, when he possessed them, were capable of acts of utmost savagery (*mainesthai* means 'to be mad'). Frenzied, they performed the ritual of *sparagmos*, tearing creatures limb from limb.

Sometimes Dionysus' victim was human. In Thrace he drove a hostile king, Lycurgus, insane. Mistaking his son for a vine, he hacked off his hands and feet. Horrified, the gods caused the harvest to fail and demanded Lycurgus' death. He was torn apart on the mountainside by man-eating horses.

Dionysus' Anger Against Thebes

At last Dionysus returned to Thebes, where he found that, while some happily embraced him, his cousin, King Pentheus, was determined to suppress his worship. Dionysus drove the Theban women mad and sent them on to nearby Mount Cithaeron, where they roamed as maenads. Meanwhile, letting himself be taken, then easily setting himself free, Dionysus hypnotized Pentheus into spying on the maenads. As Pentheus clung to the top of a high tree, the women (including his mother Agavë and aunts, Ino and Autonoë) caught sight of him, mistook him for an animal and attacked him. The description of Pentheus' death in Euripides' *Bacchae* is hair-raising:

> They stretched out their hands, all the mass of the bacchae, and tore the pine out of the earth. He was so high. He had so far to fall. And his scream seemed to go on for ever. And then the ritual of slaughter. As his mother closed in for the kill, he tore the ribbon from his hair so she would know him, so she'd spare him, and he screamed as he clawed at her cheeks in his terror.... But foam was pouring from Agavë's mouth. Her eyes were rolling wildly; her reasoning all gone. The god was riding her, and she was deaf to all his screaming. And she drove her foot hard down on Pentheus' ribcage and grasped his left elbow ... and wrenched off his arm. She never would have had the strength, but the god was in her and he gave her power. And then Ino was with her crouched, huddling over him, tearing his flesh, and Autonoë too, and the whole mob of bacchae, a bestial mass writhing, savage and feral and shredding him raw. And the noise was so deafening: Pentheus shrieking till all screams were silent, and the baying of the bacchae in triumph.

Swathed in leopard-skins, Bacchic
women tear apart a male victim, perhaps
Pentheus. (Red figure wine cup
attributed to Douris, *c.* 480 BC.)

The soothing intervention of her old father, Cadmus, restored Agavë to
her senses; but Dionysus' wrath was unappeased. He exiled Cadmus from
his city, eventually turning him and his wife into snakes. It was an ignominious end for a great hero – for Cadmus had founded Thebes.

Cadmus & the Sown Men
Cadmus was the brother of Europa, the princess carried off by Zeus in the
form of a bull to Crete, to become the mother of Minos, king of Knossos.
Cattle played an important role in Cadmus' career, too. Searching for
Europa, Cadmus consulted the oracle at Delphi. Its advice was to abandon
his quest, and instead follow a cow with moon-shaped markings on both
flanks, and, where it lay down exhausted, found a city.

The cow collapsed at Thebes. Joyfully Cadmus sacrificed it to Athene.
Then he sent his followers to fetch water. But the local spring was
guarded by a dragon, and only after the creature had slaughtered many
of his men could Cadmus himself kill it. As he was still reeling from
the fray, Athene appeared, commanding him to knock out the dragon's
teeth and sow them, like seed, across the earth. He did so. Immediately
armed men sprang out of the ground. But these Sown Men (*Spartoi*)
were so belligerent that they attacked each other. Only five were left

alive. These pledged allegiance to Cadmus and helped him build a wall round Thebes' acropolis, the Cadmeia. Many an historical Theban claimed them as ancestors.

The gods loved Cadmus, and when he married Harmonia, daughter of Ares and Aphrodite, they attended his wedding in Thebes and showered his wife with gifts. But Cadmus was not comfortable with kingship, and eventually he abdicated in favour of his grandson Pentheus – with disastrous consequences as we have seen.

Zethus, Amphion & the City of the Seven Gates

Several generations passed before the lower town was walled. A local river nymph, Antiope, was seduced by Zeus (in one of his least elegant disguises – a satyr) and gave birth to twins. When her uncle, the wolfish Lycus, found out, he exposed them on Cithaeron, and bade his wife Dirce inflict whatever punishments she chose upon Antiope. At last Antiope escaped and fled on to the mountain with Dirce in pursuit. Here she met two strapping cowherds, who initially refused to help her. Almost too late, the old man who was with them revealed the truth: they were Antiope's long-lost sons, Amphion and Zethus, whom he had reared as his own. Emboldened, the twins rescued Antiope and tied Dirce by her hair to the horns of a bucking bull. She did not survive the experience. Where her broken body fell a spring welled up, which is still called after her.

Vengefully, the brothers killed Lycus, who was ruling as regent for Cadmus' great-grandson, Laius. While Laius fled into exile, they strengthened Thebes' protective walls. As Zethus heaved great boulders, Amphion employed an easier technique. So virtuosic was he on the lyre that he could charm even rocks, which glided willingly towards the wall and slid snugly into place. Soon the ramparts were finished, a fine battlemented wall, punctured by seven well-towered gates.

Later, when Amphion's wife Niobe boasted that she had more children than the goddess Leto, Apollo and Artemis killed them all. Some say that Amphion committed suicide in grief, though the Roman Hyginus tells how, wild-eyed, he attacked Apollo's temple at Delphi and was cut down by the god. Zethus was equally unfortunate. When his one son died – perhaps in an accident, perhaps at his mother's hands – he killed himself. As late as the second century AD the mound that covered Amphion and Zethus' remains was jealously guarded, as its soil was thought to have magic properties.

Laius & the Oracle

With Amphion and Zethus dead, Laius returned to Thebes and claimed his rightful throne. He was not a pleasant man. According to late sources, while an exile in Elis he kidnapped King Pelops' son, Chrysippus, and raped him – the first instance of (human) homosexual rape in Greek mythology. In punishment the gods inflicted suffering on not just him but his descendants also.

Laius and his wife, Jocasta, were childless, so the king went to nearby Delphi to ask what they should do. The oracle's response was chilling. Better by far, she said, that Laius had no children, for his son was destined to kill his father and marry his mother. Returning home, Laius wisely shunned Jocasta, but in frustration she made him drunk and forced herself upon him. Only when she was clearly pregnant did Laius reveal the oracle's response. To try to cheat Fate, when the child was born they drove a nail through its feet and gave it to a servant to take on to Mount Cithaeron and leave it there to die. But the baby survived. Moved by compassion, the servant gave him to a kindly Corinthian shepherd, who took him in and tended his wound. As winter approached, the shepherd drove his flocks back down to Corinth, where he gave the infant to King Polybus and Queen Merope (in some accounts called Periboea). Childless, they adopted him and named him from his deformity: Oedipus ('Swollen Foot').

Oedipus grew up believing Polybus and Merope to be his parents, but when he approached manhood, a drunken party-goer jeered at him, calling him a bastard and not Polybus' son. Despite reassurances, Oedipus, by nature inquisitive, set out to discover the truth from that fount of all knowledge, the Delphic oracle. Rather than deliver a straight answer, the priestess gave devastating news: he was destined to kill his father and marry his mother.

Determined never to return to his beloved Corinth, Oedipus struck out east across the mountains, until he came to a fork in the road. In Sophocles' *Oedipus the King*, Oedipus narrates how, as he hesitated, a mule-cart drawn by colts and accompanied by outriders swept towards him on the road from Thebes. In the cart sat a troubled old man. As they approached:

> The man out front and the old man both tried to force
> me off the road. In fury I punch the driver as he shoves at
> me. The old man sees me, looks out for his moment as he
> passes by, and from the carriage lashes my face with his
> two-pronged goad. I gave as good as I got – no! Better! I
> did not hesitate. I smashed my stave hard in the middle
> of his back and sent him spinning. And then I killed
> them all.

The old man was Laius. The first part of the prophecy had been fulfilled. But crucially Oedipus was wrong: there was one survivor.

Oedipus & the Riddle of the Sphinx

Oedipus found Thebes in turmoil. As part of the gods' punishment, the land was being ravaged by the Sphinx ('Strangler') – a monster with a lion's body, eagle's wings and the breasts and head of a beautiful woman. Seated on a high cliff on Mount Phaga (or, in some versions, on a column) the Sphinx posed passers-by a riddle. If they failed to answer correctly – as they always did – she swooped down, strangled them and ate them raw.

As Oedipus approached, the Sphinx asked: 'What walks on four legs in the morning, two at noon and three in the evening?' Without hesitation the resourceful Oedipus replied correctly, 'Man', who as a baby in the morning of his life crawls on hands and knees, as a healthy adult walks upright and in old age uses a walking stick. Petulant, the Sphinx jumped to her death.

Pausanias recounts another local version of the myth in which the Sphinx was the (human) daughter of Laius. Only she and the true heir to Thebes' throne knew secrets the oracle had once shared with Cadmus about the moon-flanked cow. If anyone claimed the kingship, this Sphinx asked him to prove his legitimacy by revealing what these secrets were, killing all who failed. Oedipus succeeded only because he had been told them in a dream.

Thebes' citizens hailed Oedipus as their saviour, and – their old king having died – awarded him the throne and Laius' widow, Jocasta, as his wife. Together they had four children: two sons, Eteocles and Polyneices; and two daughters, Antigone and Ismene. Thebes prospered. Then a plague struck. In *Oedipus the King*, a priest reports:

> The land is sterile. The corn rots in the husk, and in the pasture-lands our flocks, our herds are dying of hunger. Our womenfolk – in pain, with spasms and contractions – are giving birth to still-born foetuses. And now the god of fever, of all plagues the most pestilent, has swooped down hard on us to scourge our city. So Thebes lies empty, while the black house, Hades' house of death, is rich with groans and lamentation.

Oedipus sent to Delphi for a remedy. The answer came: 'seek out the killer of Laius'. Ignorant that he was himself the killer, Oedipus launched a murder investigation, summoning the one survivor of the attack to give evidence. Sophocles shows the search interrupted by a messenger from Corinth, bearing the sad news that King Polybus has died. For a brief moment, Oedipus experiences intense relief – Polybus (he still believes) was his father; the oracle told Oedipus that he would kill his father; Polybus has died of natural causes; surely, then, oracles cannot be trusted!

However, the messenger turns out to be the very man who, as a shepherd, rescued the baby Oedipus and took him to Corinth; the sole survivor of the attack on Laius' entourage turns out to be the servant once charged with exposing the baby. Together, their evidence reveals the awful truth. Horrified at discovering that between them she and Oedipus have broken almost every taboo known to mankind, Jocasta hangs herself. Finding her, Oedipus:

> ripped the golden brooch-pins from her dress, and
> arched them high, and punched them hard into his
> eyeballs.... Not once but many times he strafed his eyes
> with blows. And at each blow, the eyeballs, bursting
> blood, kept drenching down his cheeks, not trickling
> blood-flecks, dripping, slow – no! But explosive,
> uncontrolled, a deluge of black blood burst, beating
> down as thick as hail.

In *Oedipus at Colonus*, Sophocles recounts how Oedipus wandered in exile until he came to a grove of the Furies just outside Athens. Here he was received kindly by Theseus, and met a mystical death, apparently absorbed into the earth at Colonus, where in antiquity he was worshipped as a hero.

Famous though this account of Oedipus' self-punishment is, it may have been invented by Sophocles. Homer knew another version. In the *Odyssey* 'the fair Epicasta' (as Homer called Jocasta) marries her son in ignorance, only to hang herself when the gods 'immediately revealed the situation to mankind'; in the *Iliad*, rather than blind himself and go into exile Oedipus ruled on and, when he fell in battle bravely defending Thebes from attack, lavish funeral games were celebrated in his honour. One of Sophocles' reasons for altering the myth is to compare the physically sighted hero's blindness to the truth with his subsequent clear-sightedness when blind. In this respect Oedipus mirrors another of Thebes' most memorable mythological figures, the prophet Teiresias.

Teiresias
Teiresias' early adventures took place on Mount Cyllene in Arcadia. Stumbling across two copulating snakes, he thrashed them with his stick, which made Hera so livid that she changed him into a woman. After seven years of promiscuity, Teiresias found two more snakes, similarly entwined, and thrashed them too, at which Zeus changed him back into a man. Later, when he was arguing with Hera about whether men or

women derive greater pleasure from sex, Zeus suggested they ask Teiresias. His reply – a woman's pleasure is nine times that of a man's – so angered Hera that she struck him blind. As compensation, Zeus let him live for seven generations, and gave him the power of prophecy.

Others attributed Teiresias' blindness either to divine vengeance because he had revealed more than was permitted, or to Athene's anger because – before he could foretell the future – he accidentally saw her bathing naked. Remorsefully, the goddess allowed her serpent-son Erichthonius to lick his eyelids, and so bestowed the gift of prophecy. Still others said that Aphrodite turned Teiresias into an old woman because he failed to award her first prize in a beauty contest.

Teiresias first appears in the *Odyssey*, when Odysseus consults his ghost in Hades, but he is most closely associated with the mythology of Thebes. In historical times Teiresias' 'Observatory', where he deduced the future by listening to the twittering of birds, was shown on the Cadmeian Hill, while outside nearby Haliartus was the spring where he died as he drank its waters. In Greek tragedy Teiresias regularly warns misguided heroes of the errors of their ways, be they Pentheus in *Bacchae*, Oedipus in *Oedipus the King* or Creon in *Antigone*.

Antigone & the Fourteen Against Thebes
Creon achieved his bitter reign in the fallout from a murderous dispute between Eteocles and Polyneices, whom Oedipus, their father, cursed for abandoning him to his suffering. At first the brothers agreed to rule Thebes in alternate years, but when Polyneices' turn came, Eteocles refused to surrender the throne. Angered, Polyneices took refuge in Argos, where he married King Adrastus' daughter and persuaded his father-in-law to help restore him to his rightful throne.

With six other generals, Polyneices led an army against Thebes. The city was on the point of being captured when Teiresias announced that the gods would save it if one of the royal household willingly laid down his life. When Creon's son, Menoeceus, sacrificed himself, Thebes' fortunes immediately changed. As one of the attackers, Capaneus, scaled the walls, Zeus destroyed him with a thunderbolt, and at last, with many dead on both sides, Polyneices and Eteocles challenged each other to single combat. In the vicious duel, each struck a mortal blow and with both brothers dead the invaders turned and ran. Thebes was saved, but all was still not well.

Assuming command, Creon ratified his nephew Eteocles' earlier wish that no fallen enemy should be buried – a clear defiance of the gods' unwritten laws. Opposed even by her sister, Ismene, Antigone disobeyed the edict, either dragging her brother Polyneices' body to Eteocles' already burning pyre, cremating it on a pyre of its own or scattering sufficient earth on it to free his spirit. In Sophocles' version, Creon then ordered Antigone to be walled up in a cave and left to die. However, his son Haemon (Antigone's fiancé) refused to condone such barbarity and ran to free her. Shortly afterwards, Creon, too – shown the error of his ways by Teiresias – rushed to the cave. But already Antigone had hanged herself and, seeing Creon, Haemon lunged at him unsuccessfully with a sword, which he then turned on himself. When Creon leaned that his wife Eurydice had also hanged herself, he must have hoped Thebes' sorrows were complete. They were not.

Shortly afterwards, Theseus, outraged at Creon's impiety, arrived from Athens at the head of such a threatening army that the Thebans were forced to allow the fallen attackers to be buried. Worse was to come. A generation later, the sons of the seven original invading generals launched their own attack on Thebes. Teiresias knew that these so-called 'Epigoni' were destined for success and advised the Thebans to leave city under the cover of night. The next morning the invaders broke in, ransacked its buildings and razed Thebes to the ground.

Today Antigone's story is familiar to theatregoers, but much of Sophocles' plot may be his own creation. In an older version of the story, when Antigone buries Polyneices, Creon tests Haemon's loyalty by ordering him to kill her. Haemon pretends to carry out the sentence, but in fact gives Antigone to shepherds for safe-keeping. In time their son returns to Thebes to take part in games. Creon recognizes him thanks to a genetic birthmark and, despite pleas from Heracles, vows to punish Haemon; but instead Haemon kills both himself and Antigone. Creon then gives his daughter Megara to Heracles in marriage.

The Birth & Madness of Heracles

Heracles, too, was Theban-born. His mother, Alcmene, a Mycenaean princess, fled to the city with Amphitryon, her husband, when he accidentally killed her father. Soon after they arrived in Thebes, Zeus took advantage of Amphitryon's absence on campaign to visit Alcmene by night – and no normal night at that. To prolong his pleasure, and disguised as Amphitryon, he persuaded the sun-god Helios not to rise until three days had passed and Selene, the moon-goddess, to dawdle on her journey across the sky. Only when the real Amphitryon returned did Alcmene discover Zeus' trickery.

As always, Hera was none too pleased by Zeus' infidelity, especially since, with Alcmene already in labour, Zeus announced that a son born that day to the royal line of Mycenae was destined to rule her special land, the Argolid. His boast came too soon. Not to be outwitted, Hera hurried first to Tiryns, where she eased the premature birth of Sthenelus' son, Eurystheus, then to Thebes, where she prolonged Alcmene's labour until

As his family look on and his wife, Megara, watches helplessly from the door, the maddened Heracles prepares to dash one of his sons to the ground. (Mid-fourth-century BC South Italian wine bowl.)

after dark. At last Alcmene was delivered of twins. One, Iphicles, was Amphitryon's son, the other the son of Zeus, named either ironically or in an attempt to assuage the goddess' anger, Heracles ('Hera's Fame').

Zeus' plans were thwarted, but he still managed to outwit his wife. When Hera was passing Thebes, he caused Alcmene to leave the baby Heracles outside alone. Not knowing who he was and thinking he had been abandoned, the maternal Hera was drawn to his crying. Picking the baby up, she began to suckle him. But Heracles sucked too violently. Hera tore him off her breast, and her milk splashed high into the heavens to form the Milky Way. And then she recognized Heracles. Too late. Her milk had already rendered him immortal.

Still Hera hounded Heracles. While he was a baby, she sent two serpents into the boys' nursery. Roused by Iphicles' screams of terror, their parents ran in – only to find Heracles calmly strangling the snakes in his small but powerful hands. Grown to manhood, Heracles fought valiantly against neighbouring Orchomenos, earning the Theban king Creon's gratitude and his daughter Megara's hand in marriage. Soon they were proud parents of a dynasty of sons.

But Hera, her fury undiminished, drove Heracles temporarily mad. Mistaking his sons – and those of his brother Iphicles – for the sons of his enemy, Eurystheus of Tiryns, he began butchering them. Euripides' *The Madness of Heracles* (which places the episode later in Heracles' life) tells how:

> He chased one child, circling a column in terrifying
> pursuit until his view was unimpeded and he shot him
> through the heart. The boy fell backwards, spraying the
> stone pillar as he spattered out his life.... Then Heracles
> aimed at another of his children, who was hiding,
> crouched behind an altar. The arrow drawn, the poor
> boy threw himself before him in an act of supplication,
> pleading, 'My dearest father, please! Don't kill me! I am
> not Eurystheus' son, but yours!' But Heracles scowled as
> grimly as the Gorgon ... and slammed his club down on
> the boy's fair head, crushing his skull, as a blacksmith
> hammers molten metal. Then he turned to his third son.
> Before he reached him, Megara snatched the boy and ran
> outside, slamming the doors behind them. Now Heracles
> believed that he was standing by the walls [of Tiryns that]
> the Cyclopes built. He battered down the twisted doors,
> breaking down the jambs and lintel, and with one arrow
> shot dead both wife and child.

At last, Heracles came to his senses. Although granted ritual purification from his guilt, he still needed to atone for his family's murder, and in punishment he was sent to Tiryns to serve Eurystheus and undertake twelve labours.

Narcissus

Hera was involved in another tale of destructive love located near Thebes. Learning that Zeus was consorting with nymphs on Mount Cithaeron, she set out to expose him, but each time she approached the mountain she was waylaid by the garrulous young Echo. At last, irritated by Echo's talkativeness, Hera cursed the poor nymph. No longer able to initiate a conversation of her own, all she could do was repeat the last words of others.

One day, Echo fell in love with Narcissus, a cruel but beautiful young huntsman, lost on the mountainside. Seeking his homeward path, he asked her for directions. Tongue-tied, Echo could not give them. Instead, with growing frustration on both sides, she simply reiterated everything Narcissus said, until the angry youth chased her off and collapsed in self-pity by a pool. But as he gazed into its glassy waters he saw a face gaze

On a Roman mosaic in Paphos, Cyprus, Narcissus gazes longingly at his reflection in a pool of water.

back at him, a beautiful, cruel face, the most beautiful he had ever seen. Whenever he tried to touch it, though, the face appeared to shatter, before slowly forming once again. Mesmerized, Narcissus could not tear his eyes from his reflection and in time he died. A flower grew where his body lay, called the narcissus to this day. As for Echo, she wasted away until now only her voice remains.

Alternatively, Pan so lusted after Echo and envied her sweet musicality that, when she refused his advances, he tore her limb from limb. Although her body was scattered, it could still sing, repeating every sound it heard. When Pan hears Echo's voice today, he rushes headlong in his desire to find her.

Pausanias dismisses the story of Narcissus out of hand. Instead, describing a pool near Thebes named after the dead hero, he explains that Narcissus had a twin sister. They were so devoted to each other that they wore the same clothes, sported the same haircuts and were in every way indistinguishable. When his sister died, Narcissus became obsessed with his reflection because it reminded him so much of her. After all, as Pausanias exclaims, at one stroke debunking the illogicality of myth: 'it is ridiculous – a young man old enough to fall in love, who cannot tell a human being from a reflection!'

Thebes in History & Today

Because of the circumstances of history, a detailed archaeological record of Thebes is difficult to achieve. Not only does most of ancient Thebes lie under the modern town, rendering it inaccessible, but the city was famously razed to the ground more than once, both in mythology and in history. Much of our knowledge comes from literature and the odd lucky find.

During the Bronze Age, Thebes was one of the most powerful cities of mainland Greece and traces of palaces survive on the Cadmeian Hill in its southwest quadrant. Archaeology has revealed trading and social links both with local towns, such as nearby Orchomenos (itself a wealthy centre), and with Crete, Egypt and Miletus on the western shore of Asia Minor. Like other Mycenaean sites, Thebes was deliberately destroyed around the turn of the twelfth century BC.

By the sixth century BC, thanks to its agricultural wealth, Thebes' position as the strongest city in Boeotia led to the first of many conflicts with neighbouring Attica over the border-city of Plataea. Accepting the principle that 'my enemy's enemy is my friend', Thebes sided with the Persians against Athens during the Persian Wars, earning opprobrium from the victorious Greeks. Later in the fifth century BC, it again allied itself with Athens' enemies, this time the Spartans, in the Peloponnesian War, one of the first acts of which was Thebes' siege of

Plataea. Nonetheless in 403 BC, Thebes graciously helped Athens overthrow the Thirty Tyrants imposed on it at the end of the war by Sparta.

The city's heyday came in the fourth century BC, when – after a hostile Spartan occupation in 382 BC – the politician Pelopidas and general Epaminondas built Thebes into a formidable player on the Greek stage. In 371 BC Epaminondas' defeat of Sparta at the Battle of Leuctra altered the balance of power in the Peloponnese and wider Greece, and earned him the title of 'Greece's Liberator'. However, Epaminondas' death at the Battle of Mantinea in 362 BC marked the end of Thebes' brief Golden Age.

In 338 BC, along with its allies (now including Athens), Thebes' army was defeated by the Macedonians at the Battle of Chaeronea. Its celebrated Sacred Band, a regiment formed exclusively from pairs of homosexual lovers, was cut down to a man. They were buried in a common grave – the monumental lion erected over it still guards the road into Chaeronea. Two years later the Thebans, wrongly believing Alexander the Great was dead, revolted from Macedonian rule. Alexander's response was extreme. He razed the city to the ground, sparing only its temples and the house of the fifth-century BC poet Pindar, its most famous literary son.

In 316 BC, Alexander's successor-general Cassander rebuilt Thebes, and some decades later the traveller Heracleides described it as 'lush and well-watered, with more gardens than any other city in Greece'. However, it had a reputation for lawlessness – its men were quick to pick a fight and murders were committed for the slightest motive. As for its women:

> They are the tallest, the most beautiful and the most
> elegant of any in the whole of Greece. They veil their faces
> so that only their eyes can be seen, and every one of them
> wears a white dress with purple shoes, laced to show off
> their feet. They tie their blond hair in a topknot and have
> bewitching voices – unlike the men, whose voices are
> rasping and deep.

After Rome annexed Greece in 146 BC, Thebes allied itself with Mithridates of Pontus, earning severe punishment from the Roman general Sulla. In 86 BC he sacked the city and redistributed its land. It never really recovered. When Pausanias visited, Thebes was little more than a village. It enjoyed a brief flowering in the twelfth century thanks to its silk factories, but, when the centre of production moved to Sicily, Thebes sank once more into decline. Despite its lack of loveliness, the modern town of Thivai represents a welcome return to relative good fortune.

SOME IMPORTANT DATES & REMAINS

c. 1300 BC	Thebes flourishes.
c. 1200 BC	Thebes destroyed by fire.
480 BC	Thebans fight reluctantly against Persians at Thermopylae.
479 BC	Thebans fight alongside the Persians at Plataea.
457 BC	Thebes allies with Sparta.
431 BC	Thebes' siege of Plataea stokes Peloponnesian War.
403 BC	Thebes helps Athenians to overthrow the Thirty Tyrants and reintroduce democracy.
371 BC	Epaminondas defeats Spartans at Leuctra.
362 BC	Epaminondas killed at Mantinea.
338 BC	Theban Sacred Band annihilated at Chaeronea.
336 BC	Alexander the Great razes Thebes to the ground.
316 BC	Cassander rebuilds Thebes.
86 BC	Sulla sacks Thebes, which has sided with Mithridates.
C2nd AD	Pausanias finds Thebes to be little more than a village.
AD 1146	Thebes sacked by the Normans.
C12th AD	Thebes flourishes as a centre of silk production.

Such buildings as survived Thebes' many sacks lie under the modern town, though tantalizing fragments can be seen. Among these are sparse foundations of the **Cadmeia**, Thebes' Bronze Age palace, near the modern market place, from which a trove of Linear B tablets has been unearthed; the remains of the **agora** and **theatre** on Kastelli Hill; the site of the **Temple of Apollo Ismenus** on Ismenus Hill; and some desultory remnants of the **Electra Gate** on Odos Amphionos.

The **museum** (closed indefinitely at time of writing) boasts a fine selection of Bronze Age **cylinder seals, inscriptions, armour** and **worked ivory** as well as an impressive thirteenth-century BC *larnax* (coffin) with a painting of five women tearing their hair in grief.

In the early nineteenth century AD, the Theban plain was rich in antiquities. Sadly, thanks to enthusiastic looters and developers, this is no longer the case. Close by Thebes are **Chaeronea** (with its lion-memorial to the Theban Sacred Band and rock-cut theatre), **Orchomenos** (another fine theatre and the tholos called 'The Treasury of Minyas'), the Mycenaean fortress of **Gla** to the north, and the haunting sites of **Plataea** and the battlefield of **Leuctra** to the south.

11

Tiryns & the Labours of Heracles

Heracles himself roused ancient Tiryns to arms. The city was
not without brave men nor unworthy of her great son's fame,
but fallen on harsh times, without the strength that wealth can bring.
Few live in her empty fields, but they still point out the citadel, built
from the sweat of the Cyclopes' brow. Yet still Tiryns can raise a force
of three hundred gallant men. Untrained for war they may
be, and lacking javelin-thongs or gleaming swords, but on their
heads and shoulders they drape lion skins, as befits their ancestry;
and in their hands they wield a pine staff, while their quivers bristle
with innumerable arrows. They sing the battle hymn of Heracles,
who purged the world of monsters; and far away on wooded Oeta,
the god listens to their words.

Statius, *Thebaid*, 4.145f.

Beside the straight and busy road from Argos east to Nafplio, the fortress walls of Tiryns hunker squat and grey. At first glance, the site is far from prepossessing. Contained behind a metal fence in flatland strewn with cans and plastic bags, it is flanked to the south by the local prison and, across the road, by a string of modern homes. It can all seem rather unlovely, and the roar of traffic simply compounds the disappointment.

But enter the site; walk down along the walls, the massive masonry rough and warm; climb up the ancient ramp, and through the ruined remnants of the gate; stand on the Upper Citadel; look out beyond the citrus orchards to the mountains ranging east to Nafplio, its fortress proud above the pretty town; look back to Argos with its castle perched atop Larissa Hill; look to the sea, and to the mountains of Arcadia, pale contours in the bluing haze. Half close your eyes and see the coastline closer; see Bronze Age ships at anchor jostling by the quay; half hear the creak of timber and the slap of water on the hulls, the shouts of stevedores, the quick commands, the snatch of a sea shanty learned in far-off Syrian or Cretan ports; think of the legends clinging to this place and think of Heracles. Then Tiryns comes alive. For this once-proud citadel was not only one of the most important hubs of Mycenaean trading, it was the epicentre of some of the most exuberant of all Greek myths.

Tiryns & the Coming of Heracles

Acrisius, king of Argos, had a twin brother, Proetus, with whom he quarrelled even in the womb. As adults, the two were meant to rule in alternate years, but Acrisius refused to relinquish the throne. So Proetus, aggrieved, fled east to Lycia, where he married the king's daughter, Anteia (also called Stheneboea).

With the backing of his powerful father-in-law, the Lycian army and seven Cyclopes, Proetus returned to Argos, where he fought Acrisius for the throne. There was no clear victor, so the brothers split the kingdom. Acrisius kept Argos, while Proetus took the north and east, including the port of Tiryns. Here he put the Cyclopes to work, hewing stone and heaving it into position to form impregnable defences. Today their handiwork can still be admired: with stones weighing up to nearly 14 tons, walls over 750 m (800 yd) in circumference and in places 8 m (25 ft) thick still rise to nearly 10 m (32 ft), half their original height.

Four generations later, Tiryns was the fiefdom of one of Perseus' grandsons, the cowardly Eurystheus. He was the polar opposite of his distant cousin, Heracles. While Heracles performed deeds of daring in his native Thebes, Eurystheus achieved nothing. So it was a devastating slight when, to atone for killing his wife and children (in a fit madness sent by Hera, as described), Heracles was sentenced to serve Eurystheus for ten years, performing whatever tasks the king might set him.

Even now the gods (with the exception of Hera) could not stop loving Heracles. To assist him in the approaching danger they gave him armour and weaponry, reflecting their own special attributes. Thus Poseidon provided a team of horses, Apollo a bow, Hermes a sword, Hephaestus a well-forged breastplate and Athene a woven robe, while his father Zeus gave a shield, intricately embossed with scenes from earlier mythology, from which projected twelve snakes' heads, which snapped their jaws as he advanced to battle. So, Heracles presented himself in Tiryns and bowed to his cousin's command.

Early accounts differed as to the number and identity of the 'Labours of Heracles', but by Hellenistic times there was an accepted canon of twelve. These took the hero increasingly further from Tiryns into ever more fantastical and dangerous lands.

1. The Nemean Lion

The first labour was to kill and strip the pelt from a monstrous lion, the offspring of the moon-goddess Selene, which lived in a mountain cave and was plaguing the land around Nemea (between Tiryns and Corinth). With a hide invulnerable to javelins or arrows, it had already wiped out villages and flocks. Surely, Eurystheus considered with a lazy smile, it would be more than a match for Heracles.

Following a trail of bloody devastation, Heracles tracked the lion to its lair and fired off a salvo of arrows. But even Apollo's shafts bounced harmlessly off the monster's hide and served only to anger it. Roaring,

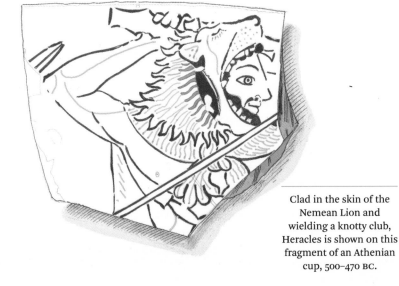

Clad in the skin of the Nemean Lion and wielding a knotty club, Heracles is shown on this fragment of an Athenian cup, 500–470 BC.

it sprang on Heracles, its sharp claws clanging on his breastplate. With no room now for subtlety, it was a trial of strength. Discarding his weapons, Heracles locked arms around the lion's neck, mercilessly tightening his iron grip until the creature slumped lifeless to the ground.

Then he heaved the carcass home to Tiryns, where he flayed it with one of its own claws. With the lion's gaping jaws set on his head like a helmet, he draped the impenetrable skin around his shoulders, snatched up an olive-wood club and sought out Eurystheus. The king was terrified. Trembling, he ordered his blacksmiths to fashion a bronze amphora and set it in the earth, where he might take refuge whenever Heracles approached; and from now on he issued orders only through his herald.

2. The Hydra

Close by to the west, at marshy Lerna lived the terrifying Hydra. With a dog's body and nine snaky heads (including one which was immortal), its breath was so toxic that anything that came close died. To kill it was Heracles' next task, so seemingly impossible that he called for help on his young nephew, Iolaus, and together they struck out along the coast. Reaching the swamp, Heracles fired burning arrows at the Hydra – to no effect. Then, taking a deep breath, he splashed into the mud, slashing at the coiling necks and slicing off its heads. But as he did so, new heads grew immediately, multiplying, jaws snapping, throats belching forth a deadly stench. Horrified and stunned, Heracles withdrew, uncertain what to do.

It was then that Athene, the goddess who most favoured him, came near and whispered her advice. Only by cauterizing the still-bleeding necks could Heracles stop new heads from growing. Again he waded out into the fetid marsh, this time with Iolaus holding blazing torches by his side. As Heracles with his golden sword lopped off each head, Iolaus plunged the firebrand into the raw, steaming neck. At last only the immortal head remained. With one final sword-stroke Heracles detached it, and swiftly buried it beneath a rock where it could do no harm. Next he dipped each of his arrowheads into the Hydra's suppurating bile, a poison he knew none might survive. Triumphant he returned to Tiryns.

3. The Ceryneian Hind

Heracles' third labour was to trap a magical wild deer, which lived in the mountains of Ceryneia to the west of Corinth. With bronze hooves and golden horns, this was the swiftest of all hinds, the only member of the herd that had escaped when Artemis harnessed its sisters to her chariot. But it was still sacred to the goddess, so Heracles dared not harm it.

To capture it became a test of stamina. For a year, Heracles chased the creature on a journey that took him north through Istria and Thrace to the Land of the Hyperboreans, where only the sun's faint glint on the galloping deer's golden horns reassured him he was still on the right track. At last even the deer tired and, exhausted too, Heracles discovered it collapsed beneath a tree. Summoning his last reserves of energy, he threw a net around it, heaved it across his shoulders and began the long trek back to Tiryns. Reporting his arrival to the cowering Eurystheus, Heracles allowed the horned hind to run free. Sparks flew from its bronze hooves as it bounded off into the mountains.

4. The Erymanthian Boar & the Tragedy of the Centaurs

Heracles' next task was comparatively easy: to capture another rampaging creature, a huge ferocious boar which lived on Mount Erymanthus in northwest Arcadia. Heracles simply pursued it into a snowdrift, where

Watched by Athene (right), Heracles presents the Erymanthian Boar to a terrified Eurystheus, who cowers in his bronze amphora. (Sixth-century BC Athenian vase painting.)

it became stuck fast. Then, in time-honoured fashion, he shouldered the snorting beast and carried it back to Tiryns.

However, this success was tinged with tragedy. On his way to Erymanthus, Heracles was entertained by a Centaur, Pholus. Years earlier Dionysus, foretelling this very meeting, had given Pholus a wineskin, to be opened only when Heracles came visiting. But the honeyed bouquet attracted other Centaurs from far and near. Maddened by its scent and desperate to taste it, they armed themselves with trees and boulders and rushed on Pholus' cave. Heracles had no choice but to retaliate. He unleashed a volley of poisoned arrows. Soon many of the Centaurs lay twitching in torment. Many more took to their hooves and galloped off to safety. Among those struck was wise old Cheiron. Immortal as he was, the arrows' toxins condemned him to eternal pain. At last, knowing he could not escape his fate, he persuaded Zeus to let him change places with Prometheus, the Titan whose punishment for giving fire to men was to have his liver pecked out every morning by an eagle, only for it to grow again before the next sunrise. Even Pholus did not survive the massacre. Intrigued by the arrows' effect, he was examining one closely when he dropped it. It grazed his leg, and immediately he collapsed, dead, to the ground.

5. The Augean Stables

For his fifth labour, Heracles returned to the northeast Peloponnese, this time to cleanse the stables – or more properly the byres – of Augeas, the cattle-rancher king of Elis. Augeas possessed so many beasts, including five hundred stud bulls and a further twelve which guarded the herd, that the amount of excrement they produced was monumental. Try as he might (and he did not try hard), nothing Augeas did could get rid of the morass of dung clogging his fields and farmyard, whose stench polluted the air for miles around.

Accompanied again by Iolaus, Heracles (wearing his trademark lionskin) had just agreed terms with Augeas – whereby the king would give him a tenth of his herd if Heracles achieved the task within a day – when one of the guard-bulls charged him, believing him to be a lion. Immediately, Heracles wrestled it to the ground, twisting its horns until it submitted.

Then the two men set to work. Rather than muck out the byres, they hit on a less unsavoury solution: they diverted two local rivers, the Alpheus and the Peneius, which flooded the fields and farmyard, removing all the ordure and rendering them clean and fragrant. However, Augeas called this cheating and, hearing that Heracles had been commanded to undertake the task by Eurystheus, he refused to make the agreed payment. So Heracles went to war, and it was to mark his victory over Augeas (some said) that he celebrated the first games at Olympia.

Heracles takes aim (here with a sling, not his usual bow) as the Stymphalian Birds rise flapping from the swamp. (Attic black figure vase, *c.* 560–530 BC.)

6. The Stymphalian Birds

Heracles went next to Stymphalia, a little north of Nemea. Here in a great swamp lived a flock of noxious birds with bronze beaks and feathers. The birds could detach these razor-sharp plumes and aim them at predators, upon whom, too, they voided themselves of acidic faeces. Heracles' mission was to drive them from the swamp, an awkward problem since it was so marshy that anyone trying to wade out became stuck fast, while its waters were so choked with weeds that no boat could navigate them.

Again, Heracles resorted to guile. Taking a rattle in his hand, he made such a din that the birds rose as one, squawking from the middle of the lake, flapping overhead in great confusion. At once, Heracles strung his bow and soon the birds were falling from the sky. The survivors wheeled in a great flock and flew off northeast, until they came to the Black Sea, where they roosted on an island sacred to Ares. Today Stymphalia still resounds to rasping squawks, not from birds but from myriad frogs, which share their murky home with writhing water-snakes.

Tiryns & the Labours of Heracles

7. The Cretan Bull

The first half of Heracles' labours were located relatively close to Tiryns; the second took him much further afield. In fact the next task necessitated a sea voyage: Heracles had to sail to Crete to fetch the white bull that Minos, king of Knossos, had vowed – then refused – to sacrifice to Poseidon and which was wreaking havoc throughout the island. After a mighty struggle, Heracles wrestled the bull to the ground, trussed it up and shipped it back to Tiryns. Eurystheus dedicated it to Hera at her shrine near Argos, but the beast escaped, rampaged through Greece and finally made its home at Marathon near Athens, where it was at last subdued by Theseus.

8. Diomedes' Mares

Next, Eurystheus sent Heracles far north to Thrace to steal the famous mares of savage Diomedes. A team of four fire-breathing horses, these were tethered in bronze stables and lived off human flesh. With him Heracles took a small band of companions – a sensible precaution as, when he did capture the mares, the Thracians pursued them.

Leaving the horses with Abderus, his groom, Heracles turned to face the enemy. But it was clear that his force was grossly outnumbered. Any battle would be costly. So instead Heracles repeated the ruse by which he had cleansed Augeas' stables. He cut a channel from the sea, through which the roiling waters inundated the low plain where Diomedes' army was assembled. The Thracians retreated. Heracles sought out Diomedes, dealt him a stunning blow and dragged him back to where he had tethered the horses.

But Abderus was nowhere to be seen. The mares' bloodied mouths revealed the truth. They had eaten him. And they still had hungry eyes. Distraught, Heracles threw Diomedes down in front of them and soon the horses were replete. Seizing his chance, Heracles muzzled the beasts and drove them back to Tiryns. Sensibly, Eurystheus removed them far away to Mount Olympus before he set them free.

9. Hippolyta's Girdle

Eurystheus now dispatched Heracles northeast towards the furthest reaches of the known world: the Black Sea coast, home to the female warriors, the Amazons. His mission was to steal the battle-belt (or girdle) of their queen Hippolyta. It meant a long sea voyage, and Heracles assembled an heroic crew, whose number included the Athenian Theseus and Peleus, the father of Achilles.

The journey was fraught with danger, but at last they reached the River Thermodon, on whose banks the Amazons lived. According to some accounts, Hippolyta graced Heracles with an audience and was so taken with his muscly manhood that she willingly removed her battle-belt and gave it to him.

Others describe a tragic sequel. Believing that Hippolyta had been abducted, the Amazons donned their armour, mounted their horses and attacked Heracles and his ship. The Greeks fought back, and in the melée Hippolyta and many Amazons were killed. In a different version the Amazons gave the battle-belt to Heracles as ransom when he captured their princess, Melanippe. In yet another, it was Theseus who captured Hippolyta, gave the battle-belt to Heracles, and in return for the queen's freedom took as his slave the Amazon princess Antiope (with whom he had fallen in love). So rich in amorous potential, it is no wonder that the episode excited the imagination of many a Classical mythographer.

Back in Tiryns, Heracles presented the battle-belt to Eurystheus who gave it to his daughter Admete – although one late version has her accompanying Heracles to the Black Sea. She was certainly feisty. A priestess at Hera's sanctuary at Argos, she later ran away to Samos with the goddess' statue. When a ship was sent to fetch it back, Hera made the statue so heavy that the vessel could not sail. Both it and Admete remained on the island.

10. The Cattle of Geryon

For his next labour, Heracles headed west towards the setting sun to distant lands, associated with death. Beyond the fringes of the continent close to Ocean lay the red island of Erythreia. Here lived Geryon (a fearsome creature with three heads, three fused bodies and six hands), the owner of a fine herd of cattle, which Heracles was to steal and bring back to Tiryns.

Where the Mediterranean debouches into the Atlantic he set two mighty rocks, named in antiquity 'The Pillars of Heracles'. Today we know them as Ceuta (on the African side) and Gibraltar (on the European). There, as Heracles gazed out across the rolling sea wondering how he could cross it, Helios gave him as a ship a large golden cup. So, running up his lion skin as a sail, Heracles was transported to his destination. He had already despatched both herdsman and guard dog (the two-headed Orthus), when Geryon stormed across the pastureland brandishing weapons in all six hands. Undaunted, Heracles strung his bow, and brought down the monster. Then he drove the herd inside the golden cup and sailed back to Europe.

The subsequent trek to Tiryns gave mythographers – and cities keen to forge a link with Heracles – a field day. Legends described his route through Spain, the south of France, across the Alps, down Italy's west coast (including to the future site of Rome), across to Sicily, back up the east coast, through Epirus, Thrace and Scythia, before finally striking south for Tiryns.

11. The Apples of the Hesperides

Soon Heracles was heading out once more for the setting sun, this time to fetch golden apples sacred to Hera from a magical garden tended by the Hesperides ('Daughters of Evening') and guarded by the hundred-headed dragon, Ladon. Heracles was warned not to pick the apples himself, but to secure the aid of Atlas (the Titan who carried the skies on his shoulders as punishment for warring with the Olympian gods). After shooting Ladon from afar, Heracles easily persuaded Atlas to let him hold the skies while Atlas stole into the orchard and picked the golden fruit.

But Atlas was loath to resume his duties. Surprisingly, Heracles agreed to the suggestion that Atlas take the apples back to Tiryns – but first he asked Atlas to relieve him for a moment, while he placed a cushion on his shoulders to ease the burden. Atlas agreed – and immediately regretted it. Now liberated, Heracles swept up the golden apples and, leaving the helpless Titan behind, strode off in triumph.

Again his journey home was tortuous, taking him west along the coast to visit Zeus' Egyptian oracle at Siwah (which later recognized Heracles' descendant Alexander the Great as a god) and found Egyptian Thebes (named after Heracles' Greek birthplace and now called Luxor), before returning to Tiryns and his final task.

Heracles presents Eurystheus (still cowering in his bronze amphora) with the three-headed dog Cerberus. (Black figure vase, *c.* 530 BC, from Cerveteri in Etruria, Italy.)

12. Capturing Cerberus

For Heracles' last labour Eurystheus devised a truly deadly mission: to bring back to Tiryns the guardian of Hades – Cerberus, the three-headed dog with a snaky mane and serpent tail. Protected once more by Athene, Heracles descended through an underwater cave at Cape Taenarum, south of Sparta and crossed the River Styx (where he menaced Charon into conveying him on his ferry) to the court of Haides and Persephone. Here Heracles pleaded his case. With unusual sympathy, Haides agreed to part temporarily with Cerberus, on condition that Heracles subdued the creature without causing it lasting harm.

Heracles grappled with the hound. Cerberus fought back, viciously lashing his tail – to no avail. Nothing could penetrate Heracles' lion skin. Exhausted, Cerberus allowed himself to be led meekly up into the sunlight, where he cringed, blinking at the unaccustomed brightness before trotting obediently at Heracles' heels all the way back to Tiryns.

The labours were complete. Heracles' enslavement was ended. But there were further traumas still to come.

A Murder & Further Enslavement

A young prince, Iphitus, was tricked into accusing Heracles of stealing his prize herd of horses. He came to Tiryns, where Heracles took Iphitus up to the highest tower, told him to scan the plain and asked if he could see the horses. He could not. But, despite his gracious apologies, Heracles was so furious that he picked up the youth and flung him to his death – an impious act, which demanded atonement.

In desperation, Heracles fled to Delphi, but the oracle refused him audience. Again the mist of anger engulfed the hero. He raged through the sanctuary causing terrible destruction before seizing the sacred tripod in Apollo's temple. Now Apollo himself intervened, and for long hours the two wrestled for control of this most sacred object. At last Zeus interceded, hurling a thunderbolt that exploded in a blinding flash and restored Heracles' sanity.

As punishment, Zeus caused Heracles to be enslaved for a further year, this time to the Lydian queen, Omphale. For the red-blooded hero this was an even more terrifying experience than his servitude to Eurystheus. The queen unmanned him: not only did she confiscate his club and lionskin, she made him dress in women's clothes, wear jewelry and make-up, and help her and her maidservants at the spinning-wheel.

The Death of Heracles

Released at last, Heracles returned to Greece, where – after many wars against cities such as Elis, Pylos and Troy – he married Deineira, Meleager's sister from Calydon, the woman who unwittingly would kill him. Leaving

Calydon, they soon came to the roaring River Evenos, swollen with melted snow from the high Vardousia mountains. Here, a Centaur, Nessus, approached them, claiming to be a god-appointed ferryman and offering to convey Deineira across while Heracles swam. It was a ruse. Nessus was intent on rape.

Reaching the far bank, Nessus galloped off with Deineira, terrified, clinging to his back. But Heracles shot at the escaping Centaur and, despite the distance, felled him. As Nessus lay dying, he whispered to Deineira to save some of his blood, and, if she ever suspected Heracles of straying, to smear it on his tunic. It would give the garment magic properties: Heracles would never be unfaithful again.

Years later Heracles returned from battle to his adopted home in Trachis (north of Delphi), with a beautiful slave girl, Iole, to be his mistress. Now Deineira recalled Nessus' words. She rubbed the Centaur's blood on a new tunic, and gave it to Heracles to wear at his victory celebrations. But the blood was infected with the Hydra's bile, in which Heracles had once dipped his arrows. Heracles' flesh began to blister and bubble. He tried in vain to tear off the tunic, and when he dived into a nearby pool he merely made the poison work more quickly. (Ever afterwards the waters boiled with sulphur, which gave them their name: Thermopylae, 'Hot Gates'.)

In agony Heracles crawled up Mount Oeta. Reaching the summit he ordered his son Hyllus – or, in some accounts, his friend Philoctetes – to burn him alive on a pyre of oak and olive branches. But before the flames caught fully, Zeus consumed the hero in a lightning flash and conveyed his soul to Mount Olympus, where, married to Hebe, the goddess of youth, Heracles lived forever, an immortal. Meanwhile in Trachis, Deineira hanged herself.

Eurystheus & the Children of Heracles
With Heracles dead, Eurystheus seized his chance to wreak vengeance on his hated cousin's children. For some time Heracles' mother Alcmene had been living in Tiryns with many of the sons whom Heracles had fathered on his travels. Now Eurystheus vowed to expel them – along with all Heracles' other children – from Greece. When Athens' king Theseus heard of this injustice, he offered them asylum in Attica and soon the sons of Heracles had formed an army.

Rousing himself to unaccustomed action, Eurystheus marched from Tiryns with his own troops, and on the coast just north of the Isthmus of Corinth the armies met head-on. In heavy fighting, the cowardly Eurystheus turned tail and fled, urging his chariot team back south along the road by the Scironian Rocks. But here the sons of Heracles caught up with him, dragged him to the ground and hacked off his head. When it was brought to Alcmene, she gouged out the lifeless eyes with brooch pins.

Now kingless, Tiryns was annexed by Atreus and Thyestes, who were ruling nearby Midea. When the brothers took control of Mycenae too, Tiryns became the main port of the Argolid.

Tiryns in History & Today

Tiryns was occupied from the mid-sixth millennium BC. Then the sea lapped close to the rocky outcrop, which rises abruptly from the plain to a height of just under 28 m (100 ft), but the shoreline gradually receded until by the second millennium BC it was 1 km (just over half a mile) away. (It is now almost twice that distance.)

Tiryns' first period of prosperity came in the mid-third millennium BC, when both the acropolis and a relatively large area outside the walls show signs of well-built houses. The most remarkable structure, on the highest part of the acropolis (the Upper Citadel), was an impressive – if now somewhat unimaginatively named – Round Building, 28 m (90 ft) in diameter. Remains of bastions suggest it rose to a significant height, sufficient to be clearly seen from afar, not least from the sea. Its purpose remains unknown: was it a fortified stronghold, a temple, a palace or perhaps a granary? Later in the third millennium much of Tiryns (including the Round Building) was burned, and only around 1400 BC did it regain its previous prosperity. The Upper Citadel was encircled by a 'Cyclopean' wall and a splendid palace was constructed, with plastered and finely painted reception rooms.

As the chief port of the wealthy Argolid, Tiryns became a rich entrepôt. Evidence suggests that merchant ships laden with foodstuffs, fabrics and precious metals reached here from Egypt by way of Syria and Crete. Towards the end of the thirteenth century BC further 'Cyclopean' walls were built around the Lower Citadel. The palace was rebuilt, its floors decorated with leaping dolphins and its plastered walls painted with scenes of elaborately coiffed women walking in procession, young men with chariots, and hunting dogs attacking a boar. The town expanded considerably, and a dam was built to contain and divert the nearby stream, which had previously been prone to flood the area to the north. But around 1200 BC an earthquake appears to have destroyed most of the town and citadel.

Unusually for Mycenaean palace settlements, Tiryns experienced renewed building in the twelfth century BC. Earthquake-damaged buildings were cleared away, a new palatial hall constructed in the Upper Citadel, and the town expanded to cover some 24 ha (60 acres). However, this prosperity came to an abrupt halt and – for reasons still unknown – by around 1060 BC Tiryns was largely abandoned.

While the Upper Citadel remained partially inhabited, Tiryns never regained its former status. In 494 BC it offered asylum to slaves escaping in the aftermath of Argos' defeat by Sparta at the Battle of Sepeia, and in 479 BC it sent four hundred hoplites to fight at the Battle of Plataea, five times the number sent by nearby Mycenae. Thanks partly to this heroic intervention, in his epic *Thebaid* (an extract from which begins this chapter), the Roman Statius imagined Tiryns' army eagerly taking part in the expedition of the Seven Against Thebes.

In 468 BC, Argos annexed Tiryns. Some inhabitants settled in Argos itself, others moved a few miles east, founding the town of Halieis (modern Porto Heli). When Pausanias visited Tiryns he found it deserted but nonetheless he marvelled:

> The wall, which is the work of Cyclopes and all that
> still remains, is made from undressed stones, each so
> large that a team of two mules could not move even the
> smallest by the slightest distance from where it is set.

He added:

> Greeks tend to admire foreign sights more than
> homegrown ones. Eminent historians have provided
> exhaustive descriptions of the pyramids of Egypt, but
> none has made even the briefest mention of the Treasury
> of Minyas [in Orchomenos near Thebes] or the walls of
> Tiryns, even though both are just as remarkable.

Because of its walls, Tiryns' location was never lost, and in 1876 Heinrich Schliemann began excavations at the site. They have been continued ever since by the German Archaeological Institute and Greek Archaeological Service.

Tiryns

SOME IMPORTANT DATES & REMAINS

c. 5500 BC	First settlements.
c. 2500 BC	First period of prosperity. Round Building constructed on Upper Citadel.
c. 2200 BC	Much of Tiryns consumed by fire.
c. 1400 BC	Walls constructed around new palace on Upper Citadel.
c. 1225 BC	Walls constructed around Lower Citadel; palace rebuilt on Upper Citadel; dam built.
c. 1200 BC	Major earthquake damage followed by rebuilding of much of town and parts of Upper Citadel.
c. 1060 BC	Tiryns largely abandoned.
494 BC	Argive slaves take refuge in Tiryns.
479 BC	Tiryns sends 400 hoplites to fight at Battle of Plataea.
468 BC	Tiryns defeated, annexed and depopulated by Argos.
AD 1876	Schliemann begins excavations.

At first sight unprepossessing, Tiryns lies on the main road 8 km (5 miles) from Argos and 4 km (2½ miles) from Nafplio. From the large car park a path leads south along the east wall to a steep ramp. At the top is the (now ruined) **monumental gateway** with postholes for folding doors. Beyond is the Upper Citadel. A courtyard leads (left) to a series of impressive **galleries** – six vaulted chambers built into the outer wall – and (left) to the foundations of a pillared **propylaion**. This gives on to a courtyard. A further **gallery** (left) set into the wall is accessed by a covered stairway; through a colonnaded courtyard (right) a series of antechambers lead to the **megaron**, the site of the earlier Round Building (no longer visible). Right is a smaller megaron, perhaps part of the women's quarters. Left is a fine **postern gate** and a secret **staircase** leading to a small gateway. The Lower Citadel contains fewer identifiable buildings. A further two staircases tunnel down into underground **cisterns** outside the walls.

Many finds from Tiryns, the nearby hilltop citadel of **Midea** and its related Mycenaean cemetery at **Dendra** (both well worth a visit) are housed in the **Archaeological Museum at Nafplio**. These include a stunning suit of **Mycenaean armour**, complete with boar's-tusk helmet and fragments of **frescoes** and **flooring**. Other artifacts (including frescoes) are in the National Archaeological Museum in Athens. The first capital of independent Greece from 1829 to 1834, Nafplio is a charming, curiously Italianate seaside town with a hilltop castle, a delightful waterfront, an island fortress, fine Venetian architecture, tempting shops and arguably the best ice cream parlour in Greece (the Antica Gelateria di Roma).

12

Iolcus & Mount Pelion: Centaurs, Weddings & the Voyage for the Golden Fleece

You would never grow bored of Pelion or of its way of life. You would never weary of its ash trees, grown strong in the breeze, which make straight spear shafts, never snapping at the spearhead. Nor would you tire of its caves – they are so beautiful! – or its springs or the female centaurs gathered round them. Overlook their equine element and they look like water nymphs; dwell on it and they seem like Amazons, for their womanly good looks are but enhanced by seeing them joined to their equine bodies.... They are so beautiful!

Philostratus the Elder, *Imagines*, 2.3

The morning is already hot and hazy. Below the low hill at Dimini, the modern port of Volos stretches its urban sprawl across the plain, its suburbs chequered with dark pine trees and lush citrus orchards. From distant highways the grind of gears and the occasional insistent blare of an alarm provide a muffled bass for the cackling concerto of cockerels squawking with increasing fervour from farmsteads closer by.

The sea once washed much nearer to our vantage point. Three and a half millennia ago the rising sun would glitter on splintering waves down there on the great inlet of the Gulf of Pagasae; though beyond, the pale folds of Mount Pelion are stippled still with shadows of tall trees and fragrant aromatic shrubs. Once Greeks believed that Centaurs lived in caves high on this wooded promontory. Intelligent and shy, half-horse, half-man, they galloped along stony tracks, as confident as any mountain goat. It was believed, too, that a white-sailed ship once cast off from the quay below, when the *Argo* slipped her moorings to sail east across the misty ocean to the very limits of the world. Even now, with the Centaurs and the *Argo* gone and a busy city booming in their stead, Volos, or Iolcus as it was known to mythology, can still be magical, a place of rare jewels and unexpected discovery.

The Centaurs

The Centaurs of Mount Pelion were the hybrid children of Centaurus, the son of Ixion. Wishing to marry princess Dia, Ixion invited her father to bring her to his palace, and then tricked him into walking over a pitfall trap into which he fell to be roasted alive. Curiously, Zeus forgave Ixion and invited him to a feast on Mount Olympus.

There Ixion plotted to seduce Hera. But Zeus found out and, to expose him, fashioned a false Hera from a cloud, with which willing substitute Ixion made love. Caught *in flagrante*, Ixion was arrested by Hermes, flogged and strapped to a burning wheel, on which he was rotated for eternity. Meanwhile Zeus took the opportunity to father a son by Dia: Peirithous, who later ruled the Lapiths.

The cloudy simulacrum, whose name was Nephele, also bore a son, Centaurus. Centaurus was unconventional. Conceiving a passion for a herd of mares which grazed near Iolcus, he mated with each one. Their offspring were the Centaurs, creatures with the torso of a human joined to the body of a horse, who, when provoked or drunk, could become barbarically wild.

One Centaur, Cheiron, did not share this lineage. Both immortal and much older, he was born when Cronus in the guise of a black stallion ravished the nymph Philyra. Cheiron's appearance was different, too – he possessed the full body of a man joined to a horse's torso and rear legs. Skilled in medicine, this wisest of all Centaurs tutored many of the

Holding a branch, from which hangs a hare, the centaur Cheiron addresses a young protégé. (Attic red figure vase, *c.* 520 BC).

greatest heroes (including Theseus, Perseus, Achilles and Jason) in the idyllic glades of Pelion.

Aeson, Pelias & the One-Sandalled Man

As the son of its founder Cretheus, Aeson was Iolcus' rightful king. However, Pelias, Aeson's step-brother by their mother, Tyro, enjoyed an even higher pedigree. As a young girl Tyro had left Thessaly when her father, Salmoneus, went south to rule Elis. But Salmoneus was overbearing, and thought himself Zeus' equal. Hurling burning firebrands as if they were lightning bolts, he drove the streets in a chariot equipped with bronze drums, which boomed like thunder. So Zeus hurled a lightning bolt of his own and put an end to Salmoneus.

Abused by her stepmother, Tyro moped by the river's edge, where Poseidon spied her, with inevitable consequences. He engulfed Tyro in a towering wave, and nine months later she was delivered of twins, Pelias and Neleus. In shame she exposed them on the mountainside to die, but a herdsman found them and reared them until they came of age. Discovering their parentage, they rescued Tyro and returned with her to Iolcus. Here Tyro married King Cretheus and bore Aeson – who subsequently fathered a son of his own and sent him to be schooled by Cheiron on Mount Pelion. While the boy was away, old Cretheus died, and it was now that Pelias showed his colours. Imprisoning Aeson and banishing Neleus (who fled in exile to the southwest Peloponnese to found Pylos), he seized the throne. Pelias could not relax, however. He lived in dread of a one-sandalled man, whom the Delphic oracle foretold would kill him.

Meanwhile, on Mount Pelion Aeson's son became well-versed in medicine and took the name Jason ('Healer'). Now twenty years old and eager to restore his father to the throne, he set off for Iolcus. In his path lay the River Anaurus, thundering in spate. As he prepared to ford it, an old woman begged him to carry her across. Without a second thought, Jason set her on his back and struggled through the swollen stream. Only when they were safely across did she reveal her true identity: she was Hera in disguise, and, because Jason had helped her so willingly, she promised to aid Jason in return.

Encouraged, Jason strode on to Iolcus. Pindar describes him as:

> a man of magnificent appearance, with two spears and a double tunic, the costume of his native land, close-fitting his magnificent physique. Around him he had slung a leopard skin to keep out the icy rain, and his uncut hair cascaded down his back in waves. Swiftly he strode, still testing his unshakeable resolve, until he came into the market place and stood there in the middle of the jostling crowd.

People were speculating whether Jason was a god when Pelias drove up in his polished mule-cart and stared in horror at the young man's feet. In the swirling currents of the river Jason had lost a sandal. Pelias' nemesis had arrived.

Jason demanded that Pelias restore Aeson to the throne. Deceitfully Pelias agreed, but first he asked Jason to 'appease the anger of the dead'. Iolcus, he said, was haunted by the ghost of Phrixus, a local prince who had fled far to the east, borne by a miraculous golden ram. The oracle had ordered Pelias to restore to Greece both the ram's fleece and Phrixus' hapless ghost, that it might rest forever in its homeland. If Jason accomplished this task, Pelias would concede the kingship.

Phrixus & Helle (a Brief Digression)
Phrixus had close ties with Iolcus' royal family. He and his sister Helle were the children of King Athamas of Boeotia (brother of Salmoneus) and the cloud-goddess Nephele. But, spurning Nephele, Athamas instead married Ino (Cadmus' daughter, a princess of Thebes) and had two further children, Learches and Melicertes.

Jealous of her step-children, Ino plotted to kill them. She commanded local women to roast the seed-corn before it was sown to prevent it from producing crops. Inevitably the harvest failed, and Athamas sent messengers to Delphi to discover why. But Ino bribed them, and on their return they announced that the gods were angry. The only way to soothe them was to sacrifice Helle and Phrixus (whom his aunt, the wife of Cretheus, king of Iolcus, had falsely accused of raping her).

The two were taken to the mountain. But before the sacrifice could be performed, their mother Nephele intervened. She sent a winged ram with a golden fleece to rescue them. The siblings climbed on to its back and it launched into the air. As it soared east across the Aegean, Helle grew tired, her grip slackened and she plunged into the sea. In her memory the Greeks called the strait where she fell the Hellespont (Helle's Sea, the modern Dardanelles). Still carrying Phrixus, the ram reached the Black Sea's furthest shores. Here, on lush plains watered by the River Phasis and bordered to the north by the snowy Caucasus mountains, King Aeëtes, son of Helios and brother of the enchantress Circe, ruled Colchis (modern Georgia). Hospitably he welcomed Phrixus, and together they sacrificed the ram and hung its golden fleece high in a tree, setting a sleepless serpent to guard over it.

Back in Greece, Hera drove Athamas and Ino mad. Believing his son Learches to be a white stag, Athamas shot him. And in a vain attempt to save Melicertes, Ino leapt into the sea with him, where she was transformed into Leucothea (the White Goddess), who helped sailors in times of trouble. Homer describes her beautiful ankles.

The Voyage of the Argo Begins

To sail to Colchis, Jason commissioned a ship, the *Argo*, named after its builder, Argus, who constructed it from pine trees felled on Pelion, while Athene fitted to its prow a talking plank, cut from the sacred oak at Dodona. For his crew (the Argonauts, 'Argo Sailors') Jason assembled the bravest heroes of his age. Most sources agree that they included Castor and Polydeuces from Sparta, Meleager from Calydon, Zetes and Calaïs, sons of the North Wind, Iphitus, the brother of Tiryns' King Eurystheus, Pelias' son Acastus, Orpheus, and Heracles, who – although the bravest of them all – conceded the captaincy to Jason.

The *Argo* first called at Lemnos, where it was greeted by a hostile army. Tensions were diffused when its leader, Queen Hypsipyle ('High Gates'), revealed the reason for her nervousness. The Lemnians had neglected their wives, complaining of their body odour, and conducted affairs with mainland girls. In consequence, Hypsipyle said, the women drove them into exile (in fact they murdered them). Finding their hostesses distinctly aromatic, the Argonauts enthusiastically embraced them, and in time Lemnos resounded to the mewls of newborn babies. Even Jason was reluctant to depart, but at last Heracles dragged the crew back to the *Argo*.

Through the Hellespont they sailed to the southern shores of the Propontis Sea, where the king of Cyzicus welcomed them to his wedding feast. Then resuming their journey, the Argonauts rounded a broad headland, before a storm forced them in to land. In the darkness they were attacked, and a bloody battle left many of their assailants dead. When the weather cleared they discovered the truth. Cyzicus was built on an isthmus, and they had been driven on to its far shore; the attackers were their friends of days before and the newly married king was among the fallen. In grief his young bride hanged herself. Mourning their error, the Argonauts returned to their rowing benches and continued east.

A Boxing King, Harpies & the Clashing Rocks

Not all the Argonauts were destined to reach Colchis. When Heracles' oar snapped, they put ashore to let him uproot a tree and make another. But when it was time to sail they discovered that Heracles' friend (or lover) Hylas had not returned from fetching water. Heracles set out to find him, but despite scouring the countryside he failed. Loath to sacrifice the breeze, but with Heracles refusing to abandon Hylas, the Argonauts set off without them. Hylas was never found – a lovesick nymph had drawn him down into her pool, where she kept him to herself forever.

Despite Heracles' absence, the Argonauts managed to defeat a savage king, Amycus, who challenged all comers to a brutal boxing match. Leaving him for dead, they sailed safely through the treacherous Bosphorus, before landing at Salmydessus on the east coast of the Black Sea (modern Kıyıköy, called in medieval times 'Medea'). Here lived Phineas, originally a Theban prophet, whom the gods punished for revealing more than was permitted. Not only was he blind, but he was plagued by Harpies – loathsome creatures, half-bird, half-woman. Whenever Phineas tried to eat, they plunged from the sky, screeching and flapping their huge wings, snatching his food and defecating prodigiously over anything they failed to grab.

When Jason sought his advice, Phineas announced that he would help only if the Argonauts chased off the Harpies. So they laid out a mouthwatering banquet. At once the Harpies swooped down. Swiftly, Calaïs and Zetes, sons of the North Wind, drew their swords and soared into the sky, slicing and lunging. Terrified, the Harpies fled squawking west, with Calaïs and Zetes flying in hot pursuit, until they came to the Ionian Sea. Here the brothers left them, turned (so giving the nearby islands their name, 'Strophades', 'Turning Place') and flew back to the *Argo*.

The delighted Phineas first feasted, then gave Jason good advice: the Symplegades ('Clashing Rocks') were high cliffs on each side of a narrow strait through which the *Argo* must sail. Not anchored to the earth, at any ship's approach they crashed together like a pair of cymbals, smashing the vessel and killing its crew. Phineas recommended that they send a dove ahead between the rocks and see how it fared. If it survived, so would the *Argo*.

As they approached the Symplegades, dull blue in morning mist, they released the bird. At once the cliffs slammed tight together in a spume of icy water – but, with just a few trapped tail feathers, the dove soared free. Immediately the crew strained at their oars, and the ship sped forward. Soon the wet crags loomed above them, motionless at first, but then with increasing momentum rushing relentlessly towards them. With a sickening crunch they slammed together – too late to harm the *Argo*. Apart from a few stern planks, the ship was safe thanks to the crew's efforts and Athene's aid, for the goddess had pledged to help Jason whenever he was in danger. The Symplegades now stayed rooted to the spot, never to move again, and the *Argo* sped on to Colchis.

At last the *Argo* nosed into the broad estuary of the Phasis. Next morning, as Apollonius of Rhodes describes, Jason and a few companions set off for the palace:

> They left the river and the ship, where it was hidden
> among tall reeds, stepped on to the shore and made their
> way on to the plain, which is named the Plain of Circe.
> Here are planted many rows of osiers and willow trees,
> and tied with ropes on to their topmost branches corpses
> hang suspended.

Met by Aeëtes and his family at the palace, they explained why they had come. Aeëtes was furious, and only just stopped himself from leaping up and killing them. Instead, he struck a bargain, setting Jason a task which he was confident the Greek would not survive.

Aeëtes possessed two bronze-hoofed, fire-breathing bulls. Each morning he yoked them and ploughed a four-acre field, then sowed it with dragon's teeth – and when angry armed men rose from the furrows he fought against this earth-born army until by evening all the warriors were dead. If Jason took his place and proved his worth, Aeëtes would give him the fleece. Fearing that to do so would mean his death, Jason accepted the challenge.

Jason & Medea

But Aphrodite was on Jason's side, and already she had worked her magic. Aeëtes' daughter Medea was a witch with the power to destroy her enemies. But now she was consumed by love. Hesiod says she was 'bashful-eyed' as she gazed at Jason; Apollonius describes her 'lifting her veil to look at Jason with her slanting eyes, her heart on fire with suffering, and, as he

left, her spirit slunk from her and fluttered after him, as if it were a dream';
while in a passage recalling real Greek magic Pindar has Aphrodite teaching Jason occult spells to woo Medea:

> The queen of the most deadly arrows, Cyprus-born
> Aphrodite, bound a wryneck woodpecker fast to a four-
> spoked wheel (the first time that mankind had seen the
> maddening bird) and taught the clever Jason charms and
> incantations, to coax Medea to forget her parents and
> burn with desire for Greece, lashed by Persuasion's goad.

Torn between respecting her parents and saving Jason, Medea crept out
to the temple of Hecate, goddess of the dead, to mix a magic salve. Here,
guided by the gods, Jason met her. Hurriedly Medea told him what to do:
he must sacrifice a sheep to Hecate at midnight before smearing the salve
over his body and his weapons to render him invulnerable. When the
armed men sprang from the furrows, he should throw a boulder into
their midst to make them fight not Jason but each other.

As he listened to Medea's words, Jason fell in love with her. If he survived, he promised he would take her back to Iolcus and marry her, so
she would be the envy of all Greece, a goddess among women. Medea

Encouraged by Athene
an oddly puny Jason
steals the golden fleece
while the serpent hisses
fiercely. (Attic red figure
vase, possibly
c. 470–460 BC.)

ardently accepted, and, in Pindar's coy words, 'they willingly agreed to join with one another in sweet union'.

Thanks to Medea's potion and advice Jason completed Aeëtes' challenges unscathed, but the king refused to honour his bargain and plotted the Argonauts' destruction. Medea discovered his intentions. Apollonius vividly describes her running from the palace, barefoot, down narrow alleyways, with one hand keeping her veil close to her face lest anyone recognize her, and lifting up her dress with the other so she could run faster. Reaching the *Argo*, she urged the crew to row with all speed to the sacred grove and steal the fleece.

Jason and Medea jumped ashore and made for the oak tree, where they saw the fleece already glowing in the light of the rising sun. But they saw too the sleepless serpent's yellow eyes. And now it was upon them, rearing its head, drool dripping from its fangs. Undeterred, Medea sang a soft enchanting lullaby and sprinkled a soporific drug on the monster's head. Its heavy eyelids closed; its neck drooped to the ground; it slept. Clutching the fleece, Jason and Medea fled back to the *Argo*. The crew cast off and, as dawn broke, they bent keenly to their oars and the ship sped out across the glassy calm of the Black Sea.

Brother-Killing & the Voyage Home

Alerted, Aeëtes ran to the shore, ordering his men to launch his fleet in pursuit of the pirates who had stolen his daughter and the fleece. At last, near the Black Sea's western shores the distance between them grew so narrow that it seemed the Colchians would overtake the *Argo*. In desperation Medea seized her brother, Apsyrtus (whom she had smuggled aboard), killed him, cut up his body and scattered the pieces into the sea. When Aeëtes saw the fingers, feet, chopped arms and head bobbing on the waves, he commanded his men to stop and collect the remains. He buried them on the shore and founded a city, naming it Tomi ('temno' means 'I cut') in his dismembered son's memory.

The Argonauts' route home excited much debate among ancient authors. Some traced a passage north up the Danube, then south down the River Rhone, and far to the west and lands associated with death. Their adventures paralleled some of Odysseus' on his journey home to Ithaca. Thus the Argonauts visited Circe, who purified them of Apsyrtus' murder; the Sirens' rock, where Orpheus saved the crew by singing more sweetly than the enchantresses; and Crete, where they defeated the bronze giant Talos by removing a pin from his ankle so that blood-like molten lead drained out and Talos crashed dying to the shore.

Returning to Iolcus, Jason presented Pelias with the golden fleece (which harboured Phrixus' ghost). But Pelias refused to hand over the throne. Again Medea intervened. Some say that Aeson was already dead

– persuaded by Pelias that Jason's mission had failed, he had drunk bull's blood and killed himself. Others maintain he was still alive, the frailest of old men, and that Medea restored him to youth. Chanting spells, she first slit Aeson's throat, then placed his body in a boiling cauldron, into which she poured a magic brew. Out stepped a comely youth: Aeson, robust once more and in the springtime of his life. Those who claim that Aeson was already dead say that Medea achieved the same results with an old ram.

Pelias' daughters, eager to make their father young again, begged Medea's help. She promised that if they slit Pelias' throat, she would perform the magic. The girls did as commanded, but Medea, triumphant, would not fulfil her promise. The people blamed the foreign princess for their king's death, rising as one to exile Jason and Medea. Far away in Corinth their love affair ended in violence. In Iolcus, Pelias' son Acastus (himself an Argonaut) claimed the throne.

The Wedding of Peleus & Thetis

Peleus, a prince from Phthia, further south on the Gulf of Pagasae, was another of the Argonauts. Acastus' wife, Cretheis, fell in love with him and, when he rebuffed her, accused him of rape. Rather than executing him, Acastus took Peleus hunting on Mount Pelion, hoping to find an excuse to kill him. In fierce competition, the two bagged a prodigious haul, but at sunset, to provoke a fight, Acastus claimed all Peleus' trophies as his own. Peleus protested. He had cut out all his victims' tongues and now exhibited them as evidence. After an uneasy banquet, Peleus fell asleep. When he awoke Acastus had disappeared, taking Peleus' weapons, and now a herd of Centaurs was surrounding him, hungry for revenge for the carnage of the day before. Only just in time Cheiron galloped up and diffused the situation.

Cheiron knew that Zeus wished Peleus to marry the sea-nymph, Thetis. (The only reason Zeus had not slept with her himself was that Thetis' son was destined to be stronger than his father.) But Thetis was unwilling to mate with a mere mortal, and when Peleus found her basking in a cave she did her utmost to resist him, turning herself first into fire, then water, a serpent, a lion and a cuttlefish. Peleus clung to her until Thetis conceded defeat.

Their marriage was celebrated near Cheiron's cave. It was a lavish ceremony. The Muses sang, the Nereids danced and the Centaurs watched in wonder. But as the festivities reached their peak, an icy chill descended. Dressed all in black a figure stalked into the glade. It was Eris, goddess of strife, whom Peleus had forgotten to invite. Now she exacted vengeance. Taking a golden apple from beneath her cloak, she rolled it across the dancing floor. Then, wordlessly, she turned and strode away.

The battle between the Centaurs and Lapiths
formed the subject matter for metopes on the south
side of the fifth-century BC Parthenon at Athens.

The apple bore an inscription: 'for the most beautiful'. Now every
woman, nymph or goddess claimed it for her own and the feast degen-
erated into acrimony. Only after many years would the apple find an
owner, when Zeus commanded Paris to make a judgment on Mount Ida,
the consequence of which would be the fall of Troy.

The Battle of the Centaurs & Lapiths

Another wedding in a cave on Mount Pelion had dire repercussions for
the Centaurs, when Peirithous (son of Zeus and Ixion's wife Dia), ruler
of the Lapiths, married Hippodameia ('Horse-Breaker'). Peirithous was
a friend of Theseus, the king of Athens, and shared many of his adventures, including the Calydonian boar hunt. So it was natural for Theseus
to be Peirithous' best man. Most of the gods attended, as well as local
dignitaries and many of Peirithous' Centaur cousins.

Wine flowed freely – which, for the normally abstemious Centaurs, was a disaster. Quickly drunk, they behaved like beasts. One tried to abduct Hippodameia; others assaulted wives of other guests. Theseus and the Lapiths sprang to Peirithous' aid; Centaurs tore up trees as weapons or hurled boulders at their hosts. It was a ghastly brawl leaving many dead, but the Lapiths were victorious.

Afterwards the Centaurs, alienated from their neighbours, left Pelion forever. Some wandered west to the high Pindus mountains; others, including Cheiron, trekked south to the Peloponnese, where a sad remnant again suffered the dire consequences of drink when Pholus entertained Heracles with a vintage skin of wine. Driven wild by its bouquet, the Centaurs stampeded, and Heracles was forced to protect himself by shooting them with his poisoned arrows. Not one Centaur survived.

Alcestis

Marriages made at or near Iolcus seemed doomed to disaster. Years earlier Admetus, the king of Pherae a few miles inland, had sought the hand of Pelias' daughter, Alcestis. Pelias set the suitor a seemingly impossible test: to yoke a lion and boar to his chariot and drive it round the hippodrome in Iolcus. Helped by Apollo and Heracles, Admetus succeeded, but in his rush he forgot to sacrifice to Artemis. When he approached his marriage bed he found that it contained a nest of serpents. Terrified, he prayed to Apollo to avert Artemis' anger, and it was a mark of the god's love that he succeeded. Moreover, Apollo agreed that, when the time came for Admetus to die, he would be spared if one of his family sacrificed themselves on his behalf.

Soon afterwards Hermes, who conveys dead souls to Hades, arrived at Pherae to announce Admetus' death. Frantically Admetus tried to find a surrogate to die instead of him, but only Alcestis agreed. Amidst bitter lamentations, the queen took her own life, while, left lonely and alive, Admetus was racked with self-blame. Euripides' *Alcestis* tells how Heracles agreed to help. At the funeral, Heracles confronts Death, rescues Alcestis and leads her, veiled, back to Admetus; without revealing her identity, he bids him take her as his wife. Admetus is indignant, but at last the truth is revealed. Death has returned Alcestis; love has triumphed; and one myth at least has a happy ending.

Iolcus in History & Today

The Mycenaean site at Dimini near Volos was first excavated at the end of the twentieth century. As a town and palace – the only Mycenaean palace in Thessaly – served by major roads, its importance soon became apparent. Finds of high-status imports from Syria and Asia Minor confirmed Dimini's strong trading links, allowing archaeologists to identify it as mythological Iolcus. Dimini's history stretches back much further. In the early fifth millennium BC a thriving Late Neolithic city was built on the hilltop above what was then an inlet on the north coast of the Gulf of Pagasae. The settlement shows signs of contact with Sesklo, an even earlier agricultural town a few miles to the west, founded around 6500 BC, at its height supporting around 3,000 people. Dimini was perhaps a coastal colony of Sesklo. For four hundred years the two were occupied simultaneously, until Sesklo was abandoned around 4400 BC.

Late Neolithic Dimini thrived. Open public spaces suggest communal activity, while up to fifty mudbrick houses were built on stone foundations next to alleyways and encircling walls. A ceramic kiln produced temperatures as high as 850°C (1562°F). In time the settlement shrank, until by around 3000 BC it was inhabited by one extended family and abandoned shortly afterwards. In the second millennium BC, the site was used as a cemetery.

It was fully reoccupied only in the fourteenth century BC, when the Mycenaean palace and city were constructed lower down the hill to the southeast. Within the Neolithic site was built one of two tholos tombs discovered so far, the other being slightly further off to the west. Meanwhile the walls and floor of the palace's megaron were covered in white plaster, with two wings (the north residential, the south containing workshops and store rooms) joined by a corridor. It was destroyed (perhaps accidentally) in the late thirteenth century BC and replaced by a bipartite palace, its walls lined with clay, with a raised clay altar near its entranceway. This palace was destroyed by fire around 1200 BC. Neither phase seems to have had protective walls, making the site vulnerable, particularly from the sea.

This time Dimini was not reoccupied. With the coastline now some miles to the south, later settlements (including Demetrias, founded by Demetrius the Besieger at the end of the fourth century BC) were closer to – or on – the site of modern Volos, of which Dimini is now a suburb.

Excavations began in 1886 when archaeologists dug the tholos tomb called 'Lamiospito' ('Haunted House'). Enthusiastic reports appeared in American newspapers extolling finds of gold jewelry, which were 'scarcely larger than a pin's head, and yet leave nothing to be desired in beauty and finish'. They added that the discoveries 'tend to the supposition that the population was seafaring'. Only six years later, historians wrote: 'Here, by the tranquil waters of the Pagasetan Gulf, were learned [the Mycenaeans'] first lessons in navigation, ere they ventured on those distant and adventurous expeditions, whose remembrance is preserved in the *Argonaut* myth.'

Today Volos is a thriving port, whose quayside boasts a proud souvenir of its heroic past: a reconstruction of Jason's *Argo*, and plans are afoot for a new 'Argo Museum'.

SOME IMPORTANT DATES & REMAINS

c. **6850 BC**	Sesklo established.
c. **4800 BC**	Dimini established.
c. **4400 BC**	Sesklo abandoned.
C15th BC	First Mycenaean settlement.
C14th BC	First Mycenaean palace at Dimini and 'Lamiospito' tholos tomb.
C13th BC	Second Mycenaean palace.
c. **1200 BC**	Dimini abandoned.
AD 1886	'Lamiospito' tholos discovered.
AD 1997	Mycenaean city and palace at Dimini first excavated.

Dimini lies on the outskirts of Volos, well signposted off the busy E92 leading into the city. The Mycenaean site (still being excavated and closed to the public) can be seen from the perimeter fence. **Neolithic Dimini**, however, with its six rings of low walls, narrow alleyways and houses, repays a visit. To the northwest is the (collapsed) Mycenaean **'Lamiospito' tholos**. From here a path leads west to a second tholos (no access).

Sesklo is reached by a country road west from Dimini, beautifully sited in rolling hills. Covering a large area, the remains of houses built of stone, clay and mudbrick are made more comprehensible thanks to an audio guide.

Further inland is **Pherae**, with foundations of the **Temple of Zeus Thaulios** and the **Hypereia Fountain**, currently being excavated in modern Velestino, as well as remains of a **stoa, walls, towers** and a **Temple of Heracles**.

The **Archaeological Museum of Volos** contains material from the Neolithic period and Bronze Age grave goods (including **gold jewelry** and a charming clay **model of a chariot with two horses**). Reconstructions of burials set objects in context. Pottery sherds bear the **image of a Mycenaean ship**. Perhaps most stunning are the third- to second-century BC **painted grave stelai**, with miraculously well-preserved colours, showing scenes of the dead taking leave of the living. One includes a poignant inscription addressing Minos and Rhadamanthus, the judges in Hades, which may remind visitors of Admetus mourning his wife Alcestis:

> Minos and Rhadamanthus! If ever you judged another
> woman to be virtuous, judge Aristomachus' daughter to be
> virtuous, too. Convey her to the Islands of the Blessed, for
> she was beautiful and pious. Tylisus in Crete brought her
> to womanhood, but now this land embraces her. Your fate,
> Archidice, has made you immortal.

13

Corinth & False Promises of Love

About Corinth I shall tell no lies. Rather, I shall tell of Sisyphus, deceptive as a god, and of Medea who married much against her father's wish.... [And of Bellerophon] who here in Corinth held the sceptre and the palace and the royal estates. He once endured great hardships, trying to harness [the winged horse] Pegasus, the offspring of the snake-haired Gorgon, until Athene, maiden-goddess, brought him the bridle with the golden brow-band. And dream became reality.

As he lay asleep in darkness, Bellerophon believed the maiden goddess of the dusky aegis spoke to him. Seizing the magic bridle, he scrambled to his feet, and in delight ran to find Corinth's royal prophet and he told him everything.... The prophet ordered him at once to heed the dream's advice: to sacrifice a strong-shanked bull to Poseidon, Shaker of the Earth; without delay to raise an altar to Athene of the Horses. Gods' power can lightly overturn man's expectations and his oaths. So great Bellerophon seized the winged horse excitedly and slipped the taming bit between his jaws. Then, armoured all in bronze, he mounted...

Pindar, *Olympian Ode*, 13.72ff.

In the lull before the town awakes and tourist buses grind and lumber through the narrow streets, the sun rises over ancient Corinth. Shadows stretch languidly. The Temple of Apollo luxuriates in golden light. The paved road leading from the sea seems pristine, while beside the Fountain of Peirene broad steps lead invitingly into the honeyed Market Place. Behind the ruins, Acrocorinth, a wall of glistening grey cliffs, rises sheer from the lush plain, its summit ringed with jagged walls, a medieval bastion encircling a plateau once sacred to the sun-god Helios. But even in antiquity his supremacy was eclipsed, and now – high on this tall acropolis, the tumbled masonry already warming to the touch – the foundations of his rival's temple sprawl in the stirring undergrowth. It is the Temple of Aphrodite, goddess of love, sex and temptation.

Prometheus, Pandora & the Pithos

Temptation lies at the heart of many of the myths of Corinth (called Ephyra in early literature), not least the temptation of Pandora and its disastrous consequences. Its origins lay almost 20 km (12 miles) west, in Sicyon: to settle a dispute between the gods and men, the trickster-Titan Prometheus made sacrifice. Butchering an ox, he wrapped the meat in its hide and the bones in glistening fat, and bade Zeus choose which portion he preferred. Zeus chose the larger – the package containing the bones. When he discovered his mistake, Zeus was incandescent. Not only had he been exposed as injudicious, he had set a precedent: ever afterwards mankind burned only an animal's bones and fat in sacrifice, reserving the flesh for feasts. When Prometheus compounded the insult by stealing fire from heaven and giving it to men, Zeus exacted punishment. He had the Titan chained to a rock, where a vulture devoured his ever-regenerating liver, and created a misleading package of his own, a 'savage beauty', beguiling to look at, destructive within: Pandora, the first woman.

Hesiod describes how Hephaestus shaped

> earth into the body of a modest girl; grey-eyed Athene
> gave her a robe and belt; god-like Seduction and the
> Graces gave golden necklaces; and the Seasons wove
> spring flowers into a garland for her hair. Hermes
> implanted lies, persuasive and cunning in her breast and
> named the girl Pandora ['All-Gifted'], because the gods
> had given her so many gifts to be the ruin of mankind.

Zeus gave her as wife to Epimetheus, Prometheus' dullard brother, together with a wedding present: a large pithos (storage jar), which he told Pandora not to open. Naturally, she disobeyed, discovering too late what it contained: tiny winged spirits, the embodiment of distress and sorrow.

Immediately they swarmed out of the jar. 'Only Hope remained beneath the rim, and did not fly out. The lid prevented her, thanks to the will of Aegis-Wearing Zeus, Cloud-Gatherer. But ten thousand plagues now jostle men. The earth is full of sorrows; and full, too, the sea.'

With which Sisyphus, the mythical founder and king of Corinth, would wholeheartedly agree.

The Myth of Sisyphus

Originally from Thrace, Sisyphus travelled to the Peloponnese with his brother Salmoneus. Both were overbearing; each hated the other; and, when Sisyphus seduced his brother's daughter Tyro, it was purely because he had learned from an oracle that a son born from the union would kill Salmoneus. Frustratingly for Sisyphus, Tyro discovered the prophecy and killed every child she bore him. In the end he simply gave up. (In another myth, as we have seen, Tyro married Cretheus, ruler of Iolcus, by whom she bore Aeson, the father of Jason – whose consort Medea would play a vital part in the mythology of Corinth.)

Sisyphus' wiles were not restricted to attempts at fratricide. He even tried to cheat death. When Zeus changed into an eagle to abduct the local nymph, Aegina, taking her to the island which now bears her name, Sisyphus (who saw everything from Acrocorinth, Corinth's acropolis) offered to reveal her whereabouts to her father, the river god Asopus, if Asopus created a well on Acrocorinth. Soon the Spring of Peirene (namesake of the fountain in the city below) was bubbling merrily and Zeus was exposed.

On Zeus' orders, Death came to Corinth to shackle Sisyphus. But Sisyphus outwitted him. Asking the god to demonstrate how best to wear them, he clamped Death in his own chains and imprisoned him. Death's power was broken; no one could die – but this was not a blessing. Warriors maimed in battle, the very old, the very ill, all begged to die and at last the gods sent Ares to set Death free and end Sisyphus' life instead. Even now, Sisyphus refused to go quietly. Before he died, he ordered his wife to leave his corpse to lie in Corinth's agora. Only the buried could enter Hades, so when Ares arrived there with Sisyphus' soul, Sisyphus argued (quite correctly) that he should not be admitted. Instead, he should return to the upper world to scold his wife for her impious behaviour and organize his funeral. His ruse worked and, once home in Corinth, he stayed put. Zeus was not amused. He sent Hermes to escort Sisyphus back to Hades, where he punished the trickster for eternity, condemning him to roll a heavy boulder up a steep hill, only for it to crash back down again before it reached the top.

However, Sisyphus was not completely impious. Once, by the sea, he discovered the body of his nephew Melicertes, whose mother, Ino, driven mad by Hera, had leapt with him into the waves, and whose corpse a dolphin had brought ashore. Sisyphus buried Melicertes at Isthmia near Corinth, establishing funeral games in his honour – the two-yearly Isthmian Games, which in antiquity were sacred to Poseidon.

Bellerophon & Pegasus

Sisyphus left several sons, both legitimate and bastard. Among the latter, some said, was Odysseus; among the former, Glaucus, father of Bellerophon. The many contradictory versions of Bellerophon's story are impossible to reconcile. In most (though not in Homer) he is master of the winged horse Pegasus, which was born from the blood of Medusa. Challenged to bridle this fabulous creature as it grazed on Acrocorinth by Peirene's spring, Bellerophon succeeded only with the help of Athene and Poseidon. (Pindar's account begins this chapter.) It was as well that he did, for he would soon owe Pegasus his life.

Having accidentally killed a man, Bellerophon was exiled to Tiryns, where the young queen Anteia (sometimes called Sthenoboea) fell in love with him. When Bellerophon rejected her advances, Anteia took revenge. In Homer's account:

> She spoke lying words to the king: 'Kill Bellerophon
> or die. He tried to sleep with me against my will.' When
> he heard these words, the king was seized with anger.
> But, a pious man, he shrank from killing him. Rather
> he sent Bellerophon to Lycia with destructive symbols
> written in a folding tablet, sufficient to unknit his life,
> and bade him show them to Anteia's father, that he
> might be destroyed.

Blissfully ignorant of the letter's contents, Bellerophon and Pegasus went east. In Lycia King Iobates tried to fulfil Anteia's request by sending him on a deadly mission to kill Chimaera, a fire-breathing beast with three heads. One was a lion's; the second, sprouting from its back, a goat's; and the third, at its tail, a serpent's. Soaring into the air astride Pegasus, too high for Chimaera's fire to harm him, Bellerophon rained down arrows. In one account, he even thrust into its lion jaws a long spear tipped with lead, which, melting in the heat, ran down Chimaera's throat and suffocated him. Then Bellerophon returned to Iobates.

The king was baffled. Why had the gods protected such a wrongdoer? His perplexity increased when, sent against fierce tribes (including the Amazons), Bellerophon constantly came back victorious. At last Iobates confronted him with Anteia's letter. Bellerophon refuted the charge and Iobates gave him his younger daughter's hand in marriage.

Mounted on (the here wingless) Pegasus, Bellerophon attacks Chimaera on a terracotta relief from Melos (*c.* 460 BC).

All did not end so rosily. Bellerophon's success went to his head and he determined to fly Pegasus to Mount Olympus, a transgression the gods could not permit. At once Zeus sent a gadfly to bite Pegasus' flanks. The horse reared up. Bellerophon fell hard to earth where, in the words of Homer: 'Hated by the gods, he wandered the plain of Aleios alone, gnawing at his spirit, shunning the paths of men.' As for Pegasus, after many journeys, when he invariably created springs by striking the ground with his hooves (*pegai* means 'springs'), he did reach Olympus, where he carried Zeus' thunderbolts and became a constellation.

Medea, Queen of Corinth

The story of Jason, sent from Iolcus to retrieve the Golden Fleece, and his wife Medea, also unfolds in Corinth. In the most well-known version, shortly after their return to Greece the couple were exiled to this city with their two sons, when Medea engineered the death of Jason's uncle, the gullible Pelias, at the hands of his own daughters.

But in Corinth, King Creon offered Jason his daughter Glauce's hand in marriage. To the now-destitute hero, it seemed a golden opportunity. Soon it was the talk of Corinth – in his tragedy *Medea*, Euripides describes old men gossiping about it as they play backgammon at the Fountain of Peirene. Incensed, Medea took revenge, killing Glauce by giving her a dress smeared with poison, which tore like acid through her flesh – and Creon's, too, when he went to Glauce's aid. Then Medea butchered her own sons. As Jason came running out too late to save them, Medea soared into the sky on a chariot drawn by serpents, lent by her grandfather Helios. Denying Jason even the chance to bury his dead children – she would bury them herself in the sanctuary of Hera on the headland at Perachora on the far side of the Corinthian Gulf – she made for Athens and the protection of its king, Aegeus.

But the Corinthians knew other, older myths, linking Medea even more closely with their past. In one she is (like Tyro) a serial child-killer. According to Pausanias, once when they had no king:

> the Corinthians invited Medea from Iolcus and granted
> her the throne. Thanks to her, Jason ruled in Corinth.
> As soon as her children were born, Medea took them to
> the sanctuary of Hera where she buried them, believing
> that if they were buried there they would become
> immortal. In the end, she discovered that her hopes were
> unfounded, and at the same time she was found out by
> Jason. She begged him to forgive her, but he refused and
> sailed back to Iolcus. Because of this, Medea, too, sailed
> away and bequeathed the kingdom to Sisyphus.

Medea's motives here are strikingly different, welcome reminders of the fluidity of Greek mythology. In fact, two mutually contradictory versions existed side by side. Pausanias also saw in Corinth the Spring of Glauce, into which the princess jumped in the belief that its waters would reverse the effects of Medea's poisons. Close by was a memorial to Medea's sons, killed not by their mother (a version probably invented by Euripides), but 'stoned to death by the Corinthians, they say, because of the gifts they brought to Glauce. Because of their violent and illegal killing, the boys caused Corinthian new-borns to die until, following an oracular command, yearly sacrifices were instituted in their honour and a female statue set up, representing Terror. It is most chilling and still exists today.'

Corinth in History & Today

Thanks to its position, Corinth was one of the richest cities in mainland Greece. Sited just south of the Isthmus, it possessed two ports – one providing access to the Gulf of Corinth and the west; the other giving access to the east. By the eighth century BC Corinth began confidently founding overseas colonies, which included Corcyra on Corfu and Syracuse in Sicily.

In the mid-seventh century BC the far-sighted *tyrannos* Cypselus further expanded Corinth's trading base. During his reign and that of his son, Periander, work began on the Temple of Apollo and Fountain of Peirene, as well as the Diolcus, a paved trackway used to haul ships across the Isthmus. At the same time, Corinth perfected the design of a new warship: the trireme.

The arts flourished in Corinth – 'proto-Corinthian' pottery was among the most sophisticated of its time, and artistic schools at Corinth and nearby Sicyon were arguably the most pioneering in Greece. During Periander's reign the court poet Arion is said to have enjoyed a miraculous escape when returning to Corinth from South Italy. Intending to steal his belongings, the crew threw him overboard, but a dolphin rescued him and brought him safe to shore. In Corinth the would-be killers, identified by Arion, were executed.

In the fifth century BC, Corinth's economic rivalry with Athens was partly responsible for the Peloponnesian War (431–404 BC). Even Syracuse, Corinth's colony, became involved in the conflict when Athens launched an unsuccessful campaign against Sicily in 415 BC. In 395 BC, less than ten years after the war ended, Corinth allied with Athens against Sparta, but civil strife and quarrels among allies, together with an inconclusive outcome, weakened Corinth, and only when it came under Macedonian influence did its star wax again. Then in 146 BC, when Rome's general Lucius Mummius defeated the Achaean League, which resisted Roman interference in Greece, he took brutal revenge on its leader, Corinth. Comprehensively plundering its artworks and destroying much of the city, he massacred many citizens and enslaved the rest.

For a century Corinth was abandoned, until in 46 BC Julius Caesar chose it as the site of a new colony for army veterans. Again Corinth flourished, quickly regaining its reputation for luxury and fine living. In the fifth and fourth centuries BC, the city had been famous for its courtesans; now Strabo marvelled at the wealth of Acrocorinth's Temple of Aphrodite, home to a thousand sacred prostitutes, dedicated by rich men (and women). It was no coincidence that it was to the Christians of Corinth that the apostle Paul (who lived there for eighteen months around AD 51) wrote a letter exploring the meaning of true love:

> Love is patient and kind; love does not envy or boast;
> it is not arrogant or rude. It does not insist on its own
> way; it is not irritable or resentful; it does not rejoice
> at wrongdoing, but rejoices with the truth. Love
> bears all things, believes all things, hopes all things,
> endures all things.

Roman emperors including Nero and Hadrian patronized and embellished Corinth, but from the mid-fourth century AD earthquakes (and perhaps looting by Alaric the Goth) led to its decline. After a brief renaissance at the turn of the first millennium, it was sacked by crusaders in 1147. The site remained inhabited, but in 1858 further earthquake damage led to the decision to relocate Corinth to the coast. For this reason, the site of ancient Corinth is less frenetic than that of (say) ancient Athens. Although many Classical buildings lie inaccessible beneath modern houses, enough remains to give a real flavour of the once bustling city.

Corinth

SOME IMPORTANT DATES & REMAINS

? 6500 BC	Early habitation (Corinth's name is pre-Greek).
C8th/7th BC	Corinth establishes colonies, including Syracuse.
658–628 BC	Cypselus turns Corinth into an economic powerhouse.
581 BC	Isthmian Games first celebrated.
480–479 BC	Corinth takes part in Persian Wars.
433 BC	Corinth fights Athens over Corinth's colony, Corcyra.
431–404 BC	Corinth takes part in Peloponnesian War against Athens.
395–387 BC	Corinth and allies (including Athens) wage Corinthian War against Sparta.
338 BC	Philip II of Macedon creates Corinthian League against Persia.
243 BC	Corinth joins Achaean League against Sparta and (subsequently) Rome.
146 BC	Destruction of Corinth by Lucius Mummius of Rome.
46 BC	Julius Caesar re-founds Corinth as a colony for Roman veterans.
***c.* AD 51**	Paul lives among Corinth's Christians.
AD 68	Nero sings at Isthmian Games and declares freedom of Greece.
C2nd–3rd AD	Further expansion and enhancements.
mid-C4th AD	First in a series of major earthquakes which last into the sixth century AD.
AD 1147	Crusaders sack Corinth.
AD 1858	Corinth relocated to the coast.

From the site entrance a track leads past the foundations of the first-century AD **Temple of Octavia** towards the impressive **agora**, dominated to the north by the sixth-century BC **Temple of Apollo,** with seven standing Doric columns, partly surmounted by entablature. Close by is **Glauce's Fountain.** At the far side of the agora is the tranquil **Fountain of Peirene** (no access), built in its current form by Herodes Atticus (second century AD). Close to the entrance but outside the enclosure is the well-preserved **Odeon** (no access). Across the road a track leads to the scant remains of the **Theatre.**

A road leads steeply up to **Acrocorinth** with its impressive **Frankish Walls.** Here are the remains of the **Upper Fountain of Peirene** and the **Temple of Aphrodite.** Little of its former glory survives, but the views north towards central Greece and south to the Peloponnese are spectacular.

Also in the environs of Corinth are the remains of **Sicyon** and **Isthmia** (site of the Isthmian Games) with its, **theatre, Temple of Poseidon** and poorly preserved **stadium.**

Further afield, travellers in Turkey can visit **Chimaera,** an inextinguishable fire fed by subterranean gases on the coast 80 km (50 miles) southwest of Antalya. Near Fethiye at **Tlos** (where the hero is said to have died) is a **tomb bearing a sculpture of Bellerophon and Pegasus.**

14

Argos: Land of Hera, Home of Heroes

The people of Argos were celebrating the Festival of Hera and it was vital that the priestess be driven to the temple by a yoked team of oxen. However, the oxen had still not returned from the fields. Time was running out, so her sons, Cleobis and Biton, shouldered the yoke and pulled the wagon with their mother inside it for five miles until they reached the temple of Hera.

Their mother was delighted with their efforts. She stood in front of the statue and prayed that, since Cleobis and Biton had shown her such honour, the goddess Hera should grant them the greatest reward which a man might have. The prayer made, the people sacrificed and feasted. As for the young men, they fell asleep in the temple, and never woke again. Their lives were over. The Argives made statues of them, which they dedicated at Delphi, to show that they had been the best of men.

Herodotus, *Histories*, 1.31

Sit in the top tier of the theatre's rock-cut auditorium, and Argos – ancient and modern – stretches before you. The view is vertiginous. Clumps of pale grasses pockmark rows of grey stone seats, whose plunging lines are scarred by brutal fissures, the work of centuries of winter rain. On either side, phalanxes of tall trees file obliquely down, drawing the eye first to the theatre's *orkhestra* and stage, and then on, beyond the Roman bath-house, its brickwork rosy-pink, across the modern road towards the agora, the flat green plain, across the bay to Nafplio, and finally to the blue hills far beyond. Rather than to modern Argos, a concrete catastrophe, bleakly unattractive, a bewilderment of busy one-way streets, it is on these hills that the eye rests. And so it was, too, in antiquity. For across the dusty riverbed of the Inachus, beyond the fields and vineyards, the most sacred shrine in all the land of Argos nestled on a low plateau below these distant hills. It was the sanctuary of Hera, the 'ox-eyed goddess', thanks to whose protection the land of Argos thrived.

Hera & the Argive Heraion

The Argolid (the region of the northeast Peloponnese named from Argos) did not hold entirely happy associations for Hera. True, it was here that she was first wooed by her brother, Zeus (though some set the scene at Knossos). After overcoming Cronus and seizing Mount Olympus, Zeus found Hera on Mount Thornax, east of Argos, and amorously pressed his suit. But Hera was unwilling and rebuffed him. Then, in a thunderstorm, she found above the bay at Hermione a cuckoo, trembling, dishevelled, its feathers dull; and gently lifting it, she cradled it inside her dress against her breasts. In an ardent flash, the cuckoo transformed into Zeus and raped her. Shamed, Hera accepted the inevitable. She married Zeus, but every year renewed her virginity by bathing in a spring at Nauplion.

Even at the Argive Heraion, her sanctuary near Argos, Zeus could cause Hera distress. As was his wont, he became infatuated with a local girl: Hera's priestess, Io, the daughter of the river-god Inachus. Io soon succumbed, and, when Hera learned of the affair, Zeus tried to conceal his misdemenour: he turned the now-pregnant Io into a cow. But Hera was not deceived. Claiming the cow as her own, she took it to her sanctuary, tethered it beneath an olive tree and set a guard over it: Argos Panoptes ('Who Sees All'), an earth-born giant with a hundred eyes, which took it in turn to close. Even when Panoptes slept, some stayed open, watching.

Zeus was loath to leave Io to her bovine fate, so he sent Hermes to abduct her. Disguised as a goatherd, Hermes ingratiated himself with Panoptes, serenading him on shepherd's pipes. So soothing and hypnotic was the melody that Panoptes' eyes began to close until, for the first time

Hermes slays the hundred-eyed Argos
Panoptes, guardian of Io whom Hera
has transformed into a cow. (Fifth-
century BC Attic red figure vase.)

ever, not one remained open. Hermes seized the moment, lopped off
Panoptes' head and untied the halter around Io's neck.

Hera saw it all and unleashed a gadfly, which attacked poor Io and
drove her, bucking, off. After many years Io reached Egypt, where Zeus
restored her to her womanly form. Here at last she gave birth to Zeus'
son, married the king and (so the Greeks claimed) was later worshipped
as Isis. As for Argos Panoptes, Hera named her land from him, removed
his hundred eyes and set them in the tail of her favourite bird, the peacock,
where they have kept watch ever since. Many Greek guard dogs (including Odysseus' on Ithaca) were called Argos after him.

The Danaids

Io's banishment was the first in a series of flights to and from Argos. In
time, a boatload of her descendants fled back from Egypt. Aegyptus, king
of Egypt (Io's great-great-grandson), had fifty sons, whom he wished to
marry to the fifty daughters of his rival, his younger twin, Danaus. But

Danaus and his daughters, fearing it was a ruse to kill them, were unwilling. So they built a ship – the first ever – and escaped across the sea to Argos.

Here (in a story dramatized in Aeschylus' *Suppliants*), they begged King Pelasgos Gelanor ('Laugher') for asylum. Pelasgos referred the matter to the Argive people, who voted to protect the girls. Pausanias writes that they also voted to make Danaus their king, a decision reached in response to an omen: while they were debating, news came of a wolf descending from the mountains and killing a bull in the pasturelands, which they interpreted as meaning that the incomer Danaus should supplant the native Pelasgos. The omen was sent by Apollo Lycaeus (the Wolf God), and they established a sanctuary in his honour, which survived to Roman times.

When Aegyptus' fifty sons arrived in hot pursuit, the Argives were unwilling to join battle. Instead, Danaus conceived a monstrous plan. Pretending reconciliation, he let the marriages proceed, all on a single day. But that night, Danaus' daughters murdered their new husbands, skewering them through the heart with their hairpins – all except Hypermnestra, whose husband, Lynceus, had respected her pleas not to sleep with her.

The other forty-nine were exonerated, purified themselves and sought new husbands. Despite their track record, many suitors came forward, so to prevent dispute Danaus arranged a footrace: the winner could have first choice of bride; the runner-up could choose next; and so on. The system worked, and the resultant families became the ancestors of the Danaans, a term Homer commonly uses for the Greeks.

Not everything ended happily, however. Some say that Lynceus murdered his father-in-law Danaus to become king of Argos, while in Hades Danaus' daughters were punished for their crime, condemned to fetch water in cracked jars to fill a leaking cauldron. It was a task of domestic drudgery that could never be completed, a fitting penalty for such unwifely women.

Perseus, Prince of Argos

Lynceus and Hypermnestra's grandson also feared death at a family member's hands. Acrisius, king of Argos, received notice from the Delphic oracle that his daughter's son would kill him. His only daughter Danaë was childless, so, to prevent her conceiving, Acrisius imprisoned her in a bronze-walled cell with just one window. This window was the king's undoing. Through it Zeus glimpsed Danaë and poured into the prison as a shower of golden rain, whose heavenly moisture impregnated her. Her resultant son was Perseus.

Refusing to believe Danaë, but reluctant to kill her, Acrisius locked her and her baby in a wooden chest, which he cast into the waves. The currents bore this latest in a line of refugees to Seriphos. There they were found by a fisherman, Dictys ('Net'), who brought up Perseus as his own. After some years, Dictys' brother, King Polydectes, became infatuated with Danaë – and to help achieve his desired ends, he plotted to do away with Perseus. As a ruse he announced his intention to woo Hippodameia, princess of Elis, and demanded from the great and good of Seriphos that each should contribute a horse as a courtship-gift. Perseus had neither horse nor the money to buy one. So he asked Polydectes to demand from him another levy. The trap was sprung. Smirking, Polydectes demanded: 'Bring me the head of the Gorgon, Medusa'.

Perseus & Medusa

There were three Gorgons, terrifying winged sisters, who lived far to the west beyond the bounds of Ocean. With grotesquely large heads, boar's-tusk teeth and lolling tongues, their hair was a nest of writhing snakes. One look at them and anything living was turned to stone. Hesiod describes how: 'Two snakes, heads bent forwards, hung suspended from their belts. Their tongues were flickering, their sharp teeth grinding in their rage, and their eyes were wildly glaring. And Terror quaked above their terrifying heads.' Two were immortal, but not the third, Medusa, and it was her head that Polydectes demanded. In fact, his choice was irrelevant: everyone knew that Perseus would never return.

When Athene found out about the quest, however, she resolved to help Perseus. First she persuaded the gods to provide him with equipment necessary to achieve his task: Hermes gave winged sandals; Zeus an adamantine sickle; Haides a dog-skin-covered helmet that made its wearer invisible; Athene herself a polished shield. But Perseus still needed one more item – a *kibisis*, an insulated bag, in which to store the Gorgon's head and prevent its venomous power from leaking out. This he must acquire in person from the Hesperides, whose home was far to the west in the realm of the setting sun.

To discover how to reach this land, Perseus first visited the Graeae. Like the Gorgons, they were Phorcys' daughters, and they, too, were grotesque. Aeschylus calls them 'three girls, but ancient, shaped like swans, with only one eye between them and one tooth. The sun with his rays does not shine down on them, nor the moon by night.'

Only by tricking them and seizing their one eye as they passed it between them in their gnarled hands was Perseus able to discover the information he needed. Quickly he set out, racing to the west, and in their golden orchard the Hesperides graciously gave him the *kibisis*. Then borne aloft by Hermes' winged sandals, he flew on to the Gorgons' lair.

As he drew near, Perseus lowered Haides' helmet over his head. Now invisible, he unsheathed his sickle and stealthily approached, holding

Encouraged by Athene, Perseus lops off the head
of Medusa, who clutches Pegasus, born at the
moment of her death, on a metope from the
c. 550 BC Temple 'C' at Selinunte, Sicily.

Athene's shield obliquely before him – for he knew that while he could
not so much as glimpse the Gorgons with his naked eye, their reflection
in the shield could do no harm. At last, with the serpents hissing round
him, he came close enough to strike, and in an instant had lopped off
Medusa's head. Hurriedly stowing it in the *kibisis*, he leapt into the air,
triumphant. Hesiod imagines the scene depicted on a shield:

> He soared as swiftly as a thought. At his back was the
> head of the terrifying beast, the Gorgon, wrapped in its
> *kibisis*, miraculous to see.... Like a man who runs in haste
> or horror, Perseus, the son of Danaë, raced at full stretch;
> and behind him raced in hot pursuit the Gorgons,
> unspeakable, whom no man might approach, stretching
> out their hands to grab him.

The Gorgons were fast, but Perseus was faster, and soon he was alone, skimming the waves towards the sunrise and the east.

Perseus, Andromeda & Home to Argos

As he passed over Ethiopia, Perseus saw a beautiful young girl tied naked to a stake beside the seashore. Even as he approached, the waves frothed and parted and a monster reared up in front of her. Perseus acted swiftly. Calling on the girl to close her eyes, he swooped down, and, averting his face, pulled out Medusa's severed head. Immediately the monster turned to stone. Carefully replacing the head, Perseus untied the girl and heard her story.

She was Andromeda, the daughter of King Cepheus and Queen Cassiopeia. Poseidon was angered when her parents boasted that she was more beautiful than the sea-nymphs, so he first flooded their land and then sent the monster to ravage it. Only by showing their willingness to sacrifice Andromeda to its appetite would they appease Poseidon's anger. Amid general rejoicing Perseus claimed Andromeda as his bride, and together they returned to Seriphos.

Polydectes, seated in his crowded hall, sneeringly enquired whether Perseus had completed his task. Silently, his eyes locked on Polydectes, Perseus lifted out the head. Its effect was inescapable and instant. Polydectes and his attendants froze like marble statues. Danaë and Dictys were overjoyed. Approving his mother's marriage to the fisherman, Perseus set off with Andromeda for Argos.

Perseus' grandfather Acrisius was now living in Larissa in Thessaly, so they made a detour to meet him. According to Pausanias:

> Perseus was in the prime of youth and excited because
> he had just invented the discus. He was giving displays to
> all and sundry when, as luck dictated, Acrisius wandered
> unseen into his discus' path. The god's prophecy was
> fulfilled, and the inevitable was not put off by his
> precautions involving his daughter and her son.

Devastated, Perseus returned to Argos, where local tradition told that he buried Medusa's head in the agora beneath an earthen mound. Others suggest he gave it to Athene, who set it into her protective snake-fringed *aegis*. In Classical times, images of Medusa's head appeared on warriors' shields to terrify the enemy, and in mosaics and sculptures to ward off evil. A running gorgon formed the centrepiece of the west pediment of the early sixth-century BC Temple of Artemis in Corcyra on Corfu.

Reluctant to rule Argos, Perseus exchanged kingdoms with his cousin Megapenthes, receiving from him Tiryns and Mycenae.

Tydeus & Diomedes

Two later military campaigns set out from the Argolid – one against Thebes, the other against Troy. Both involved the family of the hero Tydeus. Banished from Calydon for shedding family blood, Tydeus, the brother of Meleager, sought sanctuary in Argos, and in his absence his father Oineus was deposed. Argos' King Adrastus recognized Tydeus' potential, made him his son-in-law and vowed to help return him to his kingdom. He did the same for Polyneices, who had been driven out of Thebes by his brother Eteocles.

Raising a great army, Polyneices marched on Thebes with Tydeus as one of his seven generals. Tydeus won great glory, overcoming fifty Thebans who ambushed him, but after killing the Theban Melanippus, he greedily devoured his fallen victim's brains. When Tydeus died soon after, Athene, disgusted at this behaviour, renounced her intention to grant him immortality.

Ten years later, the sons of those Argives who had fallen in the Theban war mounted a successful campaign of their own. Among them was Tydeus' son, Diomedes. After conquering Thebes, Diomedes marched on Calydon and reinstated his grandfather Oineus to the throne, before returning to become king of Argos. As one of Helen's suitors, Diomedes fought at Troy, earning a high reputation among Greece's finest warriors, a wise counsellor and trustworthy lieutenant. He even fought the gods when they intervened in battle (wounding Aphrodite on the wrist and facing off Apollo) and took part in the raid to steal Troy's talismanic statue of Athene. One of those handpicked to conceal themselves inside the Trojan Horse, he was instrumental in the city's sack.

But Diomedes' homecoming was unhappy. In his absence, his wife had been prodigiously unfaithful, and she and her current lover prevented Diomedes from entering Argos. Instead, he sailed to Italy, founded many cities (including modern Brindisi) and married the daughter of the local king. Some say he did not die but vanished under miraculous circumstances, his comrades transformed into birds. He was subsequently worshipped as a god.

After a succession of disastrous kings, Argos was annexed by Orestes, Agamemnon's son, after which it passes from mythology.

Argos in History & Today

Argos played a key role in Greek history. The most powerful city in the Argolid, its location between Corinth and Sparta meant that it was constantly embroiled in war. Its historians knew of a semi-mythical king, Pheidon, credited with introducing coinage, weights and measures into Greece, but when or whether he lived remains unclear. He may have fought at the Battle of Hysiae against the Spartans in the southwest

Argolid around 668 BC, just one in a series of increasingly brutal encounters between the two states. Perhaps the most savage was the Battle of Sepeia in 494 BC, when the Spartans corralled the defeated Argives inside a sacred grove near Argos, set fire to it, and burned their prisoners alive. Argos escaped defeat only when its lyric poetess, Telesilla, distributed weapons to its women and slaves, who took up position on the city walls. Unwilling to entertain even the possibility of being defeated by women, the Spartans tactically withdrew. A commemoration to Telesilla stood near Argos' theatre.

During the Persian Wars Argos remained controversially neutral, perhaps hoping that if its Greek enemies were beaten, it would prosper. In the Peloponnesian War, Argos vacillated, allying first with Athens, then (after a change of government) with Sparta. During this period, a colossal gold-and-ivory seated statue of Hera by Polycleitus was dedicated in the Argive Heraion. In the fourth century BC Argos switched sides again, helping Thebes to defeat Sparta at Leuctra (371 BC) and Mantinea (362 BC). In the following decades it sought help against Sparta from Macedon.

In the third and second centuries BC, Argos remained an occasional war zone. Pyrrhus of Epirus was killed here, struck on the head by a roof-tile hurled by an old woman (272 BC). (He had just interpreted the memorial to Danaus in the agora, showing a wolf savaging a bull, as an omen of his death.) After Rome annexed Greece in 146 BC, Argos was an important provincial centre. In 50 BC the Nemean Games (which in previous centuries migrated between Nemea and Argos) were permanently relocated here. Although it was sacked by Alaric (AD 396), the city flourished under the Byzantines, but suffered under the Turks, who enslaved much of its population in AD 1397 and massacred the rest in 1500, replacing them with Albanians. In the Greek War of Independence (1821–29) Argos was virtually reduced to ruins. Its current concrete sprawl dates mainly from the 1960s.

_____ Argos _____	
SOME IMPORTANT DATES & REMAINS	
c. **4000 BC**	Neolithic settlements at Argive Heraion.
c. **1600 BC**	Defensive walls built around existing settlements.
1350–1200 BC	Further fortifications: the apogee of Mycenaean Argos.
? *c.* **1200 BC**	Argos falls to attack?
? **early C7th BC**	Reign of Pheidon?
668 BC	Victory over Sparta at Battle of Hysiae.
494 BC	Defeat by Sparta at Battle of Sepeia.
490–479 BC	Argos neutral during Persian Invasions.

431–404 BC	Argos vacillates during Peloponnesian War.
272 BC	Argos attacked by Pyrrhus of Epirus; death of Pyrrhus.
post-146 BC	Argos prospers under Rome.
AD 396	Argos sacked by Alaric the Goth.

Much of ancient Argos lies beneath the modern town. The most important remains lie by the Tripolis road. These include (west of the main road) the late fourth-/early third-century BC **theatre**. The auditorium, whose rock-cut seats survive, originally extended further on either side, supported on stone revetments, and seated 20,000 people. A canopy once covered at least part of it. Nearby, a smaller fifth-century BC theatre (seating around 2,500 people) was turned into an **odeon** in the second century AD. Adjoining this are scanty remains of a **sanctuary of Aphrodite**. In front of the theatre is a **Roman bath complex**, whose two-storey west end survives to roof height. East of the main road is the **agora**. Only foundations survive, but the well-signed site contains an impressive range of buildings including **nymphaia** (fountain houses), a **bouleuterion** (council chamber), a **temple** and a **tomb**.

North, on Aspis Hill, the foundations of the **temples of Pythian Apollo and Athene Oxyderkes** ('Keen-Eyed') give good views to the Convent of the Virgin of the Rock and the medieval fortress (with traces of Mycenaean and Classical masonry) on nearby Larissa Hill. Traces of Mycenaean and pre-Mycenaean houses survive on Aspis' wooded summit.

The **Argive Heraion** lies five miles northeast of Argos. Its setting is magnificent. The highest of a series of terraces housed the **'old temple'**, destroyed by fire in 423 BC thanks to the carelessness of its priestess. On the middle terrace stood the **'new temple'** (*c.* 420–410 BC), containing Polycleitus' gold-and-ivory cult statue, and a stoa. On the lowest terrace was a further (fifth-century BC) stoa. There is also a Mycenaean **tholos tomb**.

Argos' **Archaeological Museum** (currently closed) houses collections ranging from the Early Neolithic (including a *c.* 3000 BC **terracotta figure**) to Roman times. Highlights include a late eighth-century BC **bronze helmet and armour**, a seventh-century BC pottery fragment showing **Odysseus blinding the Cyclops** (among the earliest representations of mythology in Greek art) and a fifth-century BC vase showing **Theseus and the Minotaur**. There are also **fifth-century AD mosaics** showing Dionysus and the Seasons.

Cleobis and Biton's statues are housed in the Museum at Delphi.

15

Athens: Prize of Athene, Kingdom of Theseus

Glistening and violet-crowned, the subject of so many songs,
protectress of all Greece – famous Athens with your divine acropolis...

Gods of Olympus, come here to dance! Grant us sublime grace as
you come here to the city's sacred heart, so heavy with the scent of
incense, the path which leads here so well-trodden! Come to this
sacred land of Athens with its famous market place so elegantly
built! And listen warmly to our songs of garlands twined with violets
plucked in the dew of spring.

Pindar, fr. 64 & 63 (Bowra)

Possibly once holding a winged Victory in its outstretched hand, this bronze statue found at Piraeus in 1959 shows Athene as warrior and protector of her city (*c.* 360–340 BC).

Come early to the Acropolis before the crowds and heat, and you will be richly rewarded. Enveloped in the golden glow of early morning, the great sanctuary stands empty, the long shadows of the Parthenon's tall columns rippling across the polished, gleaming rock, while on the Erechtheum's porch casts of Caryatids gaze with sightless eyes, their faces ready to receive the sun's warm rays.

Walk the perimeter, look down and you can see (amid the concrete eczema of modern architecture, which chokes the once farm-studded plains of Attica) the Agora, the ancient market place, where the Temple of Hephaestus luxuriates on a low wooded knoll surrounded by pink-flowering oleander; and there the cone of Mount Lycabettus; the ridge of Mount Pentellicon, where marble for the Parthenon was hewn; and the Hymettus range, where bee-hives still produce fine honey. Look south beyond the Theatre of Dionysus and the Muses' Hill, and out across the sea, where great ships ride at anchor, past the shadowed hump of Aegina to where the mountains of the Peloponnese appear like phantoms in the early haze. Here on the Acropolis it is easy to imagine you are standing at the hub of a great wheel, whose rim embraces the mountains and the farmland and the sea. It is a place of harmony, a place of power. No wonder that gods fought so fanatically to own it.

The Birth of Athene

Athens was named from its patron goddess, Zeus' virgin daughter, Athene (though the Libyans, who said that she had sea-blue eyes, claimed her father was Poseidon). Her mother was Metis ('Cleverness'), who at first evaded Zeus by shape-shifting. But not for long. When Metis fell pregnant, Gaia, goddess of the earth, prophesied that the child would be a girl but, if Metis bore Zeus a son, the boy would defeat his father. Keen to cling on to power, Zeus followed his father Cronus' example and swallowed Metis whole.

Soon Zeus suffered debilitating headaches. At last the pressure on his skull became unbearable. By Lake Triton's shores in Libya he bellowed in pain so loudly that he was heard on Mount Olympus. The gods came running, but only Hermes knew what to do. He advised Hephaestus to take his axe to Zeus' head. The blade crashed down; the skull cracked open – and out leapt Athene, fully grown, armoured and armed, and wearing the *aegis*, a magic snake-fringed goatskin, which protected her and sowed terror in her enemies. (Others said the *aegis* was the flayed skin of one of Athene's goatish enemies, either the Titan Aex or the Giant Pallas, from whom she derived one of her epithets.) Metis, whom Hesiod calls 'cleverer than any god or mortal man', remained in Zeus' belly, where she regularly fed him good advice.

The Goddess Athene

The Homeric Hymn to Aphrodite summarizes 'clear-eyed' Athene's character and attributes:

> She takes no pleasure in the deeds of golden Aphrodite,
> but rather she delights in war and in the deeds of
> Ares – combat and battle – and the intricacies of fine
> craftsmanship. She first taught the mortal craftsmen
> of the earth to make war chariots of bronze. And she
> taught soft-skinned maidens in their halls and set the
> understanding of fine arts in every mind.

At first this polarity of interests – war and domestic harmony – seems hard to reconcile. However (unlike Ares), Athene took no pleasure in conflict in itself. Rather, in her capacity as Protectress of the City (Athene Polias), a role she enjoyed throughout the Greek world, she was more than willing to resort to combat when the need arose. Then she would lead the charge with merciless ferocity, as another epithet, 'Promachus' ('Front-Line Fighter'), attests, while her success in battle is reflected in her title Nike ('Victory').

Within the well-protected city, Athene presided over the complex craftsmanship of men and domestic skills, such as weaving, associated with women. But when the mortal Arachne was heard boasting that she was a better weaver than the goddess, Athene disguised herself and challenged her to a contest. Arachne's work was delicately beautiful. The goddess was impressed – until the girl insisted that her skill owed nothing to divine inspiration. Athene destroyed the tapestry in fury, revealed her true identity, caused the terrified Arachne to hang herself and turned the suspended victim into a spider, whose weaving remains breathtaking to this day.

As the child of Metis, Athene was also the grey-eyed ('glaukopis') goddess of wisdom, whose avatar was the owl ('glaux' in Greek). The bird appeared on Athens' coinage, often accompanied by a sprig of olive. For it was thanks to the olive tree that Athens belonged to Athene.

Athene & Poseidon Contest for Attica

The natural beauty and resources of Athens and its territory, Attica, attracted the attentions of both Athene and Poseidon. Each claimed them as their own. So they raced in their chariots to the Acropolis and leapt on to the rock. Poseidon struck the ground with his trident, and salt water bubbled from beneath the earth. In response, Athene planted a young sapling, a silver-leaved olive tree, which rustled in the breeze. As the two gods prepared to settle their quarrel by brute force, Zeus intervened, first hurling a

Wearing her
snake-fringed *aegis*,
Athene confronts
Poseidon on an Attic
black figure vase,
c. 540–530 BC.

thunderbolt, which exploded on the ground between them, then appearing in person to order that the issue be resolved in a law-court with the other gods as jurors. Called as witness, Cecrops, King of Athens, praised the usefulness of Athene's gift. In a subsequent vote, the male gods supported Poseidon, while the goddesses championed Athene. The numbers favoured Athene, and the land was awarded to her. Poseidon stalked off enraged and flooded the local Thriasian Plain, but in time he was reconciled and Athens developed a strong navy.

The olive tree thrived throughout Attica and on the Acropolis, where it was revered in historical times. In 480 BC a sacred olive tree was burned by the invading Persians, but by the next morning a new shoot 45 cm (18 in.) long had sprouted. As Herodotus records, it was interpreted as an omen of Athens' eventual victory, while Pindar describes this tree as: 'unconquered, self-reviving, a cause of terror to spear-wielding enemies. It thrives in Attica, grey-leaved, our country's caregiver: the olive tree. Neither young nor old can harm it with their hands, for Protecting Zeus keeps guard with his all-seeing gaze, and with him grey-eyed Athene.'

In the fifth century BC the stories of the birth of Athene and her contest with Poseidon over Attica were commemorated in the sculptures of the Parthenon's two pediments.

Athens: Prize of Athene, Kingdom of Theseus

Cecrops & Erichthonius

Cecrops was the first king to rule from Athens (his father-in-law, Actaeus, had his capital elsewhere in Attica). His torso, arms and head were human, but being earth-born his lower body was a serpent's. Wise and virtuous, Cecrops taught his people the art of literature as well as the rites of burial and marriage, and piously worshipped Zeus. But he refused to make blood offerings, preferring to burn cakes on the altar, a tradition which Athenians preserved in one of their rituals.

Cecrops' successor was Erichthonius. He, too, was a hybrid man and snake, and his conception was unusual. Seeing Athene walking modestly on the Acropolis, Hephaestus tried to rape her. The virgin goddess rebuffed him, but he ejaculated uncontrollably over her thigh. Athene wiped off the semen with a handful of wool, which she flung to the ground and soon forgot. But the semen soaked into the soil, where it impregnated Gaia. The resultant child was Erichthonius ('Wool-Earth').

Horrified at his appearance, Athene locked Erichthonius into a box, which she gave to Cecrops' three daughters with instructions never to open it, but, tantalized, two could not resist. They prised off the lid and looked inside. Screaming in terror at the snaky child, they dropped the box, ran to the Acropolis' edge and threw themselves to their death. Only Pandrosus ('All-Dewy'), the third of Cecrops' daughters, survived. In historical times she was honoured with a garden near Athene's olive tree and Poseidon's well on the Acropolis.

Outraged at the girls' disobedience, Athene dropped the rock she was carrying to augment the Acropolis. It remained jutting up abruptly from the soil: Mount Lycabettus. Erichthonius grew up to rule Athens. Sloughing off his human element, he was worshipped as a sacred serpent well into the Classical age and fed with honey cakes.

Pandion, Procne, Philomela & Erechtheus

Athenian mythology abounds with stories of wise kings, whose daughters met ugly or violent ends. Another was the kindly Pandion, who ruled after Erichthonius. He had two daughters, the elder of whom, Procne, he gave in marriage to King Tereus of Thrace. But when Procne's sister, Philomela, went to visit her, the savage Tereus raped her and cut out her tongue. Unable to speak, poor Philomela wove a tapestry which revealed her bitter story. Procne understood, and in revenge she and Philomela killed, dismembered and cooked Tereus' son, Itys, then served him to the king. The banquet finished, they brought in a covered platter, and revealed Itys' head. Wielding an axe, Tereus pursued the sisters through the corridors until the gods intervened and turned all three protagonists into birds. Procne became a swallow, Philomela a sweet-voiced nightingale and Tereus a sharp-beaked hawk (or a hoopoe).

In Athens Pandion was succeeded by Erechtheus (semi-serpentine like Erichthonius), who was credited with founding many of the great Athenian civic festivals. In his reign a magical, protective olive-wood statue of Athene fell miraculously from the heavens. But, during a war with nearby Eleusis, Erechtheus received an oracle that Athens would win only if he sacrificed one of his three daughters. When he obeyed, the other two committed suicide. True to the prediction Erechtheus slew the Eleusinian king, but his glory was short-lived. His victim was Poseidon's son, and the vengeful sea-god skewered Erechtheus with his trident. Despite its grisly nature, the tale was popular in Classical Athens, as a model of self-sacrifice for its citizens.

A similar message appears in the myth of Codrus, one of Athens' last mythical kings. He discovered that invading Spartans believed that Athens would fall only if its king suffered no harm. So Codrus sacrificed himself:

> He dressed as a beggar to deceive the enemy and, letting himself out of the city gates, began to collect firewood in front of the city. When two men approached from the enemy camp asking about conditions inside Athens, he killed one with his sickle. The other, thinking Codrus was a beggar, is said furiously to have drawn his sword and cut him down – at which the Athenians sent a negotiator to reveal the truth to the enemy and ask that their king be returned for burial. The Peloponnesians gave back the body and left Attica, realizing that they no longer had any hope of taking it.

Aegeus, Father of Theseus

The greatest Athenian hero was Theseus. For many years childless, his father, Aegeus, son of Pandion, had tried everything, even introducing into Athens the worship of Aphrodite, the mistress of procreation – but to no effect. Perhaps, he mused, thanks to the murderous behaviour of his sisters, Procne and Philomela, he was accursed, so he consulted the Delphic oracle. Its reply was enigmatic: 'Do not unstop the swollen wine-skin until you return to Athens.'

Perplexed, Aegeus resolved to take counsel from his friend, the king of Troezen, Pittheus son of Pelops. On his way (tells Euripides) he stopped at Corinth, where Medea had recently discovered that Jason had abandoned her. Utilizing her charms to the full, Medea persuaded Aegeus (ignorant of Medea's planned revenge) to grant her asylum in Athens.

In Troezen, Pittheus readily understood the oracle: Aegeus should refrain from sex until returning home. But rather than reveal the explanation, he sent Aegeus to bed drunk, then instructed his daughter Aethra to join him. It was an eventful night. No sooner had Aethra slept with Aegeus than she waded over to make offerings on the nearby island of Hiera, where (at the unmaidenly suggestion of Athene) Poseidon ravished her. Next morning Aegeus hid his sword and sandals under a massive rock, instructing Aethra that if, as a result of their dalliance, she bore a son strong enough to shift it, she should send him to claim his patrimony. Back in Athens Aegeus found Medea already in residence. Bewitched by her beauty, he married her and fathered a son called Medus, whom they raised as Aegeus' heir.

The Adventures of Theseus

Aethra too bore a son, and named him Theseus. Pittheus encouraged rumours that the boy's father was Poseidon, leaving Theseus ignorant of Aegeus' role in his conception. But when he reached adulthood, Aethra showed him the rock where Aegeus had hidden the tokens of his identity. Theseus easily lifted it, so she revealed the truth and bade him go to Athens; but rather than cross by sea Theseus tested his manliness by travelling overland, where (in feats of civilizing heroism mirroring the exploits of Heracles) he rid the countryside of notorious brigands.

Theseus turns Procrustes' axe on its owner, who squirms on his infamous bed. (Attic red figure vase, c. 425 BC.)

At Epidaurus a lame one-eyed beggar, Hephaestus' son, Periphetes, attacked passing travellers with a bronze-bound club. Theseus tricked him by asking if – before Periphetes killed him – he could examine the club to ensure that the binding really was bronze. When Periphetes swaggeringly handed over the weapon, Theseus smashed it over the beggar's head. Then, keeping the club, he continued on his way.

At the Isthmus of Corinth lived Sinis, a ruffian who killed passers-by with the aid of pine trees. He had two techniques. One was to ask the traveller to take hold of a tree's top branches and help him bend the trunk down to the ground – at the last moment Sinis would release his grip, catapulting his victim to his death. His other speciality was to overpower the traveller, tie him to two pines, which he had first secured in place, then cut the ropes – as the trees whipped upright, they tore the victim apart. This was the method Theseus used to despatch Sinis (after first defeating him at wrestling), thereby rendering the Isthmus safe.

Near the summit of high sea-cliffs, Theseus' path was blocked by Sciron, a towering figure seated on a rock, who forced everyone who passed to wash his feet. As they crouched before him, he kicked them over the cliff edge on to the jagged rocks below, where a turtle feasted on their raw remains. Theseus paid the bully in his own currency. The last bones the turtle chewed were Sciron's own.

At nightfall Theseus arrived in Attica and, breasting the final hills, he came to a roadside inn. Its landlord, Procrustes, possessed an iron bed, which he insisted should prove a perfect fit for every guest: if a visitor were too short he stretched him, while if he were too tall he sawed off those extremities which overhung the bed's iron frame. (Alternatively he used two beds: a long one for short people, a short one for tall.) Turning the tables on his vicious host, Theseus rid Greece of another deadly scourge.

Once in Athens, Theseus did not immediately reveal his true identity. But, as soon as she met him, Medea knew who he was. Determined that this interloper should not usurp her son, she persuaded Aegeus that Theseus was an enemy and prepared a poisoned drink. As Theseus took it, Aegeus recognized the sword he was wearing in his belt. Instantly he dashed the cup from Theseus' lips, and both watched in shocked fascination as the spilt wine caused the paving stones to melt and bubble.

While Aegeus introduced Theseus to Athens as his heir with sacrifices and a sumptuous banquet, Medea fled, travelling with her son far to the east. Here (in modern Iran) Medus gave his name to the Medes, a people whom Herodotus records were until then called Aryans. In historical times, many Greeks used the name Medes to signify the Persians.

Theseus found Athens riven with dispute. Another branch of Erechtheus' family, the fifty sons of Pallas, were challenging Aegeus' rule. Attica was on the brink of civil war. Skilfully Theseus negotiated a temporary peace, though he was later forced to go to war and kill all Pallas' sons. Before that, however, Theseus turned his attentions to an external threat. He had already slain the Cretan bull, which Heracles had brought to Tiryns and let loose to roam the mainland; now, to rid Athens of the tribute it was forced to pay King Minos of Knossos, Theseus set out on a voyage to Crete with thirteen companions. His mission: to kill the Minotaur.

Theseus, King of Athens

Returning in triumph after dispatching the monster, Theseus discovered Athens plunged in mourning. Aegeus, convinced that his son had died, had leapt to his death either from Athens' Acropolis or from Cape Sunium. Now king, Theseus made Athens the capital of Attica and introduced many constitutional innovations that would result in Athens' greatness – or so historical Athenians, keen to give their constitution an ancient pedigree, believed, and many fifth-century BC tragedies are nonchalantly anachronistic in their portrayal of Theseus as an enthusiastic proto-democrat.

Two episodes from Theseus' career were considered so significant that they were carved on the Parthenon's metopes. One was his battle with the Amazons. Accompanying Heracles on his voyage to Thermodon to steal the battle-belt of Queen Hippolyta, Theseus fell in love with the princess Antiope, brought her back home to Athens and had a son by her, Hippolytus. But the Amazons, believing that Antiope had been kidnapped, invaded Attica and occupied a rocky outcrop, subsequently called the Hill of Ares (Areopagus), just west of the Acropolis. After months of fighting and heavy losses the invaders were repulsed. Among the dead was Antiope.

Hippolytus, a Brief Digression

After Antiope's death, Theseus married the Cretan princess Phaedra. When he was temporarily exiled for killing his cousins, the sons of Pallas, Theseus took her for a year to Troezen. This was now home to his son, Hippolytus, who, an ardent devotee of Artemis, had dedicated his life to chastity, renounced carnal joys and so earned the wrath of Aphrodite. But Phaedra had already met Hippolytus at the Eleusinian Mysteries and there she had fallen in love with him. Living now in such close proximity, her infatuation grew – the daughter of Pasiphaë (who lusted after Minos' bull) and the sister of Ariadne (who had betrayed Crete for love of Theseus), she was of passionate stock. Then Theseus left to consult the oracle at Delphi. Phaedra's passion for Hippolytus became unbearable. Unable to eat or drink she propositioned him, but he rebuffed her. So when Theseus returned she told him that Hippolytus had raped her. In Euripides' innovative version, Phaedra's nurse tricks her mistress into revealing her love and tells Hippolytus. Aghast, he threatens to inform Theseus. Phaedra hangs herself, leaving a letter accusing Hippolytus of rape. When he reads it, Theseus curses his son and begs Poseidon to kill him. As Hippolytus drives off in his chariot, Poseidon sends a bull from the sea, which spooks the horses, dragging Hippolytus to his death. Too late Artemis tells Theseus the truth, and swears to take revenge by ensuring the death of Aphrodite's favourite mortal, Adonis.

But for Hippolytus death was not the end. Artemis persuaded the greatest of all healers, Asclepius, to restore him to life (flouting nature's rules so dramatically that Zeus had no option but to kill Asclepius). Resurrected, Hippolytus lived in Italy, where, worshipped in Latium as Virbius, he protected fugitive slaves. Clearly he had learned the error of his chaste ways – the location of his sanctuary, Aricia, was named after his wife.

Theseus & Peirithous

Theseus' closest friend, Peirithous, who fought with him against the Amazons, played a prominent role in another incident, which seared itself into Athens' psyche and was depicted on the Parthenon: the battle between the Lapiths and Centaurs at Iolcus. As king of the Lapiths, whose territory bordered northern Attica, Peirithous had once been Theseus' enemy – they first met when Peirithous raided Theseus' cattle herds at Marathon. But each was so impressed with the other that they swore an oath of undying friendship. Thus Theseus attended Peirithous' wedding, and when the drunken Centaurs tried to rape the Lapith women, they fought side-by-side against them.

They shared in less savoury adventures, too, which led to their undoing. Both lusted after Helen, princess of Sparta, when she was still a child. Finding her by the River Eurotas making offerings at the shrine of Artemis Orthia, they snatched her up and galloped back to Attica, where they cast lots to see which should have her. Theseus won, hid her in the village of Aphidnae in northeast Attica, and set his mother Aethra to guard her.

But Peirithous demanded that he too should have one of Zeus' daughters. So the two friends undertook a perilous adventure: to abduct Persephone from Hades. Descending from Cape Taenarum they arrived in front of Haides' throne, where they demanded that the god give up his wife. In response, Haides invited them to rest on a stone bench while he went off to fetch her. But the bench was the Seat of Forgetfulness, and it caused their bodies to fuse to the rock, where they were held so fast they could not move. For four years they sat, paralysed, until Heracles came to Hades to fetch Cerberus. He wrenched Theseus from the rock, tearing his flesh in the process. When he tried to free Peirithous, however, the ground shook, thunder rattled and, understanding that the gods forbade his liberation, Heracles left the Lapith to endure his fate forever.

The Death & Discovery of Theseus

In Theseus' absence, Helen's brothers, Castor and Polydeuces (the Dioscuri), had invaded Attica, and when they discovered her (thanks to the advice of the hero Academus, whose sacred grove became the site of Plato's Academy) they turned their wrath on Athens. Only the diplomacy of Menestheus, a great-grandson of Erechtheus, averted disaster. He welcomed the Dioscuri, made them honorary citizens, initiated them into the Eleusinian Mysteries and sent them back to Sparta with Helen. She took as her servant Theseus' mother Aethra.

Back from Hades, Theseus had few allies and little power to challenge Menestheus' authority. Instead, bowing to the inevitable, he left Athens for ever. At Scyros, the most southerly of the Sporades, King Lycomedes received him kindly. But he had murder in his heart. An ally of Menestheus, Lycomedes pushed Theseus to his death from a high cliff.

Throughout the Archaic period, Theseus languished, a minor hero, but at the Battle of Marathon in 490 BC Athenian hoplites claimed to have seen him fighting on their side. Fourteen years later the Delphic oracle ordered Athens to find and repatriate Theseus' remains. Their general Cimon conquered Scyros and scoured the island for the hero's grave. Where he saw an eagle tearing at the earth, he discovered a huge skeleton, buried with a bronze spearhead and sword. Amid pomp and ceremony Cimon accompanied the remains back to Athens, where he erected a temple in Theseus' honour.

Athens in History & Today

Athens was inhabited from the fifth millennium BC onwards, with evidence of settlements around the Agora and Acropolis dating to the fourth millennium BC. It began to flower in the late Bronze Age. Around 1600 BC a palace was constructed on the Acropolis, whose steep sides were fortified with 'Cyclopean' walls. The building apparently remained intact until the tenth century, when it was destroyed by earthquake or fire. Its location became the focus for rituals honouring kings, including Erechtheus and Cecrops, who were believed to have lived there.

By the seventh century BC the Acropolis was Athens' religious heart: in 632 BC, after a failed coup, political activists sought asylum in its temple of Athene Polias. While early sixth-century BC reforms (attributed to Solon) sought to unite the coastal, rural and urban peoples, the second half of the century was dominated by Peisistratus, a benign *tyrannos*, who increased Athens' *kudos* through building works, by enhancing the Panathenaic Festival and Eleusinian Mysteries, and by creating a new drama festival. After Peisistratus' son Hippias was expelled in 510 BC, Cleisthenes introduced *isonomia* (equality under the law), which gradually developed into *demokratia* (rule by the people).

In the early fifth century BC, Athens faced an existential threat from the Persians. Victory at Marathon (490 BC) provided temporary relief, but in 480 BC Athens was overrun and its temples burned. Days later its navy (built from revenue from silver mines at Laurium near Sunium) helped win a resounding victory at Salamis. In 479 BC, after routing the Persians at Plataea, Athens led an alliance of Greek states, the Delian League, aimed at neutralizing the Persian threat. It soon became an Athenian empire. Athens' fleet patrolled the Aegean and in 454 BC the League's treasury moved from Delos to Athens.

Under Pericles (a *tyrannos* in all but name) Athens pursued an aggressively expansionist policy. This led to the Peloponnesian War between Athens' empire and a confederacy of states led by Sparta; the eventual outcome was Athens' defeat (404 BC). It was an ignominious end to a century in which, home to many outstanding philosophers, writers and artists, Athens had shone – more than living up to Pericles' boast that it was 'an education to all Greece'.

Athens soon recovered. In the fourth century BC it resounded to philosophical debate: Plato founded his Academy, Aristotle his Lyceum and Epicurus his 'Garden' school, while Zeno taught in one of Athens' *stoas*, which gave his followers their name: Stoics. Like its allies, Athens was defeated by Philip II of Macedon at the Battle of Chaeronea in 338 BC, but it was relatively well treated by Alexander the Great and remained largely unscathed in the upheavals following his death.

When Athens supported Rome's enemy Mithridates VI of Pontus, it was sacked by Sulla in 86 BC. Rebuilt and restored to grace, it became a 'university' town, respected for its history and architecture, and patronized in the second century AD by wealthy donors such as Herodes Atticus and the emperor Hadrian. Athens was plundered in the third century AD by the Heruli and in AD 396 by Alaric the Goth, after which its importance diminished. From the ninth to the fifteenth century trade with Italy saw its fortunes rise once more, and in 1205 after the Fourth Crusade it became a Duchy. But in 1458 Athens fell to the Ottoman Empire, heralding a long period of decline, during which the Parthenon was variously used as an ammunition dump (suffering a direct hit during Venetian bombardment in 1687) and a mosque, before being stripped of its sculptures by Lord Elgin in 1801 under circumstances which are still debated today.

In 1834 after Greek independence, the nation's capital was moved from Nafplio to Athens, then little more than a village, and in 1896 the graceful neoclassical city hosted the newly revived Olympic Games. However, after the population exchange with Turkey in 1922, the Second World War and the Greek Civil War, Athens mushroomed, especially after the late 1950s. It hosted the Olympic Games of 2002, encouraging new building work and enhancing the city centre.

SOME IMPORTANT DATES & REMAINS

c. 5000 BC	First human activity in Athens.
c. 3500 BC	Settlements in areas of Acropolis and Agora.
c. 1600 BC	Mycenaean walls and palace on Acropolis.
? *c.* 1000 BC	Mycenaean Athens destroyed by fire or earthquake.
c. 650 BC	Temple of Athene Polias on Acropolis.
c. 594 BC	Solon's reforms.
556 BC	Greater Panathenaic Games inaugurated.
534 BC	Drama festival (City Dionysia) inaugurated.
507 BC	Reforms of Cleisthenes introduce *isonomia*.
490 BC	First Persian invasion; Battle of Marathon.
480 BC	Second Persian invasion; temples burned; Battle of Salamis.
478 BC	Delian League formed (leading to Athenian Empire).
476 BC	Cimon recovers Theseus' bones from Scyros.
449 BC	Pericles begins building programme, including Parthenon (dedicated 438 BC).
431–404 BC	Peloponnesian War, ending in Athens' defeat.
393 BC	Athens rebuilds fortifications.
338 BC	Philip II defeats Athens and Greek states at Chaironea.
86 BC	Sulla sacks Athens.
AD 120	Hadrian undertakes further building programmes, including completion of Temple of Olympian Zeus.
c. AD 150	Herodes Atticus (i.e. of Attica) adorns Athens, including building Odeon.
AD 267	Heruli plunder Athens.
AD 396	Alaric the Goth plunders Athens.
AD 529	Justinian closes philosophy schools.
AD 1205	Duchy of Athens created after Fourth Crusade.
AD 1458	Athens becomes part of Ottoman Empire.
AD 1687	Parthenon partially destroyed during Venetian bombardment.
AD 1801	Thomas Bruce, Seventh Earl of Elgin, receives permission from Turkish authorities 'to take away any pieces of stone with old inscriptions or figures thereon' from the Parthenon.
AD 1834	Athens capital of newly independent Greece.
AD 1896	First modern Olympic Games celebrated in Athens.

Athens is a treasure trove of archaeology. At its heart is the **Acropolis**. A steep climb leads through the **Propylaia** with the graceful **Temple of Athene Nike** on a bastion (right). Grey Eleusinian limestone forms a sacred threshold. Two temples dominate the Acropolis: the **Parthenon**, once home to Pheidias' gold-and-ivory statue of Athene; and the **Erechtheum** (or **Temple of Athene Polias**), containing several distinct chapels, the roof of whose **Porch** is supported by sculptures of six girls, the Caryatids (casts). In antiquity it was of greater religious significance than the Parthenon. The foundations of the earlier Temple of Athene Polias, burned by the Persians in 480 BC, lie between the Parthenon and the Erechtheum.

The stunning **Acropolis Museum** is housed to the south on Dionysiou Areopagitou. Further west along this street are the **Arch of Hadrian** and **Temple of Olympian Zeus,** with fine views of the Acropolis.

On the Acropolis' southern slopes are the **Theatre of Dionysus** and the **Odeon of Herodes Atticus** (still used for performances). Just west of the Acropolis is the **Areopagus** (Hill of Ares), not for the faint hearted – there is a steep climb and slippery surface. Below this is the **Agora**, dominated to the east by the **Stoa of Attalus** (reconstructed by the American School of Archaeology, now housing the **Agora Museum**) and on the west by the **Temple of Hephaestus** (sometimes wrongly called the Theseum). Further east are the **Roman Agora** and **Tower of Winds.**

West from the Agora is the **Ceramicus (Kerameikos)**, one of classical Athens' cemeteries, whose boundaries include part of the ancient wall. From the **Sacred Gate** one road led to Eleusis, another to Plato's Academy. The haunt of tortoises and butterflies, the Ceramicus is a haven for the harassed traveller. It has an excellent **museum.**

The **National Archaeological Museum** contains finds from Athens and all Greece. Innumerable treasures include **gold death masks** from Mycenae, **Cycladic figurines,** Classical sculptures including the fine **bronze Poseidon (or Zeus)**, the **Varvakeion Athene** (a marble scale copy of Pheidias' statue for the Parthenon) and a stunning second-century BC life-size **bronze galloping racehorse.**

Several days are needed even to skim the surface of Athens' sites and museums. Many close early and are popular with coach parties, so it is advisable to time visits for early morning. To avoid being overwhelmed, take frequent breaks for refreshment and reflection.

16

Knossos: King Minos
& the Labyrinth

There is a land called Crete, midpoint in the wine-dark sea, a
beautiful land and fertile, gushing with flowing water. Many people
live there – too many men to count – and there are ninety cities.
They do not all speak the same language but a variety of tongues.
There are Achaeans and big-hearted native Cretans, Cydonians
and Dorians and wealthy Pelasgians. Here is the great city of Knossos,
where Minos ruled, who every nine years spoke with mighty Zeus.

Homer, *Odyssey*, 172–79

With lazy grace a harem of peahens sashays across the palace's West Court. A peacock, his coat plumage an iridescent blue, watches with proprietary eye, fanning his tail feathers and puffing out his chest before executing an elaborately geometric dance beneath the dull red-ochre columns. From the lush valley, hens' squabbling provides an earthy counterpoint to the sighing of wood-pigeons from tall trees, their chorus punctuated intermittently by the hoarse barking of dogs.

In the strong light, edges seem razor-sharp. Palace buildings – low and rectangular, both startlingly modern and primordial – gleam in the sunshine, clean lines cleaving the profoundest shadow. Yet their regular profiles conceal an exuberant vitality. Frescoes and reliefs unfurl across their walls: griffins in a deep red landscape; blue dolphins gambolling amid a shoal of blue and orange fish; bronzed youths in pale-blue loincloths bearing vessels of all shapes and colours; wasp-waisted women with coiffed hair, kohled eyes and startling red lips.

Elsewhere a charging bull is frozen in midair, head down, hooves flying. On either side a woman, bare-breasted, bangles on her arms, with calf-length boots and hair cascading down her back, frames the animal. One seizes the bull's horns; the other stands behind it, arms outstretched; while, poised above the bull's back, lithe and sinuous, a young man somersaults towards her. It is all so tantalizing, all so pregnant with significance – for such a scene may well have spawned the legend of the Minotaur.

The Birth & Early Life of Minos

Bulls were in Minos' blood. As the Tyrian princess Europa walked wide-eyed by the shore, she saw among her father's herds a handsome bull. The second-century BC poet Moschus describes it: 'Its body was tawny. In the middle of its forehead shone a dazzling white ring, and its grey eyes flashed with desire. Its horns curved upwards, the one the mirror image of the other, as if the rim of the horned moon had been divided into two rounded arcs.'

As Europa approached, captivated, the bull allowed her to pet it and then climb on to its back. Then, with Europa riding it, it ambled into the waves. Soon it was swimming out to sea. Afraid now, Europa tried to urge it back. In vain. Turning its head, it spoke and revealed the truth – it was Zeus, disguised, intent on being Europa's lover.

They came ashore in Crete, where at Gortyn beneath an evergreen plane-tree, they made love. Europa bore three sons – Rhadamanthus, Sarpedon (who shared his name with a later Trojan hero) and Minos. Unable to wed Zeus, Europa married Asterius, the king of Crete, who accepted the boys as his own. But Minos quarrelled with Sarpedon over a young man's love, and banished him; and, when Rhadamanthus, was forced into exile after spilling a kinsman's blood, the arrogant Minos became undisputed king.

Boasting that the gods would grant whatever he asked, Minos erected an altar and prayed to Poseidon to send a bull from the sea that he might sacrifice it. As the crowds watched, a gleaming white bull rose out of the waves and walked proudly to the altar. Its beauty was so breathtaking, that – rather than destroy it – Minos ordered that it should be spared and kept among his herds, while another animal was slaughtered in its place. Deprived of his promised sacrifice, Poseidon seethed.

Minos, his Loves & his Family
With his wife Pasiphaë (the daughter of Helios) Minos had many children, including two daughters, Ariadne and Phaedra, and a son, Androgeus. But Minos was a tireless womanizer, and weary of his infidelities, Pasiphaë (an accomplished sorceress) laid a spell on him. Henceforth, Minos ejaculated millipedes and scorpions, whose sting caused his lovers unimaginable pain.

Only the Athenian princess Procris knew how to circumvent the curse. A lusty huntress, abandoned by her husband Cephalus (himself once the lover of the goddess of the dawn), she was seduced by Minos' charms and his gift of the magical hound Laelaps, which never failed to catch its prey. Before succumbing, Procris made Minos use a prophylactic drug to counteract the spell. Later, Procris returned with Laelaps to the mainland, where she was first reconciled with Cephalus, then accidentally killed by him. In mourning, Cephalus and Laelaps went to Thebes, which was being plagued by an aggressive vixen, whose fate was never to be caught. The solution seemed clear: set Laelaps to give chase. Such was the conundrum this posed – the inescapable in pursuit of the uncatchable – that the gods resolved it only by turning both creatures to stone.

Bored with Minos' embraces, Pasiphaë lusted after the white bull Poseidon had sent from the sea. So she commanded the court craftsman Daedalus to build a hollow heifer, crawled inside it and had it taken to the fields. The resultant offspring was a savage hybrid, half-human and half-bull, with a penchant for human flesh. Pasiphaë named it after its grandfather Asterius, but we know it better as the Minotaur. Determined to conceal Pasiphaë's unnatural child and protect Crete from its appetites, Minos commissioned Daedalus to build a prison for it, approached by such a maze of corridors that it could never escape. Hidden beneath the palace of Knossos, this was the labyrinth.

Theseus & the Minotaur
As for Poseidon's white bull, which was now rampaging free, Heracles abducted it as one of his labours to mainland Greece, where it settled at Marathon, near Athens. When it continued to wreak havoc, Aegeus, king

Victorious, Theseus drags the dead Minotaur from the labyrinth. (Fifth-century BC Athenian red figure wine cup.)

of Athens, promised to reward whoever who could destroy it. Among those who tried was Minos' son Androgeus, but in the encounter it was he, not the bull, who lost his life. (Another version of Androgeus' death suggests that, while in Athens to compete in games, he conspired with Aegeus' enemies, so Aegeus had him murdered.)

By chance, Minos was at that time attacking mainland Greece with his incomparable navy. When the news reached him, he called down a curse. At once earthquakes struck, crops failed, and people and animals died of starvation; and while other Greek states managed to appease the gods, in Attica the situation worsened. Urgently Aegeus consulted the Delphic oracle, which announced that the curse would be lifted only if Athens sent seven young men and seven young women every nine years to Crete as offerings to the Minotaur.

When Theseus came to Athens to claim his inheritance, he overcame the bull, dragged it up to the Acropolis and sacrificed it to Poseidon. Then, since it was time for the next consignment of Athenian youth to be sent Knossos, he announced his intention to join them and, with the gods' support, kill the Minotaur. In Crete, Minos greeted Theseus with a challenge – to prove he was the son not merely of Aegeus but of Poseidon by retrieving a gold ring that Minos hurled far out to sea. Immediately, Theseus dived off the quayside and disappeared, resurfacing after long minutes to wade ashore, the ring held high. All marvelled – and none more than Ariadne. For, as soon as Minos' daughter saw him, she fell in love with Theseus.

That night she met with him. Daedalus had taught her the secret of the labyrinth, which she agreed to share if Theseus took her back to Athens as his wife. The prince agreed, and, evading Minos' guards, they crept to the mouth of the labyrinth. Here Ariadne gave Theseus a sword. Then, placing in his hands a ball of wool, she took hold of the loose end and instructed him to let the rest unravel as he walked through the twisting corridors. By rolling the ball up again he would find his way back out.

Into the inky blackness of the low-roofed passageway Theseus disappeared, his only guide the fetid stench and ever louder bellows of the Minotaur. Finally he reached its lair, and with a roar the Minotaur attacked. Clutching at the hair between its deadly horns, Theseus lunged with his sword, calling to Poseidon to accept his sacrifice. The blade sank home. The Minotaur fell gasping to the ground. Leaving it to thrash in its own blood, Theseus escaped, rewinding the wool until he regained the entrance and the sweet night air.

Theseus and Ariadne freed the other Athenians and escaped across the low hills to the sea. Hurriedly they smashed holes in Minos' ships to prevent pursuit, boarded their own boat and set sail. By sunrise they reached the island of Dia. But here (or at Naxos), despite his promises, Theseus abandoned Ariadne as she was sleeping. When she found him gone, the princess cursed Theseus, but she was not downcast for long. Dionysus saw her, fell in love with her and – transporting her to the stars – made her his bride. (In Dionysus' rescue and transformation of the abandoned heroine some discern a distant echo of a story similar to that of Persephone or Adonis exploring the cycles of death and rebirth. In another version of the myth, Homer tells how Ariadne was killed on Dia by Artemis 'before Theseus could take pleasure in her', while Plutarch records that she died in childbirth on Cyprus.)

Theseus sailed on to Delos, where he sacrificed to Apollo and choreographed the Crane Dance, performed in historical times, whose intricate patterns retraced the winding of the labyrinth and replicated the pattern on the dancing floor which, Homer says, 'Daedalus once built for Ariadne of the lovely hair in the wide open spaces of Knossos'. Theseus set course for Athens, but because of Ariadne's curse he forgot to change his sail from black to white. When Aegeus saw it, thinking his son was dead, he threw himself into the sea.

Daedalus, Icarus & the Death of Minos

Minos' craftsman Daedalus was also an Athenian, but he had fled to Knossos when he murdered one of his apprentices. Now that the labyrinth's security was breached, he desperately needed to quit Crete. Minos' warships were repaired, so escape by sea was impossible. Instead, Daedalus crafted two sets of wings from feathers held together with wax – one pair for himself, the other for his son Icarus.

Wings spread wide, father and son launched themselves from a high cliff and were soon skimming northeastwards across the vastness of the sea. But Icarus was headstrong and eager to experiment and he ignored Daedalus' advice not to fly too near the sun. As he soared ever higher, the sun's heat grew more intense. The wax that held the feathers to the wings began to melt, and in a welter of feathers Icarus plunged headlong to his death. Today the island near where he fell is called Icaria.

Daedalus could not stop. Instead he turned west. Landing at Camicus in south Sicily, he built strong walls for Cocalus, the king, and made exquisite dolls for the princesses. Meanwhile Minos launched his fleet. At every port he offered a reward to whomsoever could pass a thread through the twisting interior of a conch shell, a problem he knew only Daedalus could solve. At last he reached Camicus.

Eager for the reward, King Cocalus set Daedalus to work. Rising to the challenge, he bored a tiny hole into the shell's tip, round which he trickled drops of honey. Then he tied a thread to an ant, and introduced it into the wider opening below. Lured by the honey, the ant navigated the shell's spiral labyrinth until it emerged – with the thread – out of the honey-smeared hole. Cocalus was triumphant. So was Minos. He had located Daedalus.

Cocalus and his daughters would not surrender him. Instead they tricked Minos, inviting him to the palace and offering every hospitality. But as Minos wallowed in his bath, the princesses opened the valves of a pipe that Daedalus had installed above it. A flood of boiling water engulfed the Cretan king. Returning his corpse to his fleet, a convincingly regretful Cocalus blamed faulty plumbing.

With Minos dead, Knossos crumbled. But his spirit lived on. In Hades, Minos ruled as one of the three judges of the dead, together with his estranged brother Rhadamanthus and Aeacus, who had once ruled Aegina.

Knossos in History & Today

Archaeology confirms Knossos' wealth – though interpretation of much of the accumulated evidence is problematic. By around 1400 BC the palace complex at Knossos was probably the largest and richest in the Aegean, the centre of a Cretan (or 'Minoan') empire. Art and traded artifacts show that its influence extended throughout the south Aegean and Near East (a Minoan interpreter may have been employed at Ugarit in Syria in the early eighteenth century BC), west to Sicily and north perhaps as far as Samothrace. There was also considerable contact with Egypt: Egyptian motifs appear in Cretan art; fifteenth-century BC Egyptian tomb paintings from the reigns of Hatshepsut and Thutmose III show Cretans bringing gifts to the Pharaoh; and a fresco at Avaris in the Nile Delta appears to show Cretan bull-leaping.

Surrounded by a city of an estimated 8,000 inhabitants, Knossos boasted an efficient civil service. Linear A and B tablets reveal that administrators were interested in everything from the allocation of labour to the revenue from wool. Although weapons have been discovered, mostly associated with burials, there is little evidence for a strong Cretan military. Knossos lacks any apparent fortifications – in stark contrast to mainland Mycenae, which probably overran Crete in the fourteenth century BC, destroying other palace sites but preserving Knossos, which survived until the early thirteenth century BC. It was once believed that the eruption of Santorini (Thera), 150 km (93 miles) to the north, brought down Minoan civilization, causing a tsunami and polluting the soil with ash. But the eruption is now confidently dated to the late seventeenth century BC, and some modern scholars suggest that climate change was a factor in Crete's demise.

Epic and lyric poetry tells of Minoan Crete, but the first historical references (albeit based on legend rather than hard evidence) come from the late fifth century BC. According to Herodotus, Minos was the first king to build a navy. Thucydides agreed, writing of how Minos established a sea-empire, ruling the Cyclades and sending his sons to found colonies. However, apart from a few fragments, we have no full record of the story of Minos, the Minotaur or Daedalus until the Roman period.

The Minotaur's popularity in Greek art owed much to the rise of Theseus as a major Athenian hero in the early fifth century BC. Scenes from his myth adorned his temple's walls in Athens, while tradition told that the sacred ship that made an annual pilgrimage to Delos was the very vessel in which Theseus sailed to Crete. Its need for constant overhaul prompted philosophical debate: since every timber had been replaced over time, when did it cease to be the original?

Questions of originality plague Knossos, too. In the early twentieth century the British archaeologist Sir Arthur Evans recreated many of its buildings (in concrete) and reconstructed the frescoes and reliefs which once adorned their walls. For some this represents an act of vandalism. For others it provides a useful template for how Knossos and other Cretan palaces would have looked, with their labyrinthine complexes of buildings – administrative, commercial and residential, including some three storeys high – arranged around wide central courtyards.

Palace life remains largely a mystery. Frescoes, showing segregated men and women watching from steps and balconies, suggest open-air festivals held in both courtyards and 'theatral' areas – perhaps similar to the dancing floor Daedalus built for Ariadne. Others (as well as fragmentary sculptures) depict bull-leaping, perhaps the inspiration for the myth of the Minotaur. The location and purpose of bull-leaping are unknown. It may have formed part of a religious ceremony. Miniature clay model bulls were dedicated at cult centres, and many buildings were adorned with 'horns of consecration', stylized bulls' horns, perhaps representing crescent moons, and possibly linked to the Egyptian hieroglyph for 'horizon'. The horns may also have been associated with the double-axe, or *labrys* (the origin of the early-Greek word labyrinth, 'place of the double-axe'). Small models of this axe were frequent ritual offerings; larger versions apparently adorned sanctuaries as totemic objects.

Caves (such as those on Mount Dicte and Mount Ida) and mountain peaks (such as Mount Juktas, clearly visible from Knossos) were important to Minoan religion – all Cretan palaces are in sight of such a cave or peak. Crete may have been a matriarchal society, whose supreme deity Linear B tablets call Potnia ('Mistress'). One even lists an offering of honey to 'Daburinthoio Potniai', perhaps 'The Mistress of the Labyrinth'. If so, it is the earliest reference to the labyrinth – though we can only conjecture what the word means in this context. Mazes appear in Cretan (and Egyptian) art, but there is no formal labyrinth at Knossos.

Knossos

SOME IMPORTANT DATES & REMAINS

c. 7000 BC	Earliest occupation.
c. 1900 BC	First palace constructed.
c. 1700 BC	Major fire destruction followed by a second palace covering over 20,000 square metres (almost 5 acres).
?1628 BC	Eruption of Santorini.
c. 1450 BC	Widespread destruction of Cretan palaces – but not Knossos – suggests invasion, probably by mainland Mycenaean Greeks.
c. 1370 BC	Knossos destroyed by fire.
AD 1900	Sir Arthur Evans begins excavating (and building) at Knossos.

A mile south of Herakleion, Knossos is easily accessible by car or public transport. A shaded path leads from the kiosk past three **kouloures** (possibly storage pits) to the **West Court**. A walkway runs round the south side of the palace to the **South Propylaion**. The **Central Court** is flanked on the east by a building complex housing a **tripartite shrine** and **Throne Room**. A monumental staircase leads to an upper level (with a view of adjacent storage rooms and Mount Juktas) giving access to the reconstructed light well above the Throne Room. The ceremonial **Grand Staircase** is across the Central Court to the east.

The **North Entrance Passage** leads to the **North Pillar Hall**. A path runs left past the **North Lustral Basin** to the **Theatral Area**, a small stepped courtyard, the terminus of the **Royal Road**. A path right from the North Pillar Hall leads to the industrial quarter, housing kilns and workshops, and the **Queen's Megaron** with the **House of the Chancel Screen** beyond. A track, affording a dramatic view up to the **Horns of Consecration,** leads to the right past pine trees in which peacocks roost to the **South House**, before returning to the West Court and site entrance.

Finds from Knossos and other sites are displayed in **Herakleion's Archaeological Museum**. These include original (but heavily restored) **frescoes** and **painted reliefs** as well as a cornucopia of artifacts: *larnakes* (burial caskets), **labrys-axes** (double-axes), **clay models of human devotees** and **clay and metal bulls**. Other highlights include a stone **bull's head rhyton** (drinking vessel) with horns of gold, a **gaming board** decorated with silver and gold leaf and inlaid with rock crystal and lapis lazuli, the **Phaistos Disk** (a small circular clay tablet stamped with symbols in a spiral) and two small **figurines of snake goddesses**. (Both disk and snake goddesses are suspected by some of being forgeries from the early twentieth century AD.) There is also a useful **model of Knossos** in its heyday and an impressive collection of later sculpture, including a seventh-century BC **frieze from Temple A at Prinias**.

Knossos' 'sister' sites at **Phaistos** and **Aghia Triadha** in the south of Crete repay a visit, as does Roman **Gortyn,** where a descendant of Zeus' evergreen plane-tree can be admired. Closer to Knossos, **Mount Juktas** affords superb views (including of Knossos itself).

17

Calydon: A Boar Hunt & Golden Apples

It is hard for men who live on earth to influence the minds of gods. If not, with prayers and sacrifices of so many goats and red-backed cattle, my father Oineus, who whipped his horses hard, would have soothed the wrath of pale-armed Artemis, whose head is garlanded with flower buds. But the anger of the maiden goddess knew no bounds. She sent a savage fearless boar to Calydon, where the dancing is so beautiful. Its strength roiled like a stream in flood as with its tusks it decimated vineyards and slaughtered flocks and cut down any man it met. And we, the best of all the Greeks, stood steadfast for six days as we fought against the beast. At last one of the gods granted us victory. We buried those the screaming boar had slaughtered in its merciless attacks .... Destructive fate had killed them. But still the anger of warlike Artemis, wild daughter of the goddess Leto, was unabated ...

Bacchylides, *Ode* 5.95f.

A brooding sky hangs heavy over Calydon. Above the terraced hilltop dark clouds press low, blanketing the mountains to the north and east, bruising what remains of the two temples as they await the deluge. It has been a short climb from the modern road, but in the lull between two storms it has already brought us far: down from the modern highway rumbling with trucks; down to the theatre, a damp, eccentric rectangle, its stone seats muddy-orange like the earth around them; past the hero-shrine and past the sanctuary of Dionysus, its tall trees dripping from the recent rain, a ruined church crumbling amid the brambles; on up the track through lustrous olive groves; and out on to the levelled bluff, once called the Laphrion, with wide views west to Messolonghi and south across the Gulf of Patras to the Peloponnese beyond. Only the foundations of the temples on the Laphrion survive. The Temple of Apollo was impressive, a colonnaded masterpiece proud above the plain, while slightly in its shadow, at the furthest edge of the escarpment, crouched the temple of his sister, Artemis. Her role was central. For it was she, the virgin huntress, who inspired the myth for which Calydon is best remembered.

Meleager, Atalanta & the Boar Hunt
When Meleager, son of Calydon's king Oineus (and brother of Tydeus), was born, the three Fates appeared miraculously in his mother Altheia's bedroom. One promised that Meleager would be strong, another that he would be noble, but the third foretold that he would die when a log already smouldering on the hearth turned into ashes. Hastily Altheia doused the log and hid it in a chest; and Meleager grew to heroic manhood.

Atalanta (far left) and Meleager (left) attack the Calydonian Boar on the sixth-century BC François Vase.

Years later, as the elderly Oineus was making offerings to all the gods in turn, he forgot to sacrifice to Artemis – so she sent a boar of supernatural size, strength and savagery to devastate his land. Homer describes it 'tearing towering trees out of the ground and flinging them about, a mess of roots and apple blossom'. Meleager swore he would slaughter it. So he invited all the greatest heroes of his age to join him in the hunt, promising the creature's pelt to whoever killed it. They included Theseus from Athens, Jason from Iolcus, Achilles' father Peleus – and one young woman, Atalanta.

Exposed at birth by her father, who wanted a son, Atalanta was reared by a she-bear, sacred to Artemis, which taught her hunting and endurance. Now a young woman, attractive, athletic and determined to preserve her virginity, she saw no reason why she should not join the hunt. Many of the men, however, were uneasy. Meleager's maternal uncles especially resented her inclusion on such a daring enterprise, while others found Atalanta dangerously irresistible. Among these latter was Meleager.

At last the hunters found the boar lazing by a stream. Suddenly alert, it charged them, killing two, hamstringing a third, and causing Peleus to scramble up a tree in terror. Atalanta's arrows drew first blood, but, despite being hacked and stabbed by Greece's finest heroes, the beast did not weaken until Meleager skewered it with his spear. Rather than keep the prize for himself (as was his right), he presented the warm, dripping hide to Atalanta. Meleager's uncles were outraged. Blows were exchanged, and in the ruckus two were killed. Two others vowed vengeance, and hurried home to rally troops.

As battle raged outside Calydon, Meleager killed his mother's two remaining brothers. In rage Altheia took the log out of the chest and threw it on the fire; as the blackened wood crumbled to red-hot ash, the young hero died. His sisters' grief caused even Artemis to pity them, so she turned them into guinea-fowl, which the Greeks called *meleagrides*.

Meleager in the Iliad

In the *Iliad*, to try to turn aside Achilles' wrath over the loss of his slave girl and persuade him to return to the fighting, a Greek delegation reminds him of the battle at Calydon. In this version, Meleager, angry with Altheia, withdraws from the conflict outside the city, and stays at home with his wife Cleopatra, 'nursing his heart-aching wrath, in fury at his mother's curses which, mourning her brothers' death, she called upon him from the gods. Repeatedly she beat her fists on the rich earth, as she stretched out on the ground, her bosom wet with tears, calling on Haides and revered Persephone to bring death to her son; and the Fury who walks in darkness, whose heart is merciless, heard her.'

Meleager's absence allows the enemy to gain the upper hand. As the situation worsens, Calydon's elders offer Meleager magnificent incentives to return to battle; next his father, sisters and even his mother Altheia beg him to fight. But only when Cleopatra adds her voice does Meleager buckle on his armour, stride on to the plain and (despite receiving none of the promised gifts) drive off the enemy.

The parallel with Achilles' situation at Troy is clear. Even the name of Meleager's wife Cleopatra ('ancestral fame') is a variant of that of Achilles' companion Patroclus. But at Troy the power of myth fails to sway Achilles, whose refusal to fight becomes a legend in itself.

Postscript: Atalanta & the Golden Apples

As for Atalanta, some claimed that she sailed on the voyage of the *Argo*, others that she bore Meleager a son, but most agreed that, a virgin, she returned in triumph to her homeland of Arcadia. Although her father welcomed her, he was determined that she should marry without delay; Atalanta was equally determined she should not. They agreed on a compromise. All suitors must compete with Atalanta in a footrace. She would marry whoever managed to defeat her; any who lost, she would kill.

As Atalanta was the fastest runner alive, fresh burial mounds soon sprang up throughout Greece, until Aphrodite took pity on a local prince, Hippomenes. She gave him three golden apples and helped him trick his way to victory. The race began. Atalanta effortlessly eased ahead. But as she did, a golden apple, dazzling in the sunlight, landed with a thud before her feet. She stopped; she picked it up; she marvelled at its beauty;

and when she resumed running Hippomenes was ahead. Then a second apple, and a third – and Atalanta watched bewitched as Hippomenes claimed victory. The two lived in chaste wedlock until one day desire overtook them at a sanctuary of Zeus, where they sacrilegiously consummated their love. So Zeus changed both into lions – mistakenly believing that lions couple only with leopards, and not each other.

Dionysus & the Spring of Callirhoe

A local Calydonian myth concerns the perils of love. Pausanias records how Coresus, a priest of Dionysus, fell in love with the beautiful Callirhoe. The more he wooed her, the more haughtily she rebuffed him. So he prayed for help to Dionysus. Immediately, the Calydonians displayed symptoms of gross drunkenness, and many died deranged. At last the oracle at Dodona revealed that the sickness came from Dionysus and would end only if Coresus sacrificed to Dionysus either Callirhoe or a willing substitute. 'When no one would save her, Callirhoe ran to her parents, but even they refused to help her. Her only future lay in death. Preparations proceeded as the oracle instructed. With Coresus presiding, Callirhoe was led to the altar – but Coresus yielded not to anger but to love. He killed himself in her place – the loftiest example of true love in all history. Callirhoe, overcome by compassion for Coresus and shame for her treatment of him, cut her throat by the spring near Calydon's harbour, which has been named in her memory ever since.' Appropriately, 'Callirhoe' means 'Fair Flowing'.

Calydon in History & Today

Despite being the setting of a well-known myth, little is known of Calydon until the time of its abandonment. Signs of occupation from the eleventh century BC suggest that it grew up round the archaic sanctuary of Artemis Laphria, an important religious centre. Briefly fought over in the early fourth century BC, in the Classical and Hellenistic periods its two temples – one of Artemis (housing a gold-and-ivory statue), the other of Apollo – were augmented by treasuries and stoas. In the third century BC, Calydon and its newly fortified acropolis were enclosed by walls, 4 km (2½ miles) in circumference. The following century a lavish shrine to a local hero, Leon, was erected, with a colonnaded courtyard and a chapel, whose vaulted crypt contained two finely carved stone beds.

In the aftermath of the Battle of Actium (31 BC), which took place not far to the north, Octavian (soon to be called Augustus) forced the Calydonians to move to nearby Nicopolis, built to celebrate his victory over Antony and Cleopatra. Calydon, which Strabo called 'an ornament of Greece', became a ghost town. Even its gods were relocated, their statues shipped south across the gulf to Patras, where their priests continued to observe ancient rituals. Here Pausanias witnessed the two-day festival of Artemis Laphria. On the first day, a young priestess rode in a chariot drawn by four deer to an altar, piled high with dried logs. Next day events were less sedate:

> Community and individuals alike take great pride in the ceremony. They hurl on to the altar living game birds and other animals (boars, deer, gazelles – some young, some fully grown). They stack fruits from their orchards on to the altar, too. Then they set fire to the wood. When they did this, I saw creatures including a bear trying to escape as the flames caught, but the people who first cast them into the fire forced them back again. There is no record of anyone being harmed by these animals.

Meanwhile, the Calydonian boar hunt was a popular subject for artists, inspiring a wealth of sculptures, vase paintings and mosaics. The sixth-century BC François Vase (now in Florence's National Archaeological Museum) shows Atalanta wielding a spear in the thick of the hunt, while on a second-century AD Roman mosaic in Patras Museum a stocky Atalanta draws her bow as dogs attack the boar.

In the second century AD, relics of the boar could still be seen. One intact tusk, three feet long, was housed in the Sanctuary of Dionysus in the Emperor's Gardens in Rome, the other at the Temple of Athene Alea in Tegea. When Pausanias visited, the priests told him that, although in their possession, this tusk was sadly broken. But they did show him the boar's hide, which he records was 'desiccated and without one bristle left'.

SOME IMPORTANT DATES & REMAINS

C8th–7th BC	Wooden temples of Artemis and Apollo on Laphrion.
C6th BC	Laphrion extended with new retaining walls.
460 BC	Gold-and-ivory statue of Artemis installed.
C4th BC	Temples of Artemis and Apollo rebuilt in stone; theatre constructed.
391 BC	Calydon briefly seized from Aetolians by Achaean Greeks.
367/66 BC	Epaminondas helps restore Calydon to Aetolians.
C3rd BC	City walls built.
219 BC	Calydon badly damaged in war with Philip V of Macedon.
C2nd BC	Hero shrine built.
30 BC	Calydon's citizens relocated to Nicopolis; religious statues and festivals transferred to Patras.

Calydon, at first sight unprepossessing, is located by the busy motorway linking Antirrhio and Messolonghi. Near the car park is the **theatre,** with foundations of stage buildings and a rectangular *orkhestra* and auditorium. From here a path leads to the fenced **hero-shrine** – the site attendant will unlock the gate and show the subterranean tomb with beautifully carved stone beds, complete with pillows and other delicate sculptural details. Further on are the foundations of a temple, identified as the **Temple of Dionysus,** from where a track (right) soon leads to the **Laphrion,** with foundations of the **temples of Artemis and Apollo**. From the Temple of Dionysus another track leads to Calydon's **acropolis,** surrounding which traces of **city walls** are visible. At the time of writing, the site had no signage and the guidebook was available only in Greek. There is no museum.

18

Sparta & the Haunts of Helen

The most beautiful of all Spartan woman had once been the most ugly. What happened was this: [as a child] her parents considered her appearance a disaster (they were wealthy; she was unsightly), so, pondering her unappealing looks, her nurse devised this plan: each day she took the child to Helen's sanctuary at Therapne, above the temple of Apollo ... placed her beside the statue and prayed to the goddess to stop the child being ugly.

One day, as she was leaving the sanctuary, they say the nurse met a woman who asked her what she was carrying in her arms. When she said it was a child, the woman asked if she could see it. The nurse refused, saying that its parents had forbidden her to show it to anyone. But when the woman kept on asking her and the nurse realized how important it was to her, she relented and showed her the child. The woman stroked its head and said it would become the most beautiful woman in Sparta. And from that day, the child's appearance changed ...

Herodotus, *Histories*, 6.61

Far below the grassy plateau studded with wild flowers, where once the shrine of Helen stood, a golden glow from the Eurotas River bathes the fertile plain. Olive groves and orchards, small-holdings and farms, the bustling town of Sparti, the road south to the sea – all seem mellow in the evening sun, though dwarfed by the mountains soaring high beyond: Taÿgetus, the great massif, a saw-tooth dragon-spine of ridges, even in early summer dazzling with snow. Sound travels effortlessly in the crystal air: the throaty barking of a dog; a tractor's sputtering; the splash of water as the river ripples past thick stands of lush bamboo. It must be the most magical location in all Greece, a perfect marriage of extremes, possessed of an almost unendurable euphoria fused with the deepest melancholy. To stand here is to stand face-to-face with the divine.

Apollo & Hyacinthus

In the Eurotas valley and its surrounding mountains the divine seems palpable. Mythology tells that at Amyclae (south of modern Sparti) god did once walk with human when Apollo fell in love with the beautiful young athlete Hyacinthus. But Zephyrus, the West Wind, also loved the youth and, shunned, was consumed by jealousy. So when Apollo and Hyacinthus were competing with each other in games, Zephyrus caused Apollo's discus to veer from its path and deliver Hyacinthus a mortal blow. Apollo could not save his lover, but in tribute caused flowers to blossom from the dead boy's blood – the hyacinth, whose petals bore, so Greeks perceived, the letters 'AI AI', the sound made in lament, in everlasting memory of Apollo's tears.

In historical times an annual three-day early summer festival was held at Amyclae. Its focus was Hyacinthus' tomb, a chamber built into the base of a colossal throne, topped by a statue of Apollo, 14 m (45 ft) tall. The Hyacinthia promised rebirth after death – ritual mourning for the fallen hero was followed by a celebration of his resurrection as Apollo-Hyacinthus.

Leda & the Swan

The porous boundary between human and divine winds through many of Sparta's myths, not least those associated with Leda's children. Leda was married to Sparta's King Tyndareus, but still Zeus desired her. Fearing (uncharacteristically) that she would rebuff him, Zeus waited until Leda was walking by the River Eurotas. Then, transforming himself into a swan and pursued by one of his own eagles, he plummeted to earth in a flurry of feathers. Leda instinctively protected the trembling bird but, as she clutched him in her arms, Zeus seized the opportunity and raped her. Nonplussed, the queen returned home, where Tyndareus consoled her by making love to her. In time Leda was delivered of two eggs, one of

The myth of Leda and the Swan as depicted on a Roman mosaic in Paphos, Cyprus.

which hatched twin girls (Helen and Clytemnestra), the other twin boys (Castor and Polydeuces). Because of their mixed patrilineage, two of the siblings (Castor and Clytemnestra) were mortal, the other two (Helen and Polydeuces) immortal.

The Heavenly Twins

Known as the Dioscuri (sons of Zeus), Castor and Polydeuces grew up to be great horsemen and bold adventurers, taking part in the boar hunt at Calydon and sailing with Jason from Iolcus to find the Golden Fleece. But they were best known for the aftermath of their destructive desire for two sisters, Phoebe and Hilaeira (great-grand-daughters of Perseus), who had been promised to the Dioscuri's cousins, the Thebans Lynceus and Idas.

When they discovered that their betrothed had been abducted to Sparta, where each had borne a son, Lynceus and Idas retaliated: to redeem their honour they would take their cousins' livestock. Feigning friendship, they joined the Dioscuri in a cattle raid, then, after unfairly beating them in a speed-eating contest, claimed all the booty. The quarrel intensified. After stealing back their cattle and rustling their rivals' herd, Castor and Polydeuces hid in ambush in a hollow oak tree. But lynx-eyed Lynceus spotted them from Mount Taÿgetus, and Idas aimed his spear unerringly. Castor was killed and, as Polydeuces leapt out to deal Lynceus a death-blow, Zeus blasted Idas with a thunderbolt. Grief-stricken, Polydeuces prayed that Zeus might let him die with Castor but, being immortal, this was impossible. Instead, Zeus told him:

> 'If you really want to champion your brother and share
> all equally with him, you may draw breath for half your
> time beneath the earth, and half in the golden halls
> of heaven.' When he heard this, Polydeuces did not
> hesitate: he opened bronze-clad Castor's eyes, and
> then set free his voice.

So, on alternate days each brother lived as a sky-god, while on the other he was honoured as a god of the underworld in his tomb-shrine at Therapne, one of the most sacred sites in Sparta. Mounted on snow-white stallions, their heads encased in egg-shell helmets, the Dioscuri were protectors of sailors, manifesting themselves as St Elmo's fire. Alcaeus of Lesbos celebrated them in a hymn:

> Leave the Peloponnese and come to me here, Castor and
> Polydeuces, brave sons of Zeus and Leda! Come with
> benevolence! You gallop on swift horses across the wide
> earth and the sea, snatching men from tearful death,
> leaping on prows of well-benched ships, a blazing light
> running high up masts and rigging, bringing brightness
> in the dark night of despair.

At Sparta the Dioscuri were worshipped in the form of two upright wooden beams, joined by two cross-bars. They were both loved and feared. In historical times, disguised as travellers, they were believed to have tested the owner of the house where they had lived, asking him to let them spend the night in their old room. The owner refused, explaining that his young daughter was asleep there. Pausanias records: 'In the morning effigies of the Dioscuri were discovered in the room, but the girl and all her servants had vanished.' Today we remember them as the Heavenly Twins, the brightest stars in the constellation Gemini, set there by Zeus as their memorial.

Helen & Menelaus

Helen's childhood had been turbulent. Already her magnetic beauty had aroused such wild emotions that her mother was rumoured to be not Leda but Nemesis, goddess of vengeance, raped by Zeus at Rhamnous when both were in the guise of swans.

Theseus, determined to possess an immortal wife, abducted Helen to Athens when she was only seven. Although the Dioscuri rescued her, when she reached marriageable age Tyndareus again realized the dangers inherent in her loveliness. Sparta was besieged by ardent, volatile admirers, the highest-born and most ambitious heroes, each offering rich gifts in exchange for Helen's hand. So passionate were they that Tyndareus feared for the stability of Helen's future marriage – until Odysseus of Ithaca (who was wooing not Helen but her clever cousin, Penelope) suggested a solution.

Taking Odysseus' advice, Tyndareus assembled the suitors on the plain just north of Sparta, and commanded each to stand on the butchered carcass of a horse and swear an oath: they would unite against any who sought to undermine the marriage. Then he gave Helen to Menelaus. Some versions of the myth suggest he also passed his kingdom to him. To Agamemnon, Menelaus' brother and king of Mycenae, he gave Helen's sister Clytemnestra (though Agamemnon had to kill her husband first).

In return for his advice concerning Helen's marriage, Tyndareus lent his support to Odysseus' efforts to win his niece, Penelope, the daughter of his brother Icarius. Odysseus was fleet of foot, so Tyndareus suggested that Icarius give Penelope to whoever won a race through Sparta's streets. The victor was Odysseus, but Icarius was loath to let the happy couple leave, and when they set out, he followed in a chariot, begging his daughter to stay. Loving her father but in love with her husband, Penelope was torn. But when Odysseus told her she must choose, she veiled her head in silence and continued on to Ithaca to be the model of fidelity.

A few years later Tyndareus forgot to sacrifice to Aphrodite, so the goddess enflamed Paris, Prince of Troy, with reports of Helen's beauty and brought him to Sparta as a reward for judging her the fairest. Foolishly, Menelaus sailed to Crete, leaving them alone. When he returned to find his palace and bed empty, he sent messengers throughout Greece to remind Helen's erstwhile suitors of their oath, and so the army sailed to Troy, and after ten years sacked the city. Helen, unbowed, returned to Sparta, where (as Telemachus discovered when he visited on his search for his father, Odysseus) she continued to assert control:

> At once into the wine, which they were drinking, she
> threw a drug, which would relax and soothe and take
> away all memory of suffering. Whoever drank the mixture

While Eros hovers overhead and Peitho (Persuasion) follows on, Paris leads Helen by the wrist from her palace at Sparta. (Red figure Attic deep wine cup, *c.* 490–480 BC.)

would shed no tears that day, not even if his mother or his father were to lie before him dead, or if his brother or dear son were to be slaughtered right in front of him before his very eyes. So clever was the drug that Zeus' daughter mixed, which Polydamna the Egyptian, Thoön's wife, had given her.

After his death, Menelaus was buried at Therapne on the plateau overlooking the Eurotas, where the Spartans honoured him as a hero and Helen as a goddess. As for the immortal Helen, a sixth-century BC Greek explorer from South Italy claimed to have met her on White Island in the Black Sea, where she was living with Achilles. She gave him a message to convey to the lyric poet Stesichorus, who had suddenly been struck blind after condemning Helen's adulterous relationship with Paris. Now Helen promised to restore his sight if he wrote a recantation, so his *Palinode* begins: 'The story is untrue! You never sailed in well-oared ships, nor reached Troy's citadel.' Immediately he wrote the lines, Stesichorus saw again. His explanation was that the gods, wishing to decimate mankind through war, yet preserve Helen's honour, substituted a phantom for Paris to abduct. The real Helen was spirited to Egypt, where Menelaus found her on his voyage home.

Sparta & the Haunts of Helen

Sparta in History & Today

Mythological Sparta is unlike the Sparta of Classical history. Early Sparta (a confederacy of villages rather than a consolidated city) enjoyed a flourishing cultural and artistic life, but in the late seventh century BC this changed. Fearing defeat by either external enemies or their own slaves, the dominant classes adopted a regime of extraordinary austerity. Loyalty to the state was paramount. Boys housed in barracks from the age of seven were trained exclusively as warriors, while girls honed their bodies to bear strong children. An eccentric constitution melded monarchy (with two kings ruling simultaneously), oligarchy and democracy (limited to the ruling warrior class), underpinned by an almost fanatical observation of religious festivals. Predictably many Spartans were sociopaths.

Despite establishing some early colonies, Spartans were reluctant to become involved in international politics. They played no role in opposing the Persian invasion of 490 BC, claiming that the Carneia (a fertility festival) took precedence. Shamed as a result, three hundred Spartans under King Leonidas died holding back the second invasion at Thermopylae (480 BC), and Sparta took the lead in every ensuing battle of the campaign until the victorious Greeks refused to follow their Spartan generals and command passed to Athens.

For the rest of the fifth century BC, Sparta and Athens enjoyed an edgy relationship, which erupted in the Peloponnesian War. In 404 BC Sparta hesitated to capitalize on victory and its power was diminished. It was even forced to build protective city walls, only to demolish them and scrap its constitution when it was conquered by a league of other Greek states under Philopoemen (188 BC).

Under the Romans, Sparta featured on the tourist trail. When Pausanias visited, almost every street corner had mythological associations. One temple even boasted a beribboned egg, said to have been laid by Leda, suspended from its ceiling. By the third century AD, Sparta's macho past was celebrated at the shrine of Artemis Orthia, where stone seating was installed to let audiences enjoy a degenerate version of an ancient initiation rite in which boys were flogged (sometimes to death) at the altar.

In AD 396, Sparta was overrun by Alaric the Goth. It never recovered. In the Byzantine era a new city was built in the foothills of Taÿgetus at nearby Mistra. After Greek independence in 1834, with Mistra in ruins, an elegant new town built on the site of ancient Sparta obscured much that was potentially of archaeological interest. Modern travellers may marvel at the prescience of Thucydides' observation two and a half millennia ago:

> Imagine that Sparta became uninhabited, with only the
> foundations of its buildings still intact. As time passed,

future generations would, I think, find it hard to believe
that it had ever been as powerful as men said it was. For
Sparta has no very striking monuments and buildings.

There would be more remains had not the French Abbé Fourmont visited
in 1730, intent on discovering inscriptions. His letters, freely describing
himself as 'a barbarian in Greece', make chilling reading:

> For a month now I have been engaged with thirty
> workmen in the complete destruction of Sparta; not one
> day passes on which I do not find something – some days
> I have discovered up to twenty inscriptions! Imagine
> my joy (and fatigue) at recovering so many marbles....
> Perhaps by my demolishing its walls and temples, so that
> no stone rests on another in even the smallest shrine,
> its location will be unknown in future, but at least I
> have some evidence by which to recognize it, and that
> is something. This is the only way that I could make my
> journey to the Peloponnese illustrious – it would have
> been quite pointless otherwise, and that would have
> suited neither France nor me.

Sparta

SOME IMPORTANT DATES & REMAINS

c. 1500 BC	Mycenaean palace (Homeric Sparta?) at Therapne.
c. 1200 BC	Mycenaean palace destroyed by fire.
c. 750 BC	Spartan expansion annexes Amyclae and much of southern Peloponnese.
late C7th BC	Spartan constitution reformed, traditionally by Lycurgus.
480 BC	Leonidas delays Persians at Thermopylae. Sparta leads Greek victory against Persia.
404 BC	Sparta and its allies defeat Athens.
371 BC	Thebes defeats Sparta at Battle of Leuctra.
331 BC	Alexander the Great forces Sparta to join 'Corinthian League'.
c. 207 BC	First city-walls built.
188 BC	Philopoemen defeats Sparta, destroying walls and constitution.
C1st BC–4th AD	Sparta features on Roman 'tourist trail'.
AD 396	Alaric the Goth overruns Sparta.

Sparta & the Haunts of Helen

| AD 1730 | Abbé Fourmont demolishes much of ancient Sparta's remains. |
| AD 1834 | Modern Sparti built on site of ancient city. |

Ancient Sparta began as a collection of villages, so (scanty) remains are relatively scattered. A car is recommended. **Mycenaean Sparta** and the **Menelaion** at Therapne lie on a bluff east of the Eurotas River. A track (15 minutes walk), signposted on the Yeraki road, leads past the chapel of Agios Ilias (on the site of a Temple of Apollo). The views are stunning. Another contender for Menelaus and Helen's Sparta is **Pellana**, 27 km (17 miles) north of modern Sparti. A complex of rock-cut tholos tombs includes one apparently with a carving of a heraldic lion. The discovery of a further Mycenaean palace in 2015 near the village of Xirocampi south of Sparti may have a significant impact on our understanding of the period.

Most of **Classical and Roman Sparta** lies on a low acropolis behind the modern sports stadium. It includes a **Roman theatre** and the **Temple of Bronze-Housed Athene**. By the banks of the Eurotas, near the bridge leading north from Sparti, are the still-atmospheric foundations of the **Sanctuary of Artemis Orthia**, complete with Roman seating.

Little remains at **Amyclae**, on the road south to Gytheion, but the site is romantic. To the west of Sparti, the **Parori Gorge** may be where Spartans exposed unwanted babies. Just to the north of this the Byzantine city of **Mistra** boasts beautifully frescoed churches and an impressive castle. In the summer this site, on a steep slope with little shade, can be arduous to visit.

Among the exhibits at Sparti's **Museum** are an **archaic relief of Helen and Menelaus** from Amyclae; a fifth-century BC (weathered) marble **torso of a warrior**, believed to be Leonidas; a Roman **mosaic of Alcibiades**, the traitorous fifth-century BC Athenian politician; and **masks** and **sickles** from the Sanctuary of Artemis Orthia.

19

Mycenae & the Curse on Agamemnon's Family

It never leaves this house, the chorus, chanting its cabbala in
unison, cacophonous, words so diabolic – and they've drunk
human blood. And so their power is growing and they're haunting
all the house now with their ghostly tarantella and they cannot
be dislodged – they're in the blood, congenital, the demons of
revenge. They are roosting in the palace, chanting psalms of blinding
madness, of the passion that began it, a polyphony of loathing for
a brother's wife debauched, detestation for the man who so seduced
her.... Look! Do you see them, roosting, huddled close beside
the house, the young dream-phantoms, arms outstretched, the
children killed – no! can it be?! – by their own family, clutching in
their hands their flesh, their guts, their entrails, sweetmeats in a
feast for their own father!

Aeschylus, *Agamemnon*, II. 1186ff.

From the rise above the whitewashed chapel of the Panagia, the All-Holy Virgin, tranquil on a low ridge riddled with remains of royal tombs, Mycenae's citadel appears to crouch, a brooding beast, between two glowering mountains. Around the low acropolis, its vertebrae of gleaming grey stones coil, clinging to the rock, whose steep cliff plunges to a chasm far below, known to the Greeks as Chaos. At times the gusting wind sweeps hard across the ruins, scouring the dry earth, and, just as suddenly, dies back – but not before a shroud of sand, an ochre cloud of dust, has lifted high into the air to drift and swell and finally subside, a spectral drizzle; and as it falls it coats once more the roofless halls, the winding lanes, the walls, the open graves.

And then the sun breaks through the scudding clouds. Quite unexpectedly the citadel is bathed in light. Yet still the feeling of foreboding lingers, a feeling rooted deeply in Mycenae's past. For this was once not just a seat of glittering empire. Legends tell how Mycenae's soil was soaked in blood as ruling families tore themselves apart, committing acts of ever-spiralling brutality.

The Foundation of Mycenae

The spilling of kindred blood flows back through Mycenae's past to its foundation. When Perseus accidentally killed his grandfather King Acrisius of Argos, he was loath to claim the throne as was his due. Instead he exchanged kingdoms with Megapenthes, ruler of nearby Tiryns. Included in his new lands was the stony outcrop of Mycenae, at the head of a fertile plain flanked by tall hills south of the Dervenaki Pass. Seeing its strategic potential, Perseus enlisted Cyclopes to build its massive walls (or so locals, marvelling at the enormous stones, told Pausanias).

But Perseus and Megapenthes quarrelled, and Perseus was killed. His death heralded a period of instability. Mycenae was attacked, its cattle stolen, and only through guile could Perseus' grandson, Amphitryon, defeat the raiders, islanders from far-off Taphos in the Ionian Sea. Still disaster dogged the royal household. When Amphitryon accidentally killed Mycenae's king, his uncle, he was exiled to Thebes with his wife Alcmene.

The new king Sthenelus restored stability, marrying the daughter of Pelops, king of Elis, but their son Eurystheus once more plunged the region into chaos. Ruling from Tiryns, Eurystheus declared war on the family of his hated and now dead enemy Heracles, and when they fled to Athens he followed with his army. But Eurystheus was killed, and, his throne now vacant, the Mycenaeans sent for Atreus and Thyestes, who were Eurystheus' uncles, Pelops' sons, and already ruling as regents in nearby Midea.

Atreus, Thyestes & a Bloody Banquet

The brothers were bitter rivals. When the elder, Atreus, was appointed king, Thyestes seduced his wife, Aerope, and plotted revolution. After Atreus vowed to dedicate his finest animal to Artemis, his shepherds discovered a miraculous horned lamb, resplendent with a golden fleece, clearly a gift from the gods. Sacrificing it as pledged, Atreus kept the fleece for himself. But his announcement that its ownership proved his right to rule backfired when Aerope stole the fleece and gave it to Thyestes, who triumphantly seized the kingdom.

Zeus, displeased, advised Atreus to challenge Thyestes: if the sun reversed its course, would Thyestes give up the throne? Thyestes agreed, and as Euripides relates: 'Zeus turned back the searing circuit of the stars and of the blazing sun, and dawn's white face ... so, while rain-clouds brooded to the north, the scorching shrine of Ammon, denied Zeus' drenching rain, withered in parching heat.' As Thyestes fled into exile, Atreus' revenge was swift. Far out to sea, he threw Aerope overboard, and calmly watched her drown. His vengeance on Thyestes took longer. After many years he tracked down his brother, assured him of his forgiveness, and invited him and his young sons to a feast of reconciliation. Thyestes was ushered into the banqueting hall and enthusiastically devoured the meal, commending Atreus' chefs. But when new platters were brought in, their covers were removed to reveal, neatly arranged, Thyestes' children's severed heads and hands and feet. Retching, Thyestes cursed Atreus and his family, and rushed from the room.

Thyestes' Revenge

Thyestes came to Sicyon, near Corinth, to find his one surviving child, his daughter Pelopia, who was priestess of Athene. His motive was eccentric – an oracle had urged him to father a child by her. So he raped her while she was bathing and ran off, dropping his sword. Soon after, Atreus arrived. When he saw Pelopia he fell in love with her, and took her as his wife back to Mycenae, where she bore a son. But recalling the circumstances of his conception, Pelopia exposed the baby on the hillside. Atreus found out and dispatched a search party. Finding him being suckled by a goat, they named the baby Aegisthus ('goat strength') and returned him to Mycenae, where Atreus reared him as his own.

Then the harvests failed. For years famine stalked Mycenae. At last an oracle told Atreus what he must do: recall Thyestes. Reluctantly Atreus obeyed, but, when Thyestes arrived, Atreus immediately imprisoned him. Determined to resolve the situation once and for all, Atreus summoned Aegisthus and ordered him to prove his worth by killing Thyestes. So the boy took a sword from Pelopia and entered the prison. He was about to strike when Thyestes recognized the weapon as his own, lost years before at Sicyon, and revealed that he, Thyestes, was Aegisthus' father. Together they killed Atreus.

With Thyestes now ruling Mycenae, Atreus' sons Agamemnon and Menelaus plotted his downfall. Supported by Tyndareus, king of Sparta, they marched on Mycenae and forced Thyestes and Aegisthus into exile. For a while all went well, and ties with Sparta were strengthened when Tyndareus selected Menelaus to marry his daughter, Helen, and inherit his throne. As for Tyndareus' other daughter, Clytemnestra: Agamemnon invaded Pisa, where her husband, Tantalus, was king, killed him, and, after a rough wooing, married her.

Agamemnon, Clytemnestra & Aegisthus

Agamemnon and Clytemnestra had four children: a son, Orestes, and three daughters, Iphigenia (sometimes called Iphianassa), Electra and Chrysothemis. Mycenae flourished, becoming the most powerful city in all Greece. But once again the shedding of family blood brought disaster.

In fulfilment of an oath, war was declared when Paris took Helen to Troy. As Menelaus' elder brother and the most powerful of all kings, Agamemnon was appointed to lead the expedition to retrieve her, so he ordered the Greek army to assemble at the Bay of Aulis, opposite Euboea in the east of Greece. While there, Agamemnon asked his prophet Calchas to foretell how long the war would last. At once, an eagle swooped from the sky and seized in its talons a pregnant hare, which it ripped apart, revealing ten unborn and bloody leverets. The omen was clear. The war would last ten years. But the pregnant hare was sacred to Artemis, and her anger knew no bounds. She caused storm winds to scream down from Thrace, so that the soldiers, huddled by the lashing sea and enduring first rains, then starvation, grew increasingly resentful.

Calchas' advice was chilling. Artemis would relent only if Agamemnon sacrificed his daughter Iphigenia. So, pretending he was giving her in marriage to Achilles, he summoned her to Aulis. Approaching the altar, her joy turned to terror when Agamemnon's guards snatched her and raised her high. Aeschylus describes the scene:

> Oh, how she begged and prayed and called out for her
> father. They did not care, though, in their lust for war,
> the generals. They did not care for all her youth and
> innocence. Agamemnon made the necessary prayer
> and told his men to hold her firm above the altar, like
> an animal, face-down, wrapped closely in her robes.
> He told them too to gag her mouth, her lovely mouth,
> to muffle any words that might bring down a curse upon
> the house by violence and the choking voiceless cord.

Her yellow robes, dyed deep in purest saffron, fell
heavy to the ground, and she looked at each man at the
sacrifice, darting looks to melt the heart, lovely as a girl
looks in a picture, wanting so to speak – as often in her
father's halls she'd sung at banquet, her virgin voice
pure, lovely, honouring in love and gentleness the third
drink offering to god, the sacred hymn, the hymn of hope
for her dear father.

As the winds dropped and the soldiers raced to their ships, Iphigenia's
mother Clytemnestra was left alone to watch her daughter's blood drying
in the warming breeze.

Others attribute Artemis' anger to Agamemnon's inadvertent killing
of a sacred deer, adding that at the moment of sacrifice Artemis relented
and substituted a deer for Iphigenia, whom she transported to Tauris in
the Crimea. Later, Iphigenia was returned to Greece by her brother Orestes,
becoming the priestess of Artemis at Brauron, near Athens, where her
hero-shrine can still be seen. Left in Mycenae alone with her resentment,
Clytemnestra turned for support to Agamemnon's enemy: Aegisthus.

At the very moment of her sacrifice, a deer is
substituted for Iphigenia. (Mixing vessel from
Apulia, Italy, *c.* 370–350 BC.)

Mycenae & the Curse on Agamemnon's Family

The Assassination of Agamemnon

To warn her of Agamemnon's homecoming when war was over, Clytemnestra arranged a chain of beacons from Mount Ida near Troy, across to Samothrace and Mount Athos, and down the east coast to Mycenae, where a sentry kept watch on the palace roof. At last the message came. Soon Agamemnon was driving triumphantly into the palace courtyard, where Clytemnestra met him. Feigning happiness, she begged Agamemnon to celebrate his victory by walking into the palace not on bare earth but over costly woven tapestries. Agamemnon hesitated, fearing this would provoke divine retribution. Then he agreed.

Inside, Clytemnestra prepared Agamemnon a hot soothing bath. But no sooner was he in it than she (perhaps aided by Aegisthus) threw a net across him, stabbing the struggling king repeatedly with a sword – or (some say) hacking at him with an axe. Bellowing like a sacrificial bull, Agamemnon fell dying in the blood-fouled bath. He had brought home with him a Trojan concubine: Cassandra, the prophetess daughter of King Priam. She sensed Mycenae's horrors past, present and future, and realizing that her death, too, was near, she was killed beside Agamemnon's corpse, her body flung into the gorge of Chaos. Agamemnon's daughter Electra hurriedly gave her young brother Orestes to a trusted slave and bundled them out of Mycenae's northern gate with instructions to escape to Phocis, where Strophius (husband of Agamemnon's sister Anaxibia) was king. Here Orestes grew to manhood.

The Return of Orestes

Later, in disguise, Orestes returned to Mycenae with his cousin Pylades. At Agamemnon's tomb, he was disturbed by a procession of women, come to make offerings to his father's ghost. Orestes recognized their leader: Electra. Clytemnestra had sent her, having dreamt that she gave birth to a serpent that sank its fangs deep in her breast. Discovering that Electra also hated their mother, Orestes revealed his identity to his sister and the two plotted their revenge.

Aeschylus tells how, driven to matricide by the god Apollo, Orestes tricked Clytemnestra into summoning Aegisthus, whom he butchered before turning his sword on his mother. Recognizing Orestes at last, she bared her breast, demanding how he could kill the woman who once suckled him. It was to no avail. Sophocles has another version. His Orestes brings false news of his own death in a chariot race and gains access to the palace by giving Clytemnestra an urn containing (he claims) her son's ashes. He then kills his mother before leading Aegisthus ominously into the palace.

The most radical retelling of the myth comes from Euripides. Here, Electra is married to a peasant, and a reluctant Orestes reveals his identity only after being recognized by an old retainer, who cajoles him into vengeance. Impiously he slaughters Aegisthus at a sacrifice. A messenger describes the scene to Electra:

> Aegisthus took the entrails and gazed at them, easing
> them apart with his fingers. And as he bent down low
> to look, your brother, rising tall up on his toes, crashed
> the cleaver heavy on his spine, smashing his back bones
> from their sockets. Aegisthus' body writhed in spasms,
> juddering, twitching, and death came hard.

Together Electra and Orestes stab Clytemnestra, whom they have first lured to the house by pretending that Electra has given birth to a baby girl. Electra and Orestes fascinated Euripides. In his tragedy *Orestes*, set just days after the matricide, he portrays the young man as a psychopath, who kidnaps Menelaus' daughter Hermione before then trying to murder Helen.

Orestes' Acquittal

With no family member left alive to take vengeance on Orestes, the gods sent the Erinyes (Furies) to pursue him. Crazed with terror, Orestes fled to Delphi, then to Athens, where Athene established the first law court. The Furies insisted that matricide must be punished, Apollo that it was Orestes' duty to avenge his father. Athene used her casting vote to acquit Orestes, insisting that fathers take precedence over mothers, as her own birth from Zeus' head showed.

Some tell how Orestes then travelled with Pylades to Tauris, where his sister Iphigenia rescued him from being sacrificed, and together they escaped to Greece. There Orestes fell in love with his cousin Hermione. That she was married to Achilles' son Neoptolemus was an inconvenient detail. Orestes arranged for the murder of his rival in the Temple of Apollo at Delphi before regaining Mycenae and conquering much of the Peloponnese, which he ruled from Sparta. He was buried in nearby Tegea, where sixth-century BC Spartans found his bones. Meanwhile Mycenae passed from mythology.

Mycenae in History & Today

Inhabited from the fourth millennium BC, Mycenae attained increasing importance and wealth in the second millennium. Funerary goods discovered in Grave Circle A, a royal cemetery later incorporated within the circuit of the citadel's walls include solid gold death masks, jewelry, cups and banqueting paraphernalia, as well as inlaid daggers, whose blades are decorated with scenes of aristocratic pursuits including lion hunts.

On stone *stelai* (grave markers), men with spears are shown hunting from chariots.

Around 1500 BC tholos tombs were constructed in the neighbouring hills. These were outstanding feats of engineering: high corbelled chambers with dressed and fitted stone, approached by long *dromoi* (processional avenues). Around 1250 BC Mycenae's citadel walls were rebuilt with massive blocks (some estimated to weigh up to 100 tons), while the palace was enlarged and enhanced. A monumental gateway was constructed and on a triangular slab above the lintel were carved two lionesses (or perhaps wingless griffins) flanking a single pillar, their forepaws resting on an altar. Possibly the earliest coat of arms in Europe, its power is palpable,

The main gate at Mycenae, built
around 1250 BC, is surmounted by
two (now headless) lionesses or
griffins flanking a column, perhaps
the oldest coat of arms in Europe.

despite the fact that the creatures' heads have not survived (they may have been originally of gold).

Bronze Age Mycenae traded widely throughout the Mediterranean and beyond, with ties to Egypt and the Hittite Empire. Linear B tablets testify to a tightly bureaucratic society. Mythology may reflect reality in suggesting that Mycenae was the most important of all Greek settlements for much of the fourteenth and thirteenth centuries BC, eclipsing the power of Knossos and taking over the Cretan empire in a period which many historians call the Mycenaean Age.

In the twelfth century BC Mycenae's power collapsed, and around 1200 BC the citadel and palace were destroyed by fire. It never recovered. A population of around 30,000 people (including those who lived in the town beneath the citadel) dwindled to almost nothing. Attempts at resettlement were only partially successful. Eighty Mycenaeans joined the Greek army fighting the Persian invasions (480–479 BC), but in 468 BC Mycenae was destroyed by neighbouring Argos. It was again inhabited in the third century BC, when a theatre was built over one of the now-forgotten tholos tombs, but again fell into such disrepair that Pausanias saw only ruins:

> Parts of the circuit wall remain, including the Lion
> Gate. They say this was built by Cyclopes, who also built
> Tiryns. Among the ruins is the spring called Perseia and
> subterranean chambers, treasuries where Atreus and his
> sons stored their wealth. Atreus' grave is there, as well as
> graves of those who returned from Troy, who were killed
> at the banquet by Aegisthus.

Pausanias' account of Agamemnon's death at a banquet is confused, and his (or his guide's) identification of the tholos tombs as treasuries is wrong. The error persists – the largest tholos is still signposted 'The Treasury of Atreus'. Mycenae's romance attracted many travellers wishing to soak up its atmosphere. One first-century AD poet wrote:

> There is but little of the age of heroes left to see – though
> still some ruins jut up from the plain. As I passed
> by, I recognized poor, suffering Mycenae, now quite
> abandoned. Not even goats go there. A herdsman showed
> the place to me. He was an old man, and he said: 'This
> was the city rich in gold, which once the Cyclopes built.'

In 1876 Heinrich Schliemann, inspired by Homeric legend and wishing to prove it true, began excavations at Mycenae. They have continued ever since.

Mycenae

c. 4000 BC	Early Neolithic settlements.
c. 1750 BC	Early circuit walls and cist graves.
c. 1500 BC	First tholos tombs.
c. 1250 BC	'Cyclopean' walls and palace constructed.
c. 1200 BC	Mycenae burned, probably by attackers.
480 BC	Mycenae sends 80 men to fight the Persians.
468 BC	Argos destroys Mycenae.
? C3rd BC	Theatre built over 'Grave of Clytemnestra'.
AD 1841	Kyriakos Pittakis discovers the Lion Gate.
AD 1876	Heinrich Schliemann begins excavations.

Approaching Mycenae, foundations of a **Bronze Age bridge** lie in the valley (right). Soon **shaft graves** can be seen cut into the rock (left). Before the main car park, is a parking area (left) for the so-called **Treasury of Atreus**, a magnificent tholos tomb, unusually containing a small side chamber.

From the main site entrance, the path leads to the **Lion Gate**. Next, right of the well-paved road, is **Grave Circle A** (no access), where Schliemann discovered many gold masks and grave-goods. A path leads upwards to the palace with its **megaron** (no access), approached through a series of antechambers. The view down the valley towards Argos is sublime. Higher up are living quarters, including bathing facilities, and the foundations of a **temple**. Near the further of **two postern gates** (through which Orestes was supposedly smuggled to safety) is an impressive **well-house or cistern**, with stone-cut steps leading deep below ground. Visitors should exercise extreme caution and not attempt descent alone, without good footwear and a torch.

Outside the walls, are further **tholos tombs**, remains of a **Hellenistic theatre** and foundations of houses. Other tholos tombs lie on the far side of the hill (behind the car park), on which stands the **chapel of the Panagia**, the view from which is well worth the short detour.

Most of the finds from Mycenae are in the National Archaeological Museum in Athens, but Mycenae's own **museum**, situated near the **Lion Tomb** contains an impressive selection of grave-goods and frescoes, as well as replicas and a model of the site.

Travellers wishing to immerse themselves more fully in Mycenae's past can stay at the Hotel La Belle Hélène, Schliemann's 'dig house' (now run by Agamemnon Dasis), the temporary home to many archaeologists and writers (including Agatha Christie and Virginia Woolf), psychologists (including Carl Jung) and composers (including Claude Debussy). They can even sleep in Schliemann's bed.

20

Troy: A City Contested
by Gods & Men

And did you then turn traitor, Zeus, betray your temple here at Troy,
your altar sweet with incense ... the wisps of myrrh that rose in
fragrance to the sky, the sacred citadel, the Pergamum, the glens of
Ida where the ivies cling, the rivers white with melted snow that froth
down to the sea and the light that bathes the far horizon with the first
pale blush of dawn, this sacred place, this shining, sacred homeland?

Your sacrifices now are gone, gone too the choral liturgy of hymns,
the all-night festivals in darkness to the gods, all gone, the icons and
the effigies all glittering with gold, yes, even the most sacred relics of
them all, the twelve gold moons of Troy. I want to know, Zeus, how I
want to know if, as you sit there on your lofty throne in heaven, you
care at all as this, my city, is destroyed and fire consumes it.

Euripides, *Trojan Women*, 1060ff.

Troy today is at once the most evocative and the most sterile of all the great centres of mythology. The site is guarded by a gigantic wooden horse towering in the trees above the coach park, its flank pierced by square windows from which tourists can grin down and wave and have their pictures taken. It is perhaps a fitting introduction to what can seem a soulless site – all cordoned walkways, joyless information boards and a tightly choreographed route that twists relentlessly across deep trenches ripping through millennia of history. It is a place which could well disappoint.

And yet this once was Troy. Stand on the low hill, where the Temple of Athene used to sparkle in the sun; look out towards the far-off Dardanelles, the tankers rippling indistinct and ghostly in the rising haze; imagine that the fertile fields are flooded, that a vast bay bellies close, its shores black, teeming with a thousand ships; think of Achilles as he dragged Hector's broken body around the sloping walls; think of Andromache weeping for her husband whom she loved more than the world; think of Cassandra, Hecabe and Priam; think of Paris; think of Helen; think of the passions that made all Greece fight for ten years to reclaim her; think of the legends clinging to these stones. And Troy becomes alive.

Foundation(s) of Troy & Divine Interventions

There are several contradictory myths about Troy's foundation. One tells that Cretans escaping famine first occupied the land. When mice overran their camp, they recalled an oracle advising them to settle where 'earth-born adversaries' attacked them. So they built a temple to Apollo Smintheus ('Mouse-God'), subdued the Troad (as the region is called), named the local mountain Ida (like the one in Crete), and thrived under their king, Teucer. Others maintained that Teucer was an Athenian, who founded a colony in the Troad and passed the crown to an Arcadian called Dardanus – but the Romans claimed that Dardanus was an Italian-born Etruscan.

Troy and the Troad were named from Dardanus' grandson Troas, himself the father of Ilus, from whom the city took its other name of Ilion. Like Cadmus at Thebes, Ilus was told by the gods to found a city where a piebald cow lay down to sleep. It chose the summit of the low Hill of Atē ('destructive infatuation'), where Ilus erected a temple to Athene. This housed the Palladium, an olive-wood statue of Athene, which had fallen from the skies and would protect Troy as long as Troy protected it.

Ilus' brother, too, the handsome, Ganymede was god-kissed. Seeing him herding cattle on Mount Ida, Zeus transformed himself into an eagle, swooped down and abducted him to Mount Olympus, to serve him as cupbearer. In the divine bedchamber Ganymede performed those boyish duties, too, associated with his Latin name, Catamitus. In compensation, Zeus gave his father Troas twelve white horses, sired by the north wind, Boreas.

Another Trojan prince, Tithonus, was less fortunate. Eos, the rosy-fingered goddess of the dawn, abducted him to be her lover, persuading Zeus to grant him eternal life. She should have asked for everlasting youth: when Tithonus was so old he could no longer move, Eos locked him in a cell, where he 'chattered on incessantly, the strength of his once lissom limbs all gone'. In sympathy, Zeus transformed him into a cicada.

The gods were less content with another Trojan king. When Ilus' son Laomedon built walls around Troy's citadel, he hired two tireless workmen for a modest daily rate – Poseidon and Apollo, sentenced to serve him for a year as punishment for trying to topple Zeus. While Poseidon laboured (helped by Aegina's King Aeacus), Apollo tended Troy's flocks, but in the end Laomedon refused to pay them. In retribution, Poseidon sent a sea-monster to ravage the Troad, demanding that Ilus sacrifice his daughter, Hesione.

Enter Heracles. On his way back to Tiryns from one of his labours, he found Hesione, richly bejewelled but otherwise naked, chained to a rock, awaiting the monster. Chivalrously, he released her, agreeing with Laomedon to kill the creature in return for Hesione's hand in marriage – and the white horses that Zeus had given Troas. Then Heracles attacked the creature, leaping down its throat, hacking at its innards until it died. But when he demanded payment from Laomedon, the king reneged.

So Heracles returned to Greece, raised an army, sailed in six ships back to Troy and attacked the city. Led by Telamon, the son of Aeacus (who had built this section), they stormed Troy's western walls where they were weakest and (in Homer's poignant words) 'made desolate her streets'. The only survivor was the young prince Podarces, who had championed Heracles when Laomedon refused to pay him. Now he became Troy's king, changed his name to Priam ('Redeemed'), and rebuilt the city. As for Hesione, Heracles gave her to Telamon; but he kept the horses.

The Children of Priam

With his wife Hecabe (whose own parentage was famously obscure), Priam had fifty sons and fifty daughters, among them the warriors Hector and Deiphobus, the handsome Troilus and the prophetic twins Helenus and Cassandra.

When Apollo wooed Cassandra with promises that, if she slept with him, he would grant her the gift of prophecy, the princess agreed and the god breathed his power into her. But at the last moment Cassandra changed her mind and haughtily rebuffed him. There was little that Apollo could do. He could not withdraw his gift. So instead he added a curse: none of Cassandra's prophecies would be believed.

Predictions of disaster already haunted Troy. When Hecabe was pregnant with her second son, she dreamt she bore a baby with a hundred hands, each holding a blazing firebrand. The meaning was clear: if allowed to live, the boy would ruin Troy; only his death would save the city. Reluctantly Hecabe wrapped the newborn in a fine embroidered cloth and gave him to a herdsman to expose on nearby Mount Ida. Here, though, the child was suckled by a she-bear. Finding him still alive nine days later, the herdsman pitied him and took him in his knapsack (in Greek, *'pera'*) to his steading, where he reared him as his own. The boy grew strong and handsome. When he fought off a band of cattle-rustlers, the herdsmen called him Alexander ('Protector of Men'), though – in memory of the knapsack – he had already been named Paris.

The Judgment & Triumph of Paris

Paris had two passions: the mountain nymph Oenone, a skilful healer; and battles between bulls. His prize beast could beat any rivals, until a wild bull thundered into the ring. After a vicious duel it won, and Paris ungrudgingly placed the victor's garland on its head. At once it changed its form, revealing its true identity: it was the war-god Ares. He had been searching for an honest judge to arbitrate a vexed dispute. He had found the perfect man.

So, carrying the golden apple inscribed with the words 'for the most beautiful', with which Eris had once disrupted Peleus and Thetis' wedding

On Mount Ida, Hermes leads the three goddesses
– Hera, Athene and Aphrodite – to Paris for his
judgment. (Attic red figure wine cup, *c.* 440 BC.)

on Mount Pelion, Hermes descended to Mount Ida with three goddesses: Hera, Athene and Aphrodite. Each claimed the apple for herself. Euripides' *Andromache* tells how they came 'to win the prize for beauty, dressed for war, equipped for horrid strife, to the steading, to the isolated homestead, to the lonely shepherd boy. When they reached the dappled glen, they bathed their dazzling bodies in the mountain streams, and trading promises (so fulsome yet deceptive), they faced Priam's son.'

Paris could not choose between them. So each made him an offer. In Euripides' *Trojan Women*, Helen of Sparta summarizes their terms:

> The gift Athene promised Paris was to lead an army
> out from Asia and destroy Greece. Hera promised
> kingship over all of Asia and Europe, if Paris chose
> her. But Aphrodite, who admired my beauty and my
> body, promised that she'd give him me if he awarded
> her the prize.

Aroused by the bewitching goddesses, seduced by the prospect of Helen, and forgetting his love for Oenone, Paris awarded Aphrodite the apple and struck out for Troy.

He found the city celebrating games in memory of the royal baby exposed on Mount Ida twenty years before. Magnanimously Priam let Paris compete, and to widespread surprise he emerged as champion. Deiphobus was incensed and, with Hecabe, plotted Paris' murder. But Cassandra recognized him – or perhaps the herdsman revealed his true identity – and, dismissing her dream as superstition, Hecabe with Priam welcomed their son Paris back to Troy.

Then, at the head of a magnificent flotilla and accompanied by his cousin Aeneas (the son of Aphrodite by Anchises), Paris sailed to Sparta to claim his prize. He rode inland from Sparta's port to the royal palace. The late fifth-/early sixth-century AD epic poet Coluthus imagines Helen:

> unlocking the doors of her welcoming chamber, running
> into the courtyard, seeing him standing there before the
> palace gates. At once she called to him, and led him in,
> and sat him on a new-made silver chair. And she gazed on
> him and could not satisfy her eyes with gazing.

Helen's husband Menelaus entertained his guest lavishly. Then he departed for Crete. Within hours, Paris and Helen crept from the palace and that night on tiny Cranaë, a stone's throw from the coast, they made love. Then they set sail for Troy.

The Coming of the Greeks

When Menelaus learned the news, he reminded Helen's suitors of their oath to her father Tyndareus to help him should anyone abduct her. So they assembled a mighty army, led by Agamemnon, king of Mycenae, and containing the greatest heroes of the age. Some, such as Achilles (from Phthia near Iolcus), joined reluctantly.

Achilles' mother, the sea-nymph Thetis, coddled him from birth, purifying him in a fire, immersing him (held tightly by the right heel) in the River Styx to make him invulnerable, and sending him to Cheiron the Centaur to be educated. Now, knowing that he might die at Troy, she persuaded him to hide on Scyros at the court of King Lycomedes. But Odysseus of Ithaca, Nestor of Pylos and Ajax son of Telamon heard rumours of his whereabouts. Arriving at Scyros, they laid out a wealth of jewelry as gifts of friendship. As the women crowded round excitedly, Odysseus sounded the alarm as if the palace was under attack, at the same time throwing a sword high in the air. Instinctively a hand shot up and caught it. It was Achilles, dressed in women's clothes. Sulkily he joined the expedition. (His mood was not improved when, at Aulis, Agamemnon used him as bait to lure Iphigenia to her death.)

The fleet attempted to make landfall at Tenedos, the island close to Troy, but it met with opposition. In the fighting Achilles showed his bravery, killing Tenedos' ruler, Tenes. But when he discovered that Tenes' father was Apollo, he remembered Thetis' warning: if he killed Apollo's son he would one day perish at Apollo's hand.

From captured Tenedos the Greeks sent a demand for Helen's return. It was refused. War was inevitable. So the Greek fleet nosed into Troy's bay, where, after a brief skirmish, the Trojans withdrew behind the walls, the Greeks built a stockade around their ships, and both sides settled down for a long siege. For already Agamemnon's prophet Calchas had predicted that Troy would be captured in the tenth year.

Nine Years of Attrition: Troilus & Palamedes

Troy's fate was governed by a number of preconditions. The first said that the city could not be defeated if its young prince Troilus reached his twentieth birthday. So Achilles plotted Troilus' death. In one myth he ambushed Troilus as he and his sister Polyxena fetched water from a fountain house. Achilles killed Troilus, and although Polyxena escaped, she aroused a desire in Achilles, which would prove her undoing. In a variant version Achilles ambushed Troilus as he exercised his horses on ground sacred to Apollo – having already provoked Apollo's anger, Achilles had no longer anything to lose. A third, darker version has Achilles fall in love with Troilus and arrange to meet him at Apollo's shrine. When the boy refused to yield to his advances, the frustrated Achilles murdered him. But it was the fact, not the means, of Troilus' death that was important. The first stipulation for Troy's downfall had been met.

The Greeks spent much of the war's first nine years raiding nearby cities. While here, too, Achilles shone, among other Greek leaders arguments festered, breeding bitter hatreds. Thus Odysseus loathed the brilliantly clever and creative Palamedes, king of Nauplion and inventor of writing, dice and lighthouses. So, planting a letter on a dead Trojan's corpse and a bag of gold in Palamedes' tent, Odysseus convinced the Greeks that Palamedes was an enemy agent. Enraged, the army stoned the innocent Palamedes to death. When his father Nauplius found out, he took revenge, encouraging Agamemnon's wife Clytemnestra to be unfaithful with Aegisthus. Then, when Troy had fallen, he positioned false beacons, causing the homecoming Greek fleet to run aground on rocks.

The Iliad & Achilles' Wrath

In the tenth year hostilities broke out in earnest. But there was further internal conflict in the Greek camp. Angered by Agamemnon's refusal to restore the captured daughter of Chryses, his priest, to her father, Apollo sent a plague against the Greeks, lifting it only after they complied. But when, as compensation, Agamemnon took Achilles' slave girl, Briseis, Achilles refused to fight. Instead, with his comrade Patroclus, he sulked in his tent, singing moodily of the famous deeds of men.

Achilles' absence encouraged the Trojans. Even Paris swaggered in the front line:

> Draped across his shoulders was a panther skin, and
> buckled fast a sword and quiver. In his hand he shook
> two spears, bronze-headed, as he called out all the
> bravest of the Greeks to fight in single combat. When
> Menelaus, whom the war-god Ares loved, saw him
> striding out among the ranks, he delighted in his heart
> as a hungry lion delights to find a fallen carcass – an
> antlered stag or goat – and ravenously he tears at it,
> although swift dogs and eager huntsmen crowd around.

The outcome of this single combat between Paris and Menelaus was meant to end the war. But when Paris was wounded, Aphrodite intervened, wrapping him in mist and transporting him to his bedchamber. Battle was rejoined, and when more warriors were killed or wounded, even the gods took pity. So at the bidding of Apollo (who supported Troy) and Athene (who supported the Greeks), Troy's greatest champion, Hector, issued a challenge to the greatest of the Greeks to fight him. He meant Achilles, but since he still refused to fight, Ajax took his place. When neither man won they agreed instead to exchange gifts. Ajax gave Hector his sword-belt; Hector gave Ajax his sword.

The Trojans were ascendant, but, when it was announced that their ally, the Thracian king Rhesus, was nearby with reinforcements, the fulfilment of another condition of their city's capture helped seal their fate still tighter. A prophecy foretold that Troy could not fall if Rhesus' horses drank from the River Scamander. So Odysseus and Diomedes, king of Argos, crept out by night, intercepted Rhesus, killed him and stole his horses.

But the next day Hector and the Trojans breached the Greek stockade, fanned out across the beach and torched the fleet. Achilles could stand by no longer. Still, though, he would not fight. Even when Agamemnon offered him great riches, he rebuffed him. Instead, he lent Patroclus his armour, and let him lead his men to battle. Unleashed, Patroclus slew Sarpedon, the son of Zeus, and chased the Trojans back inside their walls. But then Apollo intervened. He punched Patroclus so hard on his back that his helmet flew off, revealing his true identity. As Patroclus stood there stunned, Hector drove a spear through his belly.

> As a lion defeats a tireless boar in battle, when they fight
> enraged on a high mountain ridge, each thirsting for a
> trickling spring; the boar snorts loud, but the lion defeats
> him with his strength. Thus Hector, Priam's son, deprived
> the brave Patroclus of life, although he had killed many,
> impaling him at close quarters with his spear.

Then he stripped Patroclus' armour. Somehow the Greeks retrieved the body and brought it to Achilles. Racked with self-blame, he mourned his friend and promised retribution.

That night Sleep and Death flew down to Troy to claim Sarpedon's corpse. Back home in Lycia he was buried with great honour. The same night, Thetis brought armour freshly fashioned by Hephaestus to Achilles' tent. She had already warned her son that one of two destinies awaited him: either to grow old in Phthia, where his bravery would be forgotten; or to die at Troy and enjoy 'unwithering fame' (*kleos*). Achilles knew, too, that if he killed Hector, he would die soon afterwards. He did not care. He yearned only to avenge Patroclus.

Next day Achilles rejoined the fight. No one could resist him. Even the river-god Scamandrus felt his anger, as he wrestled vainly with Achilles to stop him reaching Troy. At last Achilles found Hector. For a moment they faced each other. Then Hector turned and fled. Close on his heels Achilles followed: 'As a hawk high in the mountains, the fastest of all birds, swoops hard to catch a trembling dove; she flees from him, while he, shrieking shrilly, presses hard and his heart drives him on to snatch her.' As the gods watched enthusiastically, Athene, disguised as Deiphobus, persuaded Hector to stand his ground. Hector launched his javelin. Then:

> he called to white-shielded Deiphobus, and asked for
> a long spear. But Deiphobus had vanished. And Hector
> understood and said, 'The gods have called me out to die.
> I thought Deiphobus stood near me, but he is inside the
> walls, and Athene has deceived me. Now hateful death is
> close and there is no escape. I think this has long been
> the will of Zeus and of his son Apollo, who shoots from
> afar, who helped me until now with willing hearts. But
> now my share in life is over.'

As Hector lay dying, his throat transfixed by a spear, he begged Achilles to return his body for burial. Instead, he tied Hector to his chariot with the sword-belt Ajax had once given him, and dragged the corpse around the walls of Troy before returning to his tent. Then he organized Patroclus' funeral, with athletic games and sacrifices (including twelve Trojan prisoners); and every day he dragged Hector's corpse three times around the funeral mound.

Devastated at the treatment of Hector's body, Priam visited Achilles in his tent by night. With profound humanity and using simile to devastating effect, Homer relates how:

> Great Priam ... clasped in his arms Achilles' knees and
> kissed his hands, his terrible man-killing hands, that had
> slain so many of his sons. And just as blind infatuation
> [atē] grips a man, who kills another in his father's house
> and so flees to a wealthy stranger's home, and wonder
> seizes all who look on him, so was Achilles seized with
> wonder as he looked on godlike Priam.

As Priam described his desolation at the loss of so many sons, imagining Achilles' father Peleus in Phthia anxiously awaiting news, Achilles was moved to compassion. In a moment of sublime humanity both wept together for the tragedy of war. So Priam took his son's body back to Troy and buried him.

The Death of Achilles & its Consequences
Achilles continued to harry his Trojan enemies and their allies. In single combat he killed both the Amazon queen Penthesilea and the Ethiopian

king Memnon, the son of Eos and Tithonus. At last, death came to Achilles, not at the hands of a great warrior, but through the skill of the archer, Paris. As Achilles fought beneath Troy's Scaean Gates, Apollo guided Paris' arrow. It struck the one place where Achilles was not invulnerable: his right heel. The Greeks and Trojans fought hard over his corpse, lying 'in the swirling dust, huge and heroic but no longer caring for his battle-skills'.

Ajax took Achilles' body to the Greek ships, where Thetis and her nymphs rose from the waves, 'and the sound of their other-worldly lamentation rippled across the surface of the sea'. As the Muses sang their requiem and the army clashed their weapons on their shields to honour him, Achilles was cremated. His bones were laid in a gold urn with Patroclus' remains, and a mound was raised on the headland, 'to be seen far off from sea by those alive today and those still to come'. As the ghost of Agamemnon, who provides this description in the *Odyssey*, concludes: 'Even in death your name is not forgotten, but your fame [*kleos*] will live for ever among men.'

Some claimed that Zeus made Achilles immortal. An early traveller, Leonymus of Croton, even claimed to have seen the spirits of Achilles (now married to Helen) and other Greek heroes on White Island near the Danube's mouth. Others said that Achilles spent eternity in the Islands of the Blessed, the husband of Medea. Late mythographers, keen for a romance between Achilles and Polyxena, had him consider betraying the Greeks in return for her hand in marriage.

Ajax believed that by right he should inherit Achilles' armour, but out of spite – or brainwashed by Athene – the Greeks awarded it to Odysseus. In god-lashed fury Ajax stalked the Greek camp, intent on massacring all who had humiliated him, but at sunrise he awoke surrounded by the corpses of not men but cattle. Athene had deluded him. Humiliated, he killed himself with the sword he had received from Hector. Only his half-brother Teucer (son of the Trojan princess Hesione) honoured Ajax's corpse, until Odysseus persuaded Agamemnon to bury it.

Final Conditions Fulfilled

Four last conditions controlled Troy's fate. The first was that Achilles' son, Neoptolemus, a brave but brutal warrior, be summoned from Scyros. (In early tradition the siege of Troy may have lasted not ten but twenty years, which makes Neoptolemus' age more plausible.)

Neoptolemus helped in the fulfilment of the next precondition, too. Only with Heracles' bow and arrows could Troy be taken. These were owned by Philoctetes, a Greek hero, who, before reaching the Troad, was bitten by a snake. The stench from his wound was so obnoxious that he was abandoned on Lemnos (an island associated in the Argonaut myth, too, with unpleasant smells). Now when Odysseus arrived, demanding his presence at Troy, Philoctetes gave him short shrift. Only Neoptolemus' pleas – and those of Heracles' ghost – persuaded Philoctetes to rejoin the army. At Troy he was cured by Machaon, the son of the healing god Asclepius.

Watched by Athene, Greeks and Trojans clash shields fighting for possession of the 'huge and heroic' body of Achilles. (Chalcidian amphora, *c.* 540 BC.)

Troy: A City Contested by Gods & Men

Philoctetes proved his worth, soon shooting Paris in the wrist and ankle and blinding him in one eye. The prince crawled to Mount Ida, where Oenone had once promised to cure him should he ever be mortally wounded. Still piqued by Paris' infidelity, however, the nymph refused – though later in remorse she hanged herself. Meanwhile Helen tried to leave Troy, lowering herself down on ropes, but she was caught and given as wife to Deiphobus.

The penultimate condition, that one of Pelops' bones be brought to Troy, was easily fulfilled, but the last took guile and planning. Ownership of Athene's statue, the Palladium, guaranteed Troy's safety. So Odysseus plotted to steal it. In a disguise made more realistic when he was voluntarily beaten by his comrades, he undertook a reconnaissance mission, presenting himself at Troy as a Greek deserter. Helen recognized him, but, longing to escape Deiphobus' unwelcome clutches, she kept quiet. Then Hecabe too discovered his identity. When Odysseus desperately supplicated her, Hecabe's piety forbade her from exposing him and he escaped – only to return that night with Diomedes and steal the statue.

The Sack of Troy

The war might still have dragged on indefinitely had not Epeius (from Mount Parnassus) conceived an ingenious plan: to build a massive firwood horse, conceal hand-picked Greeks inside it, and cause it to be taken into Troy. Soon the horse, its belly pregnant with armed men, was standing proudly on the othwerwise empty shore. For the Greeks had sailed away, leaving only the smoking ruins of their tents. And the wooden horse.

Jubilant, the Trojans raced out of the city to read the inscription on the horse's flank: 'From the Greeks to Athene, a thank-offering for a safe homecoming.' But some doubted this Greek gift: 'There were three views: one to hack the hollow wood with merciless bronze; another to drag it to the highest point and throw it on to the rocks; and the third to let it stand there as a pious offering to the gods.'

As they debated, a Greek was brought before them. He was Sinis, a spy, and his lying message was convincing: tired of the war, the Greeks were sailing home; if the Trojans took the horse inside their city, Athene would favour them, but if they left it on the beach, they would excite her wrath. While the priest Laocoön counselled caution, two serpents slid across the sea from Tenedos and coiled around him and his two sons before, abandoning their strangled corpses, they glided through the gates and on to Troy's acropolis.

Ascribing Laocoön's death to his opposition to the gods, the Trojans knocked down a section of their walls and pulled the horse into the city, where they feasted long and hard. Later, when the city slept, Helen walked the starlit streets. She knew the horse was a ruse, and she knew who was

A Greek gift: one of the earliest representations of the Trojan War appears on a Cycladic relief vase, *c*. 675–650 BC.

hidden there. Coquettishly she taunted each in turn, flawlessly imitating their wives' voices. Inside, the unnerved Greeks kept perfect silence.

At last they opened the trap door, let down ropes and slid noiselessly to the ground. While some ran to unbar the gates, others signalled to their comrades. For the fleet had merely hidden in the lee of Tenedos, and now it had returned. Suddenly the streets were filled with armed men. Neoptolemus butchered Priam on the palace steps. Another general (the 'Lesser' Ajax) tried to rape Cassandra as she clung to Athene's altar, while Odysseus and Menelaus slaughtered Deiphobus, and in a fit of anger mutilated his corpse.

Striding through the smoke and carnage, Menelaus sought out Helen. But when he saw her standing there in front of him, her breasts bare, her face so radiant and still so beautiful, he was overcome once more by love. He dropped his sword and took her in his arms. Soon they were sailing back to Greece – with Aethra, Theseus' mother, Helen's slave, whom she had brought from Sparta. (Her grandsons later restored her to Athens.)

When the massacre was ended, the Greeks led off Troy's womenfolk to slavery. Only Polyxena remained: Achilles' ghost demanded her as a sacrifice. The others' fate was just as grim. Cassandra fell to Agamemnon (though she knew that at Mycenae both would be killed by Clytemnestra). Hector's wife, Andromache, whose father, brothers and husband had all been killed by Achilles, was given to Achilles' son Neoptolemus, while to prevent him avenging Troy, her son Astyanax was thrown to his death from Troy's walls.

Assigned to Odysseus, Hecabe discovered that Polymestor, a Thracian guest-friend, greedy for Troy's gold which he had been given for safe-keeping, had murdered Polydorus, her one remaining son. With Agamemnon's help, Hecabe lured Polymestor to her tent, killed his children in revenge and blinded him. By now she had become so savage that it was little wonder that before she could sail for Greece she turned into a dog.

Only the Trojan prince Aeneas escaped, carrying on his shoulders his father Anchises and tightly clutching the hand of his son Ascanius (known to the Romans as Iulus). With the last remnant of Trojans they sailed to Italy to found the city which in time would be called Rome. Storms and shipwrecks meant that few of Troy's conquerors were destined to return home. Like Troy itself their time was over.

Troy in History & Today

Troy enjoyed a commanding position. Although today alluvial deposits from the River Karamenderes Çayi (probably Homer's Scamander) mean the coastline has moved almost 6 km (4 miles) away, in the early Bronze Age (c. 3000 BC) Troy was by the sea. Sited near a wide, shallow bay just south of the entrance to the Dardanelles, it controlled the shipping lane between the Aegean and the Black Sea. Moreover, brisk westerly winds meant that sailing ships could voyage east along the Dardanelles only by rowing, but even this was difficult. The west-flowing current runs at up to 3 knots, so to maintain headway oarsmen needed to achieve a constant speed of at least 5 knots. Where better to rest and wait out the winds than in the bay at Troy? The city enjoyed great prosperity. Archaeologists have identified nine phases of development, some of which are subdivided for greater precision.

In the early third millennium BC Troy I was a village of stone and mudbrick houses, but already by its second phase (Troy II) around 2550 to 2300 BC, stone-crowned ramparts pierced by monumental gates surrounded a citadel with large (40-m/130-ft long) buildings, used for public gatherings or religious purposes. A further palisade enclosed a lower town covering 9 ha (22 acres). Troy II was destroyed by fire, perhaps in war, for its people did not salvage their riches, which included artifacts made from gold, silver, bronze, electrum, carnelian and lapis lazuli. When Heinrich Schliemann discovered Troy II's exquisite items of jewelry, he identified them as the 'Jewels of Helen'. They were a thousand years too early.

Excavating between 1871 and 1879, Schliemann wrongly identified Troy II as 'Homer's Troy', digging out much of what lay above and badly damaging three phases of Troy's history. This compounded destruction wrought by Hellenistic Greeks, who flattened the mound for the foundations of their Temple of Athene.

Enough survives to tell that the citadel of Troy VI, founded around 1700 BC, was magnificent. Limestone walls, 5 m (16 ft) wide, angled gently inwards as they rose, their line softened by subtle vertical offsets. Fine towers soared high. A paved and well-drained road led through the city, where on terraces two-storeyed buildings stood, many with defensive ground-floor walls and pillared halls. Outside the citadel was a thriving town, covering 30 ha (75 acres), protected by a ditch and palisade and provided with water by a sophisticated system of artificial shafts and tunnels. Finds suggest that Troy VI traded with the Greek world rather than Anatolian Hittites, but around 1300 BC this changed – perhaps exacerbated by Troy VI's partial destruction, by earthquake or plunder. The discovery of one arrowhead has excited more speculation than it perhaps deserves.

In the citadel smaller houses now crowded once open spaces. New towers were added, and the Lower Town expanded. We know this bustling metropolis prosaically as Troy VIIa, but the Hittites called it Wilusa (linguistically close to the Greek 'Ilion', originally 'Wilion'). Thirteenth-century BC Hittite correspondence reveals that an attack on Wilusa by south Anatolian Arzawans prompted its king Alaksandu ('Alexander'?) to bring his city under Hittite rule. Another mid-thirteenth century Hittite document (the 'Tawagalawa Letter') is written to the king of the Ahhiyawa – probably the Hittite form of 'Akhaioi', as Homer calls the Greeks – confirming 'an agreement regarding Wilusa, over which we went to war'. Around 1200 BC the Hittites intervened once more when the Wilusan king Walmu was ousted from his throne. Then around 1180 BC Troy VIIa was destroyed by fire.

While these fragmentary references suggest tensions and even warfare, neither they nor archaeology confirm the historicity of the Trojan War. It is not surprising. Mythology and epic are not history. Both rely on invention and exaggeration, and disappointment that Troy was not the scene of a ten-year war over Helen must be tempered by reflecting on its influence on our imagination and creativity over three millennia (for the *Iliad* contains material which seems to date at least to 1000 BC). Inspired by a brief war over Wilusa which ended in a treaty between Greeks and Hittites, poetic vision fused with reality to form a masterpiece.

The quickly rebuilt Troy VIIb shows signs of cultural continuum, but subsequent building techniques and ceramics suggest a new, immigrant population. Unlike mainland Mycenae or Tiryns, Troy was inhabited throughout antiquity. With the receding shoreline, ships waiting to enter the Dardanelles abandoned Troy to shelter in the lee of Tenedos, but as the city's commercial star waned its cultural importance grew.

In 480 BC, Persia's Great King Xerxes sacrificed a thousand cattle at Troy's Temple of Athene before launching his unsuccessful invasion of

Greece (partly to avenge the sack of Troy). In 334 BC Alexander the Great, who kept a copy of the *Iliad* under his pillow, landed at Troy, where he too sacrificed before invading Persia, and ran naked to Achilles' grave mound. When Athene's priests presented him with ancient armour claimed to date back to the Trojan Wars, and offered to show him the lyre belonging to his namesake (Paris-Alexander), he replied that he preferred to see the lyre to which Achilles sang the famous deeds of men.

Alexander planned to build the largest temple in the world to Athene at Troy, but it was never begun. Nonetheless, his successors enhanced and enlarged the city, restoring the existing Temple of Athene with sculptures mirroring those of the Parthenon in Athens. A theatre was constructed and festivals inaugurated. Troy prospered, assuming renewed significance under Julius Caesar, his adopted son Augustus and subsequent Roman emperors. As Caesar's family, the Iulii, traced their descent through Iulus (Ascanius) to Aeneas and Anchises, so the ruling Romans lavished money on the city they perceived as their ancestral home.

Constantine considered making Troy his capital before settling instead for Constantinople. Under the Byzantines, Troy's importance diminished, and in AD 1452 their nemesis, Mehmet the Conqueror, paid one last visit to the site to mark his victory over the crusading infidels, now couched as the successors to Homer's Greeks.

For 400 years the site lay almost forgotten, but in 1865 a British expatriate, Frank Calvert, believing reports that Hisarlık ('The Place of the Fortress') was Homer's Troy, bought the land and began digging. Six years later a chance conversation in nearby Çannakale so enthused the romantic German Heinrich Schliemann that he took over, ploughing much of his wealth into unwittingly destroying valuable archaeology. Excavations have continued ever since.

--- Troy ---

SOME IMPORTANT DATES & REMAINS

3000 BC	Troy I: first settlements.
2550–2300 BC	Troy II's Citadel and Lower Town (destroyed by fire) show signs of wealth.
1750–1300 BC	Troy VI: fine houses on the Citadel and a Lower Town covering 30 ha (75 acres). Partially destroyed by fire.
1300–1180 BC	Troy VIIa: further houses on the Citadel and an expanded Lower Town.
***c.* 1300 BC**	King Alaksandu of Wilusa signs treaty with Hittites.
***c.* 1250 BC**	?War between the Greeks and Hittites over Troy.
***c.* 1200 BC**	King Walmu of Wilusa temporarily overthrown.

1180–950 BC	Troy VIIb: signs of immigrant occupation.
480 BC	Xerxes sacrifices at Temple of Athene.
334 BC	Alexander the Great sacrifices at Troy.
85 BC	Roman general Fimbria sacks, and Sulla restores, city.
48 BC	Julius Caesar visits Troy and inaugurates building works.
20 BC	Augustus visits Troy and rebuilds Temple of Athene and theatre.
c. AD 318	Constantine considers making Troy his eastern capital.
AD 1452	Mehmet the Conqueror visits Troy.
AD 1865	Frank Calvert buys site and begins excavations.
AD 1871	Heinrich Schliemann takes over excavations.

Troy is situated off the E87 southwest of Çannakale in a gated compound amid flat wheat fields. From the car park (dominated by the replica wooden horse) the path leads past the old dig house (now a museum containing models and photographs) before forking (right) to a vantage point. Steps (left) lead down to the fine **city walls** and **eastern gate** (from Troy VI). From here the designated walkway climbs to the **Temple of Athene** with its Roman altar and good views towards the Dardanelles. After traces of **early walls** (Troy I) and **houses** (Troy II), the path skirts Schliemann's trench before reaching the magnificent **ramp** into the citadel of Troy II and a stretch of city walls from **Troy VI**. Beyond is a sanctuary. The track now curves back past the **Roman Odeon** and **Bouleuterion** (Council Chamber), between which is a narrow **towered gateway fronted by altars**, identified as Homer's Scaean Gates. The Lower City lies beneath wooded terrain, from which can be seen the tumulus known as the **Grave Mound of Achilles**. At the time of writing, plans are afoot for an Eco Park, which will integrate the site more sympathetically with the surrounding countryside.

Some finds from Troy are housed in **Istanbul's Archaeological Museum**. Others, including the 'Jewels of Helen', enjoyed a peculiar and very modern adventure. Taken by Schliemann to Germany, they were kept in the Royal Museums in Berlin until the Second World War, when they were hidden for safe keeping in vaults beneath Berlin's zoo. At the end of the war they disappeared, but in 1993 it was revealed that the Red Army had spirited them to Russia, where they can now be seen in Moscow's Pushkin Museum.

21

Ithaca & the Wanderings of Odysseus

I am Odysseus, the son of Laertes, known to all men for my cunning, and my fame has reached the skies. I come from clear-seen Ithaca. There, on the island, is a mountain, Neriton, with rustling trees, quite visible even from far-off. Nearby are many other islands, all close to each other: Dulichium and Same and forested Zacynthus. Ithaca itself is generally low-lying, the furthest out towards the sunset, while the others lie apart to the east, towards the rising sun. It is a rugged island, but a good nurse for young men.

Homer, *Odyssey*, 9.21f.

Lapping water; rigging slapping rhythmically against the tall masts of sleek yachts moored by the harbour wall; cafés; salt-blistered wooden tables draped with ochre cloths and crowned with crisp white linen; the clink of plates and cutlery; fine, solid houses freshly painted; pale blue walls and deep blue shutters; orange roof tiles gleaming in the noon-day sun; the town hall with its clock tower and its Greek flag dragging lazily in the warm breeze; the music drifting from the open doors of tourist shops: the seafront of Vathy, the capital of Ithaki, nestles in the arms of an idyllic bay embraced by gentle wooded hills.

A statue stands beside the sea, a ragged figure, hollow-cheeked, gazing out across the gulf towards Mount Niritos. He is Odysseus, exhausted from long voyages, exuding defiant confidence that at last he has found his home. But Ithaki and the Ithaca of Greek mythology may well be different places. The island's location and topography bear arguably scant resemblance to the description in the *Odyssey*. The harbour restaurants of Vathy may offer fine havens for contemplation but, like Odysseus as he struggled with the foam-lashed sea, we too may have some way to go before we can be certain that we have truly reached his Ithaca.

The Kings of Ithaca

Odysseus belonged to a dynasty of island kings, all only sons. Most were of doubtful parentage. His (supposed) grandfather, Arcesius, was said to be the son of either Zeus or the hero Cephalus. The Athenian Cephalus had been the reluctant and temporary paramour of Eos, goddess of the dawn. Then, in a hunting accident, he tragically killed his true love, Procris (who had returned to him after an affair with King Minos of Knossos). As Cephalus mourned her fate, an oracle advised him to mate with the first thing he came across. This turned out to be a she-bear, but no sooner was the deed done than it changed into a beautiful young woman, Arcesius' mother. Later, in gratitude for helping Amphitryon defeat Taphians raiding Mycenae, Cephalus received the island which now bears his name – Cephalonia, just west of modern Ithaca.

Arcesius married Chalcomedusa ('Cunning with Copper'), fathering Laertes, a king who, as he reminisces in the *Odyssey*, expanded Ithacan rule to include Nericus, 'the well-built citadel on the mainland shore'. In turn Laertes married Anticlea, the daughter of Autolycus, a notorious trickster (a human Hermes), but when she bore a son gossips suggested that Laertes was not his father. They remembered how, when Anticlea still lived with her father near Delphi, Autolycus stole cattle belonging to Sisyphus the king of Corinth, himself an inveterate deceiver. Sisyphus traced his beasts to Autolycus' byres, where, while finessing their release, some claimed he slept with Anticlea, either with or without her consent.

Now Autolycus sailed to Ithaca to see his grandson. Homer tells how:

> After supper, Eurycleia [the boy's nurse] placed the baby
> on his knees and said to him: 'Autolycus, you must find
> a name for the grandson you have longed for for so many
> years.' Autolycus replied: 'My daughter and my son-in-
> law, give him the name that I shall tell you. I hold such
> anger against so many people, men and women, across
> the bounteous earth. So let him be called Odysseus ['The
> Angry One']. And when he reaches manhood, send him
> to his maternal home on Mount Parnassus, where I store
> my possessions, so that I may give him some and send
> him home rejoicing.'

In due course, Odysseus travelled to Mount Parnassus, where he took part in a boar hunt with his uncles. But when Odysseus ran in close and speared it, the dying boar sliced Odysseus' leg with its tusk, inflicting a dangerous, deep wound. His uncles ran to help him, binding his wound and singing spells, before carrying him back home. The wound healed, but its scar (in Greek, *oulē*) remained, a physical reminder, lending him another name: Ulysses.

The Reluctant Hero

Odysseus was renowned for his intellect – his Homéric epithet is 'very cunning' (*polymētis*). Thanks to his advice, King Tyndareus of Sparta made his daughter Helen's suitors swear an oath to aid her future husband, should she ever stray – which led to the Trojan War and Odysseus' own prolonged absence from home.

As a reward, Tyndareus helped Odysseus marry his niece, Penelope, whose childhood was not without adventure. Some say that her father Icarius tried to drown her at birth by throwing her out to sea. But when she was rescued by a flock of ducks, Icarius relented and named her from the birds that saved her (*pēnelopes* in Greek). Others suggest that the ducks saved Penelope when she tried to drown herself, having been wrongly told by Nauplius (embittered by his son Palamedes' death at Troy) that Odysseus was dead.

Odysseus envisaged a life of marital bliss, even building his own bed – a wondrous creation inlaid with gold and silver, strung with ropes and covered in crimson oxhide – around a vigorous young olive tree. Lopping off its upper branches he used the trunk as the bedpost. In time, the couple had a son, Telemachus ('He Who Fights from Afar'). But soon the drums of war beat throughout Greece. Helen had run off to Troy with Paris; Agamemnon had assembled an army to retrieve her; and now he, Menelaus and Palamedes, the clever king of Nauplion near Argos, had arrived in Ithaca to recruit Odysseus. But Odysseus knew that the war would be protracted. So he pretended to be mad. Yoking an ox and ass to a plough, he carved furrows in the beach and sowed them with salt. Suspicious, Palamedes stole Telemachus from his cradle and laid him in the ploughshare's path. Odysseus reined in his team, accepted the inevitable and – as his puppy, Argos, whined to watch him leave – set off for Troy.

Ithaca in Odysseus' Absence

The Trojan War finally over, the Greeks' homecoming – particularly that of Odysseus – was plagued by storms and sabotage. After many years, when he did not return, most thought that Odysseus was dead. Only Penelope still hoped, but her resolve was tested when a plague of bachelors descended upon Ithaca demanding her hand in marriage. These suitors behaved abominably, eating voraciously, drinking copiously and cavorting with the maidservants.

Penelope refused them all, until, pestered to distraction, she agreed to reach a decision, but only after she had woven a winding-sheet for Odysseus' father Laertes, who now lived on his country farm – another possible meaning of Penelope's name is 'Weft-Face' (from *pēnē*, 'weft' and *ops*, 'face'). Progress was slow, and after three years a maidservant revealed why. Weaving at her loom by day, by night Penelope was unpicking all the stitches. Torn between her desire to save the house from ruin by remarrying and a wish to stay faithful to Odysseus' memory, Penelope despaired.

Or so Homer tells us. Pindar was less convinced, asserting that she slept with Apollo, and so bore Pan, god of the countryside. A different myth has Hermes fathering Pan by her. Another went further, claiming that she slept with all 112 suitors – hence name Pan's name ('All') – and that, returning to Ithaca, Odysseus consequently banished her to the mainland. For most, though, Penelope remains a beacon of fidelity.

With Telemachus nearing manhood, the suitors, seeing him as a threat, plotted his murder. But Athene intervened in the guise of his guardian, Mentor, suggesting that he make one last attempt to learn Odysseus' fate. So Telemachus hoisted a white sail and put to sea, 'and the dark waves sang loud around the keel'. His journey took him first to Pylos and then to Sparta. Back in Ithaca he rushed to tell his news to the swineherd Eumaeus, who, fostered in the palace, was treated with considerable respect. Eumaeus embraced him:

> Kissing his head and his lovely eyes, and both his hands,
> and letting fall a great tear. As a loving father greets his

beloved son, returning from a distant land in the tenth
year, his only son, his darling son, the cause of so much
sorrow – so did the noble swineherd embrace godlike
Telemachus, and kiss him as if he had escaped death.

Sitting by Eumaeus' fire was a ragged, weather-beaten man, who revealed his true identity only when he could be sure that he could trust Telemachus. It was Odysseus, returned at last. The story of his homecoming is legendary.

The First Wanderings of Odysseus

Following the sack of Troy, Odysseus sailed with twelve ships to the land of the Cicones. Here he sacked the city and enslaved its women, but, not for the last time, his crew disobeyed him, raucously partying instead of making a swift escape. Cicones from the country's heartland launched a dawn raid, inflicting heavy losses before the Greeks could flee.

Sailing south, a storm which wrecked so many other Greek ships forced them ashore; and later, trying to round Cape Malea, the wind and currents drove them off course. When they next made landfall, they had put the real world behind them and entered the realm of mythology. A brief visit to the laid-back land of the Lotus-Eaters saw many of Odysseus' crew so stupefied by the narcotic effects of the 'honey-sweet lotus fruit' that they had to be forcibly dragged back to the ships.

Their next port of call was much less welcoming: a land of Cyclopes. Polar opposites of civilized urban Greeks, these Cyclopes lived in isolated families without laws or decision-making assemblies. Nor did they honour the Greek concept of *xenia* ('guest-friendship'), whereby strangers received hospitality when far from home. With twelve men, Odysseus entered one of their caves, where, overruling the suggestion of a quick raid and hasty departure, he stayed and feasted on the cheeses he discovered there. It was a rash decision. When the Cyclops Polyphemus ('Garrulous') returned with his flocks, he closed the cave's mouth with a huge boulder. Then, spying the Greeks, he brusquely interrogated them, seized two, dashed out their brains and ate them. Odysseus was helpless. Because of the boulder, escape was impossible, but next morning, after Polyphemus (breakfasting on human flesh) departed, leaving them still trapped, Odysseus hatched a plan.

That evening after Polyphemus consumed two more of his companions, Odysseus offered him a skinful of potent red wine, which he had fortuitously brought with him. The normally abstemious Cyclops accepted, asked Odysseus his name, and happily accepted his strange reply, 'My name is No one.' Then he collapsed in a stupor. Hurriedly the Greeks retrieved the sharpened stake they had hidden earlier, and heated its point in the fire. Then they rammed it into the sleeping Cyclops' single eye 'and the boiling blood surged out around it. As the eyeball burst it singed his eyebrow and both eyelids, and the roots crackled in the fire.'

With Polyphemus bellowing in pain, his fellow Cyclopes outside the cave demanded to know what was happening. 'No one is attacking me', he shouted, to which they replied: 'If no one is confronting you and you are alone, Zeus must have caused your sufferings, and you must endure them. So, pray for help to our father Poseidon!' Odysseus' ruse defies translation. 'No one' in Greek is *outis*, but sometimes (as here) the form changes to *me–tis*, which in turn sounds like (though is not cognate to) the word for 'cunning' – part of Odysseus' epithet *polymētis*. So the Cyclopes' reply could mean: 'If cunning is confronting you...' It is the first pun in Western literature.

Next morning, when Polyphemus let his flocks out to graze, the Greeks made their escape by clinging underneath the bellies of his sheep to avoid his fumbling grasp. Once out to sea, Odysseus taunted

Odysseus drives the sharpened stake into the eye of the Cyclops, Polyphemus. (Black figure vase, *c.* 530–510 BC.)

Polyphemus, announcing himself as: 'Odysseus, sacker of cities, the son of Laertes, whose home is Ithaca.' Unwittingly he thus provided all the details necessary to formulate a curse, which Polyphemus duly did, calling on Poseidon either to prevent Odysseus' homecoming or to cause him to reach Ithaca after many years, in a stranger's ship, having lost all his men.

Odysseus' Wandering Continues

The voyage became a nightmare of increasingly surreal encounters. Visiting Aeolus, King of the Winds, Odysseus was given a leather bag in which were confined every wind except the benign westerly that would waft him safely home. But close to Ithaca – so close they could see the islanders tending their fires – his men (thinking that it contained riches) opened the bag while Odysseus slept, unleashing a squall which swept them back out to sea.

Bound to his ship's mast, Odysseus alone hears the song of the Sirens and survives. (Attic red figure vase, *c.* 450 BC, from Vulci, Italy.)

They next came to the island of the Laestrygonians, a land of midnight sun and terrifying giants, who trapped Odysseus' ships in a high-cliffed harbour, spearing his men like fish and carrying them off to their 'bitter banqueting'. Only Odysseus and one ship escaped to reach Aeaea (its name linked to the Greek lament 'AI AI'). Unaware that this was the island home of Helios' daughter, the sorceress Circe, Medea's aunt, Odysseus sent men to reconnoitre. Only one returned. Surrounded by tame lions and wolves, Circe had turned his comrades into pigs. As Odysseus ran to investigate, Hermes met him, giving him a magic herb called 'moly' as protection from Circe's spells. Following Hermes' advice, Odysseus made Circe promise not to harm him, and to restore his men. For some time they enjoyed her hospitality, but when they left she advised Odysseus to consult the soul of the Theban prophet Teiresias – in Hades.

Across the boundaries of Ocean they sailed to a land of mist, where they poured libations, made sacrifice and summoned the spirits of the dead. Materializing, Teiresias warned Odysseus that to kill any cattle on Thrinacia, an island sacred to Helios, would bring disaster. It was a prohibition waiting to be broken.

Returning briefly to Aeaea, Odysseus sailed on to face fresh challenges. The first was to survive the half-bird, half-women Sirens, who 'sit in a meadow, while all around lie heaps of bones from rotting corpses, whose flesh has shrivelled in the sun'. The Sirens sang a song so irresistible that: 'whoever in his ignorance approaches them and hears their voice will never return home to bring joy to his wife and little children as they crowd around him, but the Sirens bewitch him with their ethereal melody'. Following Circe's advice, Odysseus bade his men lash him to the mast, while they plugged their ears with wax. So the ship passed safely by, and Odysseus, though tormented by desire to leap on to the rocks, became the only man still alive to have heard their heavenly voices.

Next they reached straits bounded on one side by Charybdis, a deadly whirlpool, and on the other by the monstrous Scylla, who crouched in a cliff-face cavern feeding on passing sharks, dolphins – and sailors. Trying to avoid Charybdis, the helmsman steered towards Scylla's jaws. Suddenly six dogs' heads arcing with unerring aim hauled six crewmen high into her bloody lair. But the rest rowed on until from distant Thrinacia they heard the bellowing of oxen.

The weary crew insisted on making landfall, but that night a storm blew up. It lasted a whole month. Supplies dwindled. In the end, as Odysseus slept, his men slaughtered Helios' finest oxen, but even as they cooked them 'the skins crawled and the spitted meat, both raw and roasted, thundered like the bellowing of cattle'. A week later, the storm abated, and they set sail once again. But in mid-ocean, as Zeus piled dark clouds above the ship, the tearing storm wind snapped the mast, and a thunderbolt exploded in the ship. Only Odysseus survived, clinging to the wreckage. Nine days later he was washed up on Ogygia, home to the nymph Calypso.

Odysseus in Limbo

The daughter of Atlas, Calypso ('Concealer') spent her days weaving at her loom, singing in her cave surrounded by:

> alders and poplars and sweet-scented cypress, the
> nesting-place of long-winged birds – owls and hawks
> and chattering sea-crows, which work the ocean's face.
> Around the hollow cave there trailed a garden vine,
> fecund and thick with grapes; and four springs bubbled
> with sparkling water, each beside the other, but flowing
> in different directions. And all around lush meadows
> blossomed, a riot of violets and parsley.

In this island paradise Calypso kept Odysseus for seven years, offering immortal youth in exchange for his exclusive love. But Odysseus still longed for Ithaca and Penelope. He sat for long hours brooding by the shore, until Hermes arrived with a message from Zeus. Calypso must let Odysseus go. His wanderings were almost at an end.

So Odysseus built a raft and made good headway until Poseidon returned from a festival in his honour in Ethiopia. Seeing Odysseus he unleashed a storm. Only Leucothea (the White Goddess, who had once been Ino, princess of Thebes) could save Odysseus. Disguised as a gannet, she wrapped him in a magic veil. Diving from the broken raft, Odysseus swam for two days and nights until he came ashore, crawled up the beach, sank into a bed of leaves and fell asleep.

Next morning a group of girls came to the beach to wash clothes and play ball. Awakened by their shrieking, Odysseus rose, naked, and approached them. Only one stood firm: Nausicaa, the daughter of Alcinous ('Strong-Minded'), king of the seafaring Phaeaceans, whose peaceful island, Scherie, was sacred to Poseidon. Responding to Odysseus' flattery (she reminded him, he said, of a young palm tree on Delos) she offered to help him. So at the palace, after supplicating Queen Arete ('Virtue'), while still not identifying himself, Odysseus was given food and wine and invited to compete in games. When Odysseus wept as the blind court bard, Demodocus, sang of the sack of Troy, Alcinous, suspecting the truth, asked his identity – and Odysseus recounted his adventures.

Despite being offered Nausicaa as his bride, Odysseus yearned for home, so Alcinous put him on a ship, heaped him with gifts (including thirteen tripods) and sent him on the final stage of his long odyssey.

Arriving at Ithaca, the sailors carried the sleeping Odysseus ashore and hid the gifts in a cave. Then they returned to Scherie, where, angered because they had helped Odysseus, Poseidon turned their ship to stone as it neared the harbour. Meanwhile, dressed as a vagabond, Odysseus reached Eumaeus' hut to be reunited with Telemachus.

Odysseus on Ithaca

Still disguised, Odysseus entered the palace. Only his dog Argos – now old and frail – knew him. Laying back his ears and wagging his tail joyfully he died, content to have seen his master one last time. Inside, Odysseus asked the suitors for alms, but received only abuse and blows. But Penelope was curious about the newcomer and granted him an audience in her private quarters. Despite his longing, Odysseus did not reveal his true identity. Instead, as Penelope wept 'for her husband, who was sitting beside her', he claimed to be a Cretan prince, who knew Odysseus before the Trojan War, adding that Odysseus would soon be home.

Instructed by Penelope, Odysseus' old nurse Eurycleia bathed him – and, as she did, she recognized the scar inflicted on the boar hunt on Parnassus. Warning her to keep silent, Odysseus rejoined Penelope, who related a dream in which an eagle killed her pet geese. Its interpretation was clear: the geese were the suitors, the eagle Odysseus.

Next day, Penelope, wearied by the suitors' demands, promised to marry whoever strung Odysseus' bow and fired an arrow through the eyes of a row of axes. Not one suitor could even string it. Then the beggar asked to try:

> And as a singer, virtuosic on the lyre, effortlessly
> stretches a new string around a peg, fastening each end
> with twisted sheep-gut, even so without effort Odysseus
> strung the great bow. Then holding it in his right hand he
> tested the string, and it sang like the voice of a swallow.

With Telemachus and Eumaeus at his side, Odysseus shot down the defenceless suitors. Then he ordered the colluding maidservants to scrape and scrub the hall, before they too were hanged.

After an emotional reunion with Penelope, Odysseus hurried to Laertes' farmstead, where he fought off an attack by the suitors' relatives. The *Odyssey* ends with Athene's intervention, forcing the warring sides to reach an agreement.

An Inland Odyssey

But Odysseus' wanderings were not over. Teiresias' prophecy and later sources tell that, as reparation for killing the suitors, Odysseus was exiled for another ten years, leaving Telemachus to rule Ithaca. As Teiresias instructed:

> You must set out on a journey, taking a well-shaped oar,
> until you come to a land of men who know nothing of the
> sea, eat nothing seasoned with salt and know nothing of
> red-cheeked ships or well-shaped oars, which are to ships
> as wings are.... When another traveller approaches you,
> remarking on the winnowing fan that you are carrying on
> your shoulder, you must plant your well-shaped oar hard
> in the earth and make rich offerings to Lord Poseidon
> – a ram, a bull, a rutting boar. Then return home and
> offer a hundred victims to the deathless gods, who live
> in the broad heavens, making sacrifice to each in order.
> Death will come to you from the sea, a peaceful death,
> in glistening old age with your people rich around you.

A prophecy proclaimed that Odysseus would die at his son's hand, so before his return Telemachus was banished. Then unexpectedly Telegonus, whom Circe had borne to Odysseus, arrived at Ithaca searching for his father. In his ignorance Odysseus thought Telegonus was a pirate; Telegonus thought Ithaca was Corfu (and so fair game for plunder); blows were exchanged; Telegonus speared Odysseus with a sting-ray's spine; and by the sea, as his muscles cramped, the hero's life ebbed from him.

A fragment of the lost epic poem, the *Telegony*, completes the story. When he realized his error, Telegonus transported his father's body along with Penelope and Telemachus (now recalled from exile) to Aeaea, where Circe made them all immortal. Telegonus married Penelope, while Telemachus married Circe. What happened next is lost even to mythology.

Ithaca in History & Today

There are two Ithacas – one the modern island of Ithaki, the other the Ithaca of the *Odyssey*. Many have tried to reconcile them, for, if Mycenae and Troy really existed, why not Odysseus' palace at Ithaca?

Archaeological and topographical surveys show some similarities between Homer's descriptions and Ithaki. Thus in the south of the island, the bay where the Phaeacians put Odysseus ashore corresponds to Dexia Bay (just west of Vathy Bay), while Eumaeus' hut may be located on the Marathia Plateau above Raven's Crag (*Stephani tou Korakou*). Two sites in the north of Ithaki claim to be Odysseus' palace – Alalkomenai (Schliemann's favoured location) and Platrithias. Both have Mycenaean remains, but nothing on the scale of mainland palaces.

At Polis Bay in northwest Ithaki in the 1930s the remains of twelve tripod-cauldrons from the ninth or eighth century BC were found in a collapsed cave. Decorated with Geometric motifs, their handles were topped by miniature dogs and horses. Sixty years earlier, another tripod-cauldron had been uncovered, making a total of thirteen – the number Alcinous gave Odysseus. Also found was a second- or first-century BC fragmentary terracotta mask inscribed, 'A Prayer to Odysseus'. Probably the cave was associated with a hero cult to Odysseus from at least 800 BC. Some even suggest that Homer heard of (or saw) the dedicated tripods, and wove them into his narrative.

Unlike Homer's Ithaca, however, Ithaki is not the 'furthest out towards the sunset' of the Ionian Islands (although some argue that from certain locations Ithaca *appears* to be further west than the others). A host of other candidates are suggested, including Lefkas (now a mainland promontory but once an island) – whose champions explain its location east of Ithaki by claiming that Homer meant it was 'closest to the mainland' – and Paliki (now a promontory of Cephalonia but also once an island), which is, indeed, the furthest west. In antiquity Ithaca's identity worried Strabo, who was confused as to whether it was Ithaki or Lefkas.

The *Odyssey*'s wider geography was even more problematic. Herodotus attempted to anchor episodes in real locations – the Land of the Lotus Eaters in western Libya, for example – and Apollodorus states that 'some interpret the *Odyssey* as an account of a voyage round Sicily'. Scylla and Charybdis are still commonly sited in the Strait of Messina, while Scherie has been identified with Corfu. In the 1980s, Tim Severin's voyage in a reconstruction of a Bronze Age ship placed the first adventures in North Africa and Crete and many of the remainder in and around the Ionian Islands.

While the identification game is fun, it disregards the fact that the *Odyssey* is not history but a blend of mythology, sailors' yarns and heroic epic. It can also be read as a 'parable', a journey from life to death and subsequent rebirth, an odyssey that is as much spiritual as geographical. The early twentieth-century poet Constantine Cavafy expressed it best in his poem 'Ithaca', concluding:

> Keep Ithaca always in your mind. Your goal is to reach
> it. But do not hurry your voyage – better to let it last for
> many years, to drop anchor only when you are old, rich
> with experiences, not expecting that Ithaca will give
> you wealth. Ithaca has furnished the delightful voyage.
> Without her you would never have set out. But she has
> nothing else to give you. And if you find her poor, Ithaca
> has not deceived you. You have gained great wisdom.

You have experienced so much. Surely by now you must know what Ithacas mean.

In Classical times Ithaki was poor and insignificant. The island was taken by Sicilian Normans in 1185, then ravaged by Turks in 1479 and resettled by Venetians in 1504. Together with the other Ionian islands it became part of Greece only in 1864 (thirty-three years after the foundation of the modern state), when it was ceded by the British, who had ruled it for fifty years.

Ithaca (Ithaki)

SOME IMPORTANT DATES & REMAINS

C13th BC	Mycenaean buildings in the north of Ithaki.
c. **1200 BC**	Possible destruction of Mycenaean sites.
C9th/8th BC	Hero-shrine to Odysseus in Polis Cave?
C2nd/1st BC	Votive 'Prayer to Odysseus' inscribed on terracotta mask at Polis Cave.
AD 1185	Sicilian Normans capture Ithaki.
AD 1479	Turks capture Ithaki.
AD 1504	Venetians capture Ithaki and build settlement above Vathy.
AD 1814	Ithaki part of British protectorate.
AD 1864	Ithaki part of Greek state.

There is little convincing archaeology to enjoy on Ithaki, and many will prefer to imagine what Homeric parallels they can at the evocatively renamed sites.

From **Vathy** a road leads south to the **Marathia Plateau**, perhaps the site of Eumaeus' hut. Another leads north, past **Dexia Bay** (perhaps where Odysseus was set down by the Phaeacians) to the spectacularly sited **Alalkomenai** (which Schliemann identified as Odysseus' palace) before reaching the pretty village of Stavros, with fine views across the sea to Cephalonia/Kephallonia. Further north is Mycenaean **Platrithias**, currently promoted as the genuine location of Odysseus' palace. Southeast of Stavros is **Polis Bay** with its (collapsed) **Cave of the Tripods**.

22

Hades: Ephyra & the Gateway to the Underworld

Install your mast, hoist the white sail and take your seat! The breath of the North Wind will guide your ship. Across the boundaries of Ocean, you will find a fertile headland and groves sacred to Persephone with tall black poplars and willows which yield fruit. Here you must beach your ship by the shores of deep-eddying Ocean, and go on foot to the dank house of Haides. Here the Periphlegethon and the Cocytus flow into the River Acheron, which is itself an offshoot of the waters of the Styx; and here, where the two raging rivers meet, there is a craggy rock ...

Homer, *Odyssey*, 10.508f.

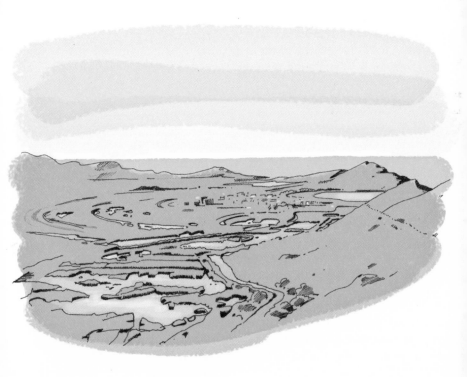

Across fertile plough-land the early sunlight pours obliquely through the lush green mountains of Thesprotia. Crows caw lazily from distant clumps of trees, their conversations interspersed by the atonic clack of sheep's bells in the pastureland below and the bark of dogs nearby in sleepy gardens. To the north, the mound whose tumbled masonry was Cichyrus, the region's ancient capital, is thrown into sharp focus by the slanting light, while to the west, beyond the cliffs, the limpid sea melts to the far horizon. Just inland are lagoons, the home of languid turtles and iridescent dragonflies, which skim coquettishly above the glassy water. It is all so peaceful.

But hunters' gunshots startle suddenly. All is not always as it seems. Even the rivers gliding through the reeds have a darkly haunting past. The Acheron is still the Acheron, but the Mavros was once called Periphlegethon and the Vouvos was Cocytus. In antiquity they were the rivers of Hades. And here, on the crag beneath the Church of St John the Baptist, a slippery iron ladder leads deep into the gloom to a vaulted chamber, its atmosphere fetid with the hot breath of decay. It is an earthy place, a stifling place. To climb back to the sunlight feels like a rebirth. In antiquity this may have been the Necromanteion, 'Oracle of the Dead'; some say Odysseus communed with spirits here. For at Ephyra, in northwest Greece, may be a gateway to Hades.

Haides & Persephone

Haides, Zeus and Poseidon, the mighty triad, ruled creation. In the *Iliad*, Poseidon outlines the arrangement:

> We are three brothers, born of Cronus and Rhea – Zeus,
> myself, and Haides, who rules beneath the earth. So all
> [creation] is divided into three, and each of us has been
> apportioned his own area. When the lots were shaken,
> I won dominion over the grey sea, Haides the misty
> subterranean gloom, and Zeus the broad heavens in the
> upper air and clouds. But the earth and high Olympus
> are shared between us all.

Haides' name ('Unseen') was considered so unlucky that by the fifth century BC people commonly refered to him as Plouton ('Wealthy'), perhaps because of the rich minerals which, like his kingdom, lay beneath the earth.

Haides' court included other deities. Chief was his wife, Persephone, who lived with him for only four months out of twelve. Lonely, Haides amused himself with Minthe (a nymph of the River Cocytus), but Persephone found out. She trampled her rival underfoot. Poor Minthe was transformed into a herb (mint) and a mountain near Pylos was named after her, with a sanctuary to Haides on its slopes. Another paramour was luckier. Leuce died a peaceful death and was changed into a white poplar.

From earliest times, Haides' lieutenant was Thanatos (Death), the twin brother of Hypnos (Sleep), described by Hesiod as having: 'An iron heart and a spirit as pitiless as bronze. He possesses whatever mortal he takes hold of and is hateful even to the gods.'

Hateful Thanatos may have been, but both he and Haides were considered to be as central to human experience as any other god: neither virtuous nor wicked, just inevitable. Only mortals were good or bad. Classical Greeks believed that in the Underworld each soul was judged to decide its fate and that the dead were punished or rewarded for their behaviour while alive. Plato's Socrates playfully describes Zeus explaining:

> I have appointed my own sons as judges: two, Minos
> and Rhadamanthus, are from Asia; one, Aeacus, is from
> Europe. When they are dead, they will sit in judgment
> in the field beside the crossroads. From here one road
> leads to the Islands of the Blessed, the other to Tartarus.
> Rhadamanthus shall judge the Asiatics, Aeacus the
> Europeans, with Minos as final arbiter, if the others
> have doubts.

When Plato wrote this in the fourth century BC, an 'official' geography of Hades was evolving – but it was very different from Homer's vision.

Homeric Hades

In the *Iliad*, none of the action takes place in Hades, but we do learn about it. Sited beside the River Styx's icy waterfall and protected by a grim dog, Hades lies just below the surface of the earth. When Poseidon causes an earthquake, Haides 'ruler of the dead, sprang up in terror from his throne and bellowed loud in fear lest – up above – Poseidon, who encircles the dry land, might crack open the earth and expose to men and gods the houses of the dead, so hideous and mouldering that even the gods shudder as they see them.'

We learn, too, that being dead was not of itself sufficient qualification to enter Hades. Rather, corpses needed to be buried or cremated. Thus at Troy Patroclus' ghost (the mirror of the hero when alive, with the same physique, eyes, voice and clothing) begs Achilles:

> Bury me as quickly as you can and let me enter through
> the gates of Hades. The souls, which bear the image of

The three-headed dog Cerberus, guardian of the Underworld, sits at the feet of his master, Haides. (First-century BC statue from Gortyn, Crete.)

the dead, are shunning me and will not allow me across the river to join them, but I am wandering just as I am by Haides' house with its wide gates.

The *Iliad* also tells of a special area in Hades, called Tartarus, reserved for whoever disobeyed the gods' will. Zeus threatens that if anyone defies him: 'I shall hurl him down to the mists of distant Tartarus, in the deepest pit beneath the earth with its iron gates and brazen threshold, as far below Hades as earth is beneath the skies.' The *Odyssey* fleshes out this subterranean landscape, revealing more about how the spirits journeyed there. Before Hermes conducts the souls of the dead suitors from Ithaca to the Underworld, using his *kerykeion*:

> he roused them from their sleep, and, gibbering, they followed him. As gibbering bats flit back and forth in the darkest corners of a cave, when one falls from the cluster where they cling on to each another and the rock, so they went with him, gibbering, and gracious Hermes led them down the dripping path. Past Ocean's streams, past the White Rock, past the gateway of the sun they went and past the Land of Dreams, and soon they came to the Asphodel Meadow, where the spirits live, which bear the image of those men who work no more.

The geography tallies reasonably well with the *Odyssey*'s description of Odysseus' voyage to consult the spirits of the dead in a setting that bears some similarity to Ephyra. Here, Odysseus digs a pit into which he pours libations of milk, honey, wine and water, sprinkles white barley meal, slits the throat of sacrificial sheep, and lets the blood gush down. Greedily the spirits jostle to eat and drink. Homer describes them by category: first heroic women – Odysseus' mother, Anticlea, Jocasta (called here 'Epicasta'), Leda, Phaedra and many more; next heroic warriors, including Agamemnon, Patroclus and Ajax (who even in death blames Odysseus for his suicide). Grimly, Achilles, who at Troy preferred everlasting fame to long life, comments: 'I would rather be a hired labourer, working in a poor man's house, but alive, than the king of kings among the dead.' Nonetheless when Odysseus tells him of Neoptolemus, 'Achilles' ghost strode off across the meadow thick with asphodel, rejoicing at the news of his son's glory'. As, dreamlike, the scene shifts from the sacrificial pit, Odysseus witnesses the torture of the damned before the sheer volume of spirits and their blood-chilling screams cause him to flee, 'terrified lest Persephone send up from Haides' house the head of the grim Gorgon'.

Homer's Hades is a place of monochrome monotony, where souls remember their past lives with aching nostalgia, a vision captured by Sappho: 'When you are dead, you will lie forgotten. No one will mourn you, no one bring roses for you from Pieria. In death as in life you will be quite anonymous, wandering vaguely, with the aimless, nameless dead.'

Hesiodic Hades

Homer's contemporary, Hesiod, imagines Haides' realm more like a city than a single house. Thus the goddess of the River Styx has her own home, roofed with huge stones and supported with silver pillars, while her stream, 'eternal and primordial', 'the famous icy water which trickles from a high and overhanging cliff', spouts through the rocks.

Night (Nyx) too has a house:

> swathed in dark cloud. Before it stands Atlas, rigid and immobile, holding the broad heaven on his head and tireless hands. Here Night and Day come close and greet each other as they pass the mighty brazen threshold.... Here, too, Night's children have their homes – Sleep and Death, both terrifying gods.... And before them stand the echoing halls of mighty Haides, ruler of the Underworld, and dread Persephone.

In the *Iliad* 'the hound of the hateful death god' guards Haides' house. Hesiod provides more details. He is 'a monster which cannot be tamed or spoken of – Cerberus, who eats raw flesh, the hound of Haides, with a harsh bark, fifty-headed, merciless and strong':

> He has a vicious trick. He fawns on all who enter, wagging his tail and setting back his ears, but he will not let them leave. Rather, he keeps watch and feasts on any he finds leaving through the gates of mighty Haides and dread Persephone.

Charon

In the fifth century BC one of the most memorable of all Hades' inhabitants is first mentioned: Charon, the ferryman who punts dead souls across the Acheron. Again, local geography may mirror that of Hades: east of Ephyra in antiquity was the Acherousian Lake, into which flowed the Acheron and Cocytus. It has since been drained, but some argue that pilgrims visiting the Necromanteion were rowed across the lake as if they were approaching Hades.

The first surviving work to name Charon ('Keen-Sighted') is Euripides' *Alcestis*. Anticipating death, Alcestis herself exclaims: 'I can see him sitting at the oars in his rowing boat in the lake – Charon, the ferryman of the dead. He is sitting at the oars and calling me: "Why are you waiting! Hurry! You are delaying us!" He is calling to me angrily, impatiently.' Aristophanes provides a further detail. In *Frogs*, Heracles informs Dionysus that before crossing the Acheron he must pay Charon a fare of two obols. Usually it was half that sum, and from the fifth century BC the dead were regularly buried with an obol (a low-denomination coin) in their mouths. Only the dead of Hermione, the city in the Argolid, were exempt. Strabo explains that they knew a short-cut to Hades, which bypassed the Acheron.

The fifth-century BC artist Polygnotus depicted Charon in a wall-painting which adorned the *Lesche* ('Club Room') at Delphi. Elaborating on Odysseus' visit to the Underworld, he could not resist including Charon. Pausanias describes:

> a reedy river, clearly the Acheron, containing outlines
> of fish so indistinct that you might think them shadows.
> A boat is on the river with the ferryman at the oars ...
> Charon, a man weighted by age.... By Charon's boat on
> the Acheron's banks is a large group, including one man
> who in life had not been dutiful to his father, and is now
> being strangled by him ...

Eternal Punishment

The idea that the virtuous were rewarded in Hades while wrongdoers were appropriately punished became increasingly popular. Supervising these punishments were demi-gods, or *daimones* (though, unlike 'demons', the Greek word has no pejorative overtones). Polygnotus' painting included:

> Eurynomus, whom the guides at Delphi say is one of the
> *daimones* of Hades. He devours the flesh from corpses,
> leaving only bones.... His colour is the colour of meat
> flies, somewhere between blue and black; he is baring
> his teeth and squatting with a vulture's skin spread out
> beneath him.

In the *Odyssey*, Odysseus witnesses some of these punishments: two vultures perch on Tityos (who attempted to rape Leto near Delphi), constantly tearing at his liver; Sisyphus (who tried to cheat death) forever pushes a boulder uphill, which always rolls back down just before reaching the top; while Tantalus, who fed his son Pelops to the gods is:

standing in a pool. The water almost reached his chin. He was thirsty but he could not drink. Whenever the old man bent down and tried to drink the water, it was swallowed up and disappeared, and at his feet was only the dark earth. A god had made all dry. Above his head were tall leafy trees, all thick with fruit – pear trees and pomegranates, apple trees with shining fruit, sweet figs, fat olives. But whenever the old man reached up to seize them in his hands, a wind blew, sweeping them all away towards the massing clouds.

Homer and Hesiod knew the place of punishment as Tartarus, setting it apart from Hades, reserving it specifically for the Titans. Hesiod described its location:

> Falling from heaven for nine days and nights, a bronze anvil would reach the earth on the tenth. Similarly a bronze anvil falling from earth for nine days and nights would reach Tartarus on the tenth. A bronze barrier surrounds it. Night spreads in three circlets like a necklace all around it, and high above it grow the roots of earth and the barren sea.... It is clammy, at the very limits of the earth.

Elsewhere Hesiod says that anyone who entered Tartarus' bronze gates and fell into the yawning chasm would plummet for a year, buffeted by winds, before he reached the ground.

By the fourth century BC Tartarus was included within Hades, a place of torture for not only Titans, but mortal criminals, too, a blueprint for Hell and Purgatory. The irredeemable stayed there forever, but each year lesser criminals were granted temporary release so they could beg their victims for mercy. If pardoned, their suffering ended. If not, the felon was led back to torture.

One of our earliest sources to imagine Tartarus, the late sixth- /early fifth-century BC Anacreon admitted his terror: 'Often I shed tears in fear of Tartarus. The descent to Hades is racked with pain. Only one thing is for certain: once that descent is made, there's no return.'

The Elysian Fields

As Tartarus became more 'democratic', so Elysium (or more properly the Elysian Fields), once the exclusive domain of heroes, increasingly admitted the souls of the mundanely virtuous. Its location too shifted over time. Hesiod sited it near Ocean's shores on the Islands of the Blessed, where:

happy heroes live. Wheat-bearing earth produces for
them fruit as sweet as honey, which ripens three times
every year, far from the immortal gods. Cronus rules
them – Zeus, the father of gods and men, released him
from his chains – and they enjoy equal honour and glory.

To Homer, the Elysian Fields were equally remote: 'There men live lives
completely free from labour. There is no snow, no gale, no thunderstorm.
Rather, Ocean cools men with soft-singing breezes from the west.' Pindar
imagined a similarly idyllic scene, where his patrician patrons could continue to enjoy their earthly pleasures: 'In meadows outside their city red
roses bloom and trees, fragrant with incense, weighed down with golden
fruit. Some amuse themselves with riding and wrestling, others with
draughts and the lyre...' Developing the relatively common idea of metempsychosis (the transmigration of souls, where the dead are reborn as
humans or animals), Pindar suggests that the virtuous experience the
cycle of death and rebirth three times before being automatically admitted to the Islands of the Blessed. The idea probably evolved in Mystery
religions, such as those at Eleusis. Indeed, 'Elysium' and 'Eleusis' may
both come from *eleusō,* 'I release' (from suffering). In *Frogs*, Aristophanes
explores this concept, imagining a party of dead Eleusinian initiates
singing hymns to Iacchus, the god who is leading them to Elysium.

Leaving Hades
Plato's Socrates believed in reincarnation, too. Advocating a virtuous life,
he agreed that 'man's soul is immortal. At one point it reaches a conclu-
sion, which we call "dying"; at another it is reborn; but it never perishes.'
However, to experience rebirth, the soul must first leave Hades and erase
all memory of its time there and its former lives. This it achieves by drinking from another of the rivers of the Underworld: Lethe ('Forgetfulness').

Metempsychosis and reincarnation, however, belong to the worlds
of metaphysics and philosophy more comfortably than to mythology. In
Greek legend only a very few return from Hades with their memories
intact. These are the heroes who have made the journey to the Underworld
while still alive: Heracles and Theseus, as well as Odysseus. And Orpheus,
who emerged from Hades to sing beside the waters of the Helicon beneath the snow-capped peaks of Mount Olympus at Dion, where this
book began.

Ephyra in History & Today
Pausanias identifies Ephyra as the inspiration for Homer's Hades in the
Odyssey. 'Here', he writes, 'is the Acherousian Lake, the River Acheron
and the noxious stream called the Cocytus. It seems to me that Homer

---

The underground chamber at Ephyra is thought by
some to be associated with the Oracle of the Dead.

must have visited this area and in his bold description of Hades gave its
rivers the names of those in Thesprotia.' If so, Homer also gave himself
license: elsewhere in the *Odyssey* he tells how Odysseus visited the city
of Ephyra 'in a swift ship, in search of man-killing poisons that he might
smear on to his bronze-tipped arrows'.

While in more common versions of another myth, Theseus and
Peirithous try to abduct Persephone from Hades, Pausanias records a
tradition setting it at Cichyrus (as Ephyra was also known), while Plutarch
elaborates (using the alternative names Epirus and Molossia for this
region of Thesprotia and Aidoneus for Haides):

> Theseus travelled with Peirithous to Epirus in his quest
> for the daughter of the Molossian king Aidoneus. This
> man called his wife 'Persephone', his daughter 'Kore' and
> his dog 'Cerberus'. He instructed his daughter's suitors

to fight with this dog, and promised her to anyone who defeated it, but when he discovered that they were there not to woo but to steal his child he seized them both. He killed Peirithous (by means of the dog) and kept Theseus locked up in solitary confinement.

Bronze Age pottery has been found at Ephyra, but the Necromanteion ('Oracle of the Dead') first enters the record in a racy story by Herodotus (the raciest elements of which are omitted below). He writes of Periander, the early sixth-century BC *tyrannos* of Corinth:

> One day he stripped all the Corinthian women naked because of his wife Melissa. He had sent envoys to the Necromanteion on the River Acheron in Thesprotia to ask about a monetary deposit which a friend had left him, but Melissa's ghost refused to reveal its location because she was cold and naked and unable to wear the clothes she had been buried in, since they had not been burned in the fire.... So on Periander's instruction, all Corinth's women went to the sanctuary of Hera dressed in their finest clothes as if for a festival. There Periander posted guards and stripped them all, freeborn and servants alike, and heaping the clothes in a pit he burned them as he prayed to Melissa. When he sent a second envoy, Melissa's ghost told him where the deposit had been left.

Ephyra flourished thanks to its proximity to the port at Glykis Limen ('Sweet Harbour'), with capacity for 150 to 200 ships. In the fourth or third century BC the hill of the Necromanteion was flattened, erasing all traces of previous structures, and some of the buildings whose foundations still survive were erected. Burned by the Romans in 168 BC, the site was largely abandoned until in the eighteenth century AD a Church of St John the Baptist and a fortified two-storey house were built.

Debate bedevils the site. The remains are inconclusive – a series of outer rooms cluster round a central hall, beneath which is a vaulted chamber accessible only by ladder. Convinced that it was the Necromanteion, Sotirios Dakaris, excavating from the late 1950s to the mid-1970s, identified the outer rooms as dormitories, where pilgrims slept before undergoing initiation. The rituals (he said) included eating hallucinogenic lupin seeds and broad beans, whose remains he discovered. Dakaris claimed that initiates were led through a dark labyrinth (whose foundations survive), reminiscent of Plato's description of the path to Hades: 'There seem to be many forks and turnings, as I infer from the rites and rituals, which we perform here on earth.'

These preliminaries accomplished, initiates were lowered into the underground chamber. Encouraged by the discovery of seventh- to fifth-century BC terracotta figurines and some pieces of machinery (iron blocks, bronze rings and ratchet wheels), Dakaris identified a sanctuary to Haides and Persephone and further claimed that, using the machinery, their priests staged illusions (levitations and raising the dead). Many disagree. For them the building is a fortified farmhouse, the food found in its amphorae were everyday supplies and the machinery belonged to six catapults. Quite why the farmer needed six catapults, however, remains unclear.

Ephyra

SOME IMPORTANT DATES & REMAINS

C14th BC	Ephyra settled.
C6th BC	Periander consults Necromanteion.
C4th/3rd BC	Necromanteion hill flattened and buildings erected.
168 BC	Romans burn Ephyra.
C18th AD	Church of St John the Baptist and farmhouse built.
AD 1958–77	Dakaris excavates Ephyra.

The Necromanteion sits on a low hill above the agricultural village of Mesopotamos, beside the main highway between Preveza and Igoumenitsa. The Church of St John the Baptist dominates the site, now precariously supported above the excavations on girders. Facing the entrance and ticket office, a central courtyard lies west of the eighteenth-century two-storey house. An arch (left) leads to the **north corridor** with foundations of rooms confidently labelled '**ritual dormitories**' and '**purification room**'. From its furthest point, another corridor leads off (right) before turning sharply (right) into the '**labyrinth**'. This accesses the '**main sanctuary**', beneath which a **vaulted chamber**, best avoided by the faint-hearted, is accessed by a slippery steep ladder atmospherically lit. The 'main sanctuary' is flanked by **storage rooms**, some of which contain fine amphorae.

Not only can visitors sail up the Acheron to Ephyra from the coastal town of Ammoudia, but they may also dine in the evocatively named Necromanteion Taverna in nearby Mesopotamos, pondering the words of one online 'smart travel guide': 'Acheron is soppy with soul's tears for loosing [*sic*] their lives and their relatives' for missing their beloved persons'.

Acknowledgments

The concept for this book emerged during a discussion over the kitchen table at the house of Colin Ridler, Thames & Hudson's commissioning editor. The idea was mostly his and in the months which followed he offered me both guidance and encouragement – so it is to Colin, first, that my warm thanks are due. It was his proposal, too, that the text should be illustrated by specially commissioned drawings. These have been brilliantly and evocatively executed by Lis Watkins, and throughout the process I have particularly enjoyed receiving intriguing batches of her drawings, some based on my own site-photographs.

As ever, there has been an outstanding team at T&H to steer the book safe to its completion: Colin's assistant, Jen Moore, who has fielded emails and enquiries with grace and efficiency; Sarah Vernon-Hunt, who, keen-eyed, has edited my text with patience, expertise and equanimity; Aman Phull, the imaginatively creative designer; Celia Falconer, who has overseen the production with her usual skill and proficiency; and the splendid publicity guru, Kate Cooper. I thank them all profoundly.

Thank you, too, to Jennifer Ogilvie and Isobel Pinder for allowing me to quote the Shillingstone poem at the end of the Introduction. I have lived with it, and with fond memories of my one-time mentor, Robert Ogilvie, since I was a student.

To research the book, I needed to travel to the sites which it covers, a study trip that was possible only thanks to the support and generosity of my mother, Kate. Her encouragement of me and confidence in me mean more to me than I think she knows, and I thank her profoundly. I am grateful, too, to the staff at the British School at Athens, and especially Vicki Tzavara, for their help – as I am to all those (but especially to Ioanna Karamanou and Robin and Kathryn Waterfield) who offered kindness and hospitality on my journeys.

Accompanying me for some of them was my wife, Emily Jane, without whose support, patience and belief this volume could not have been written. In a book about heroes, it is right for me to acknowledge her as my heroine and inspiration. These pages are dedicated to her – and to two old friends, with whom many years ago I travelled in Greece: Mark Grant and Alex Zambellas. Finally, a big thank you to the home study team, our two cats, Stanley and Oliver, who firmly believe that keyboards are for sitting on and paper is for chewing.

Recommended Reading

There are numerous books about Greek mythology. Among them are:

Buxton, R., *The Complete World of Greek Mythology*, London and New York, 2004
Graves, R., *The Greek Myths*, 2 vols, London, 2011
March, J., *The Penguin Book of Classical Myths*, London, 2008
Matysak, P., *The Greek and Roman Myths*, London and New York, 2010
Waterfield, R. & K., *The Greek Myths*, London, 2011

Similarly there are many books tracing the reception of Greek mythology, including:

Graziosi, B., *The Gods of Olympus: A History*, London, 2014
Woodard, R. (ed.), *The Cambridge Companion to Greek Mythology*, Cambridge, 2007

Some recent books introducing ancient Greek history and culture are:

Hall, E., *Introducing the Ancient Greeks*, London, 2015
Cartledge, P., *Ancient Greece: A Very Short Introduction*, Oxford, 2011
Rhodes, P., *A Short History of Ancient Greece*, London, 2014
Stuttard, D., *A History of Ancient Greece in Fifty Lives*, London and New York, 2014

Particularly useful volumes exploring latest discoveries about the Bronze Age, when many of the myths are set, are:

Cline, E. (ed.), *The Oxford Handbook of the Bronze Age Aegean*, New York, 2010
Shelmerdine, C. (ed.), *The Cambridge Companion to the Aegean Bronze Age*, Cambridge, 2008

Of the many travel guides to Greece and the eastern Mediterranean, arguably the most useful are the Blue Guides, which contain brief histories of most of the sites mentioned in this book, as well as many useful site plans.

Many of the Classical authors quoted in this book are available in English translations. They include:

Greek Lyric Poetry: The Poems and Fragments of the Greek Iambic, Elegiac, and Melic Poets (Excluding Pindar and Bacchylides), trans. West, M. L., Oxford, 2008
Homeric Hymns, trans. Cashford, J., London, 2003
Aeschylus, *Oresteia*, trans. Collard, C., Oxford, 2008
Aeschylus, *Persians and Other Plays*, trans. Collard, C., Oxford, 2009
Apollodorus, *The Library of Greek Mythology*, trans. Hard, R., New York, 1997
Apollonius, *Jason and the Golden Fleece*, trans. Hunter, R., Oxford, 2009
Euripides, *Bacchae and Other Plays*, intro. Hall, E., trans. Morwood, J., Oxford, 2008
Euripides, *Electra and Other Plays*, intro. Easterling, P., trans. Raeburn, D., London, 2008
Euripides, *Medea and Other Plays*, intro. Hall, E., trans. Morwood, J., Oxford, 2008
Euripides, *Orestes and Other Plays*, intro. Hall, E., trans. Waterfield, R., notes Morwood, J., Oxford, 2008
Euripides, *The Trojan Women and Other Plays*, intro. Hall, E., trans. Morwood, J., Oxford, 2008
Herodotus, *The Histories*, trans. Holland, T., London, 2013
Hesiod, *Theogony* and *Works and Days*, trans. West, M., Oxford, 2008
Homer, *The Iliad*, intro. Graziosi, B., trans. Verity, A., Oxford, 2012
Homer, *The Odyssey*, intro. Kirk, G., trans. Shewring, W., Oxford, 2008
Ovid, *Metamorphoses*, trans. Raeburn, D., London, 2004
Pausanias, *Guide to Greece*, trans. O. Levi, 2 vols, London, 1979
Pindar, *The Complete Odes*, intro. Instone, S., trans. Verity, A., Oxford, 2008
Sappho, *Stung with Love: Poems and Fragments of Sappho*, trans. Poochigian, A., London, 2009
Sophocles, *Antigone; Oedipus the King; Electra*, intro. Hall, E., trans. Kitto, H., Oxford, 2008
Sophocles, *Electra and Other Plays*, intro. Easterling, P., trans. Raeburn, D., London, 2008

Index

Mythological characters appear in Roman type, historical figures in *italics*, place names in SMALL CAPITALS and Classical terms, buildings and institutions in *ITALIC SMALL CAPITALS*.

Page numbers in *italics* indicate illustrations.

Abderus, Heracles' groom 128
Academus, Athenian hero 180
Acastus, Argonaut 140, 145
ACHERON, River 249, 250, 254, 255, 257, 259, 260
Achilles, Greek hero at Troy 8, 9, 24, 60, 69, *70*, 128, 138, 195, 196, 205, 212, 215, 220, 224–29, *228*, 231, 234–35, 251, 253
Acrisius, Argive king 122, 162, 165, 210
ACROCORINTH 33, 151–53, 156, 158
ACROPOLIS (ATHENS) 12, 43, 83, 171–74, 178, 180, 182–83, 187
Actaeon, Theban prince, huntsman 67, *67*
ACTIUM, Battle of (31 BC) 197
Admete, daughter of Eurystheus 129
Admetus, king of Pherae 147, 149
Adonis, huntsman, beloved of Aphrodite 82–83, *82*, 86, 179, 188
Adrastus, Argive king 113, 166
Aeacus, king of Aegina, judge of the dead 189, 221, 251
AEAEA 243, 246
Aeëtes, king of Colchis 140, 142, 144
AEGAE (Euboea) 29, 31
AEGAE (Macedonia) 24
AEGEUM, MOUNT 17
Aegeus, Athenian king 33, 155, 175–78, 186–88
AEGINA 33, 152, 171, 189, 221
Aegina, nymph 152
Aegisthus, usurper of Mycenaean throne 211–15, 217, 225

Aegyptus, king of Egypt 161–62
Aeneas, Trojan hero 9, 81, 223, 232, 234
Aeolus, king of the winds 242
Aerope, Mycenaean queen 211
Aeschylus (525–455 BC), Athenian tragedian 40, 59, 162–63, 209, 212, 214
Aeson, prince of Iolcus, father of Jason 138–39, 144–45, 152
Aethra, mother of Theseus 175–76, 179–80, 231
Aex, Titan 171
Agamemnon, king of Mycenae 93, 166, 204, 212–14, 217, 224–26, 228, 229, 231, 232, 238, 253
Agapenor, Paphian king 85
Agavë, Theban princess 107–8
Ahhiyawa 233
Ajax, Greek hero at Troy 224, 226–28, 253
Ajax ('Lesser'), Greek hero at Troy 231
Alaksandu, 13th-century BC Hittite king 233, 234
ALALKOMENAI 246, 248
Alaric (c. AD 370–410), Gothic leader 27–28, 43–44, 102, 157, 167–68, 181–82, 206
Alcaeus, 7th-/6th-century BC lyric poet 203
Alcestis, queen of Pherae 147, 149, 255
Alcibiades (450–404 BC), Athenian politician 102–3, 208
Alcinous, king of Scherie 244, 247
Alcman, 7th-century BC lyric poet 11
Alcmene, Mycenaean princess 114, 116, 132–33, 210
Alexander I (r. 498–454 BC), Macedonian king 24
Alexander the Great (356–323 BC), Macedonian king 9, 11, 27–28, 61, 73–75, 119–20, 130, 181, 207, 234, 235
Alexandros *see* Paris
Allat, near-Eastern fertility goddess 47

ALPHEUS, River 89, 91, 94, 96, 97, 100, 102, 126
Altheia, queen of Calydon 194, 196
ALTIS 100, 103
Amazons, tribe of warrior women 67–70, 69, 72, 73, 128–29, 136, 153, 178–79, 227
AMMOUDIA 260
AMNISUS, River 66
Amphion, Theban prince 109
AMPHISSA 59
Amphitrite, sea-nymph 32
Amphitryon, Mycenaean prince 114, 116, 210, 237
AMYCLAE 12, 201, 207
Amycus, boxer-king 141
Anacreon (c. 582–485 BC), lyric poet 79, 256
ANAURUS, River 139
Anaxibia, Phocian queen 214
Anchises, Trojan prince, father of Aeneas 9, 81–2, 223, 232, 234
Androclus, Athenian prince 72, 74, 76
Androgeus, Cretan prince 186–87
Andromache, Trojan princess, wife of Hector 220, 231
Andromeda, Ethiopian princess 10, 165
Anteia, *aka* Stheneboea, Lycian princess 122, 153
ANTHESTERIA 40
Anticlea, Ithacan queen 237, 253
Antigone, Theban princess 111, 113–14
Antilochus, Greek hero at Troy 24
Antiope (i), Amazonian princess 69, 129, 178
Antiope (ii), Theban river-nymph 109
Antipater of Sidon, 2nd-century BC poet 73
Antony, Mark (83–30 BC), Roman general 74, 197
APHIDNAE 179
Aphrodite, goddess of love and sex 12, 16, 22, 32, 69, 77–84, *78–79*, *82–83*, 86, 109,

113, 142–43, 151, 156, 158, 166, 168, 172, 175, 178, 179, 196, 204, 222, 223, 225

Apollo, god of light, healing and prophecy 10, 12, 21, 24, 25, 33, 45–57, *48*, *51*, *55*, 59–65, 86–89, 97, 103, 105, 106, 109, 120, 123, 131, 147, 151, 156, 157, 162, 166, 168, 188, 194, 197, 199, 201, 206, 214, 215, 220, 221, 224–28, 239

Apollodorus, mythographer 11, 247

Apollonius of Rhodes, 3rd-century BC epic poet 11, 142, 144

Apsyrtus, Colchian prince 144

Arachne, weaver-turned-spider 172

ARCADIA 23, 32, 66, 85, 88, 112, 122, 125, 196, 220

Arcadius (AD 378–408), Byzantine emperor 34

Arcas, son of Zeus and Callisto 66

Arcesius, grandfather of Odysseus 237

Archelaus I (r. 413–399 BC), Macedonian king 26, 28

AREOPAGUS (ATHENS) 178, 183

Ares, god of war 22, 46, 69, 79, 80, 83, 97, 109, 127, 152, 172, 178, 222, 225

Arete, queen of Scherie 244

ARGIVE HERAION 160, 167, 168

ARGO, ship of Jason and the Argonauts 12, 90, 137, 140–42, 144, 148

Argonauts, sailors seeking the Golden Fleece 11, 140, 141, 144, 145, 148, 229

ARGOS 21, 26, 32, 33, 63, 113, 122, 128, 129, 134, 135, 159–68, 210, 217, 218, 226

Argos, Odysseus' dog 161, 239, 245

Argos Panoptes, hundred-eyed giant 160, 161, *161*

Argus, builder of the *ARGO* 140

Ariadne, Cretan princess 10, 178, 186, 188, 191

Aricia, wife of Virbius 179

Arion (i), talking horse 32,

Arion (ii), 7th-century BC poet 156

Aristotle (384–322 BC), philosopher 181

Arsinoë (d. 41 BC), Egyptian princess 74

Artemidorus, 2nd-century BC writer on dreams 68

Artemis, goddess of hunting, virginity, childbirth and the moon 12, 45–50, *48*, 56, 62, 63–74, *67*, 76, 109, 124, 147, 165, 178, 179, 188, 193–99, 206, 208, 211–13

ARTEMISION, temple of Artemis at Ephesus 70, 72–76

Asclepius, healing god 179, 222

ASOPOS, River 105

Asopus, river-god 152

Asteria, sister of Leto 46

Asterius (i), Cretan king 185–86

Asterius (ii) *see* Minotaur

Astyanax, Trojan prince 231

Atalanta, Arcadian princess 194–98, *194*

Athamas, Boeotian king 139, 140

Athene, goddess of wiles, wisdom and womanly crafts 10, 12, 18, 32–35, 43, 62, 63, 79, 87, 106, 108, 113, 123–25, *125*, 140, 142, *143*, 150, 151, 153, 163–66, *164*, 168, *170*, 171–76, *173*, 180, 182, 183, 198, 203, 211, 215, 220, 222, 223, 225, 227, *228*, 229–35, 239, 245

ATHENS, 10–12, *19*, 33–35, 37, 40, 42, 44, 48–50, 59–61, 66, 69, 90, 95, 102, 103, 112, 114, 118, 119, 128, 132, 135, 146, *146*, 155–57, 167, 169, 171–83, 186–88, 190, 195, 204, 206, 210, 213, 215, 218, 231, 234

ATHOS, MOUNT 214

Atlas, Titan rebel 18, 32, 130, 244, 253

Atreus, king of Argos 133, 210–12, 217

Attalus III (c. 170–133 BC), king of Pergamum 74, 183

Augean Stables, 5th Labour of Heracles 126

Augeas, king of Elis 99, 126, 128

Augustus (63 BC – AD 15), Roman emperor 9, 74, 197, 234, 235

AULIS 212, 224

Autolycus, grandfather of Odysseus 237, 238

Autonoë, Theban princess 107

Ba'al, Phoenician god 50

Bacchylides, 5th-century BC lyric poet 21, 193

Bellerophon, prince of Corinth 10, 69, 150, 153, 154, *154*, 158

Biton, Argive youth 63, 159, 168

Blegen, Carl (1887–1971), archaeologist 93–95

BOEOTIA 118, 139

Boreas, wind-god 221

BOSPHORUS 141

BRAURON 66, 213

Briareus, giant 17, 21

BRINDISI 166

Briseis, Trojan princess 225

Bruce, Thomas, Seventh Earl of Elgin (1766–1841) 181, 182

BUTO 47

CADMEIAN HILL 113, 118

Cadmus, founder of Thebes 10, 24, 108, 109, 111, 139, 220

Calaïs, Argonaut 140, 141

Calchas, Greek prophet at Troy 212, 224

Callimachus (?310–240 BC), Alexandrian poet 11, 65, 66, 68

Calliope, Muse (of epic poetry) 23, 24

Callirhoe, Calydonian maiden 197

Callisto, nymph 66

Calvert, Frank (1828–1908), archaeologist 234, 235

CALYDON 8, 12, 90, 131, 132, 140, 166, 193, 194, 196–99, 202

Calypso, nymph 244

CAMICUS 189

ÇANNAKALE 234, 235

Capaneus, one of the Seven Against Thebes 113

Cassander (c. 350–297 BC), Macedonian general and king 119, 120

Cassandra, Trojan princess and prophetess 214, 220, 221, 223, 231
Cassiopeia, Ethiopian queen 165
CASTALIA, spring at Delphi 60, 61, 63
Castor, Spartan prince 140, 180, 202, 203
Catamitus *see* Ganymede
Cavafy, Constantine (1863–1933), Alexandrian poet 247
CAYSTER, River 74
Caystus, river-god 72
Cecrops, king of Athens 173, 174, 180,
Celeus, king of Eleusis 38, 39
Centaurus, horse-loving prince 137
Centaurs (half-horse, half-man) 40, 126, 132, 137, *138*, 145, 146–47, *146*, 179, 224
Cephalus, Athenian prince 186, 237
Cepheus, Ethiopian king 165
Cerberus, three-headed guard-dog of Hades 25, *130*, 131, 179, *252*, 254, 258
Ceryneian Hind, 3rd Labour of Heracles 124
CHAERONEA 119, 120
CHAERONEA, Battle of (338 BC) 28, 102, 119, 120, 181
Chalcomedusa, grandmother of Odysseus 237
Chandler, Richard (1738–1810), antiquary 102, 103
CHAOS (gorge, Mycenae) 210, 214
CHAOS, primordial void 9, 15
Charon, ferryman of the dead 131, 254, 255
CHARYBDIS, whirlpool 32, 243, 247
Cheiron, centaur 126, 137, 138, *138*, 145, 147, 224
Chimaera, fire-breathing monster 17, 153, *154*, 158
Christie, Agatha (1890–1976), writer 218
Chrysaor, giant 32
Chryses, Trojan priest 225
Chrysippus, prince of Elis 109
Chrysothemis, Mycenaean princess 212

Cicero (106–43 BC), Roman statesman 43
CICHYRUS 250, 258
Cicones, Thracian tribe 25, 240
Cimmerians, Black Sea tribe 73
Cimon (510–450 BC), Athenian politician 180, 182
Cinyras, Paphian king 82
Circe, sorceress 32, 140, 144, 243, 246
CITHAERON, MOUNT 107, 109, 110, 117
CLADEUS, River 97
Clarke, Edward (1769–1822), traveller 43
Cleisthenes (*c.* 570 – *c.* 507 BC), Athenian statesman 180, 182
Clement of Alexandria (*c.* AD 150 – *c.* 215), theologian 83
Cleobis, Argive youth 63, 159, 168
Cleopatra VII (69–30 BC), Egyptian queen 74, 197
Cleopatra, Calydonian queen 196
Clio, Muse (of history) 23
Clytemnestra, Mycenaean queen 202, 204, 212–15, 225, 231
Cocalus, Sicilian king 189
COCYTUS, River 249, 250, 254, 257
Codrus, king of Athens 175
Coeus, Titan 45
COLCHIS 140–42
COLONUS 112
Coluthus, 5th-/6th-century AD epic poet 223
CONSTANTINOPLE 102, 234
CORCYRA 155, 157, 165
Coressus, co-founder of Artemision 72
CORFU 155, 165, 246, 247
CORINTH 33, 110–12, 123, 124, 132, 145, 150–58, 166, 175, 177, 211, 237, 259
Coronis, Apollo's lover 57
CORYPHASION 88, 94, 95
Costobocs, Caucasian tribe 44
CRANAË 223
Creon (i), king of Corinth 154, 155
Creon (ii), king of Thebes 113, 114, 116

Cretan Bull, 7th Labour of Heracles 128, 178, 186, 187
CRETE 17, 47, 56, 98, 106, 108, 118, 128, 133, 144, 149, 178, 184–92, 204, 220, 223, 247
Cretheis, queen of Iolcus 145
Cretheus, king of Iolcus 138, 140, 152
Creusa, Athenian princess 60
CRIMEA 69, 213
CRISA 57, 61
Croesus (595–547 BC), Lydian king 61, 73, 75
Cronus, erstwhile king of the gods 12, 16–19, 21, 31, 54, 59, 78, 79, 97, 137, 160, 171, 250, 257
Cteatus, prince of Elis 99
Curetes 17, 98, 106
Cybele, Asiatic mother goddess 68, 69, 71
CYCLADES 31, 34, 46, 52, 190
Cyclopes, Titan blacksmiths 16, 18, 66, 116, 121, 122, 134, 168, 210, 217, 240; *see also* Polyphemus
CYLLENE, MOUNT 88, 89, 112
CYNOSCEPHALAE, Battle of (197 BC) 27
CYNTHUS, MOUNT 46, 47, 52
Cypselus, 7th-century BC Corinthian tyrant 156, 157
CYZICUS 141

Dactyls 98
Daedalus, inventor 186, 188–91
Dakaris, Sotirios, archaeologist 259, 260
Danaë, Argive princess, mother of Perseus 10, 162, 163
Danaids, Egyptian princesses 161, 162
Danaus, king of Argos 161, 162, 167
DANUBE, River 144, 228
DARDANELLES 140, 220, 232, 233, 236
Dardanus, king of Troy 220
de Coubertin, Baron de (1863–1937), founder of modern Olympics 102, 103
Death *see* Thanatos
Debussy, Claude (1862–1918), composer 218

Decius (*c.* AD 201–251), Roman emperor 72

Deineira, Calydonian princess 131, 132

Deiphobus, Trojan prince 221, 223, 227, 230, 231

DELOS 10, 45–50, 52, 55, 65, 68, 181, 188, 190, 244

DELPHI 10, 12, *17*, 19, 48, 53–57, *55*, 59–63, 68, 72, 100, 108–11, 131, 132, 139, 140, 159, 162, 168, 175, 178, 180, 187, 215, 237, 255

Demeter, goddess of the earth and harvest 17, 28, 32, 36–40, *41*, 43, 44, 99

Demetrius the Besieger (337–288 BC), Macedonian general and king 148

Demodocus, Homeric bard 8, 9, 80, 244

Demophoön, Eleusinian prince 38

Demosthenes (d. 413 BC), Athenian general 94, 95

Despoina, fertility goddess 32

Deucalion, son of Prometheus 23, 59

DEXIA BAY 246, 248

DIA 188

Dia, wife of Ixion 137, 146

DICTE, MOUNT 17, 191

Dictys, fisherman 163, 165

DIMINI 137, 147–49

Diomedes (i), Thracian king, owner of mares 128

Diomedes (ii), Greek hero at Troy 166, 226, 230

DION 14, 15, 21, 24–28, 257

Dione, goddess at Dodona 79

Dionysus, god of wine, drama and transformation 20, 25, 27, 40, 52, 57, *58*, 59, 62, 80, 104, 105–8, *106*, 126, 188, 194, 197, 255

Dioscuri, the Heavenly Twins (Castor and Polydeuces) 180, 202–4

DIRCE 104

Dirce, queen of Thebes 109

DODONA 79, 140, 197

Echidna, snake-girl 17

Echo, repetitive nymph 117, 118

EGYPT 11, 27, 47, 50, 85, 86, 90, 118, 130, 133, 134, 161, 190, 191, 205, 217

Eileithyia, goddess of childbirth 46, 65

Electra, Mycenaean princess 212, 214, 215

ELEUSINIAN MYSTERIES 37, 39, 40, 42–44, 178, 180

ELEUSIS 10, 36–38, 40, *41*, 42–44, 175, 183, 257

ELIS 91, 94, 97–102, 109, 126, 131, 138, 163, 210

ELYSIAN FIELDS 18, 256, 257

Emmerich, Sister Anne Catherine (1774–1824), visionary nun 71, 75

Endymion, shepherd, beloved of Selene 72

Eos, goddess of the dawn 221, 228, 238

Epaminondas (*c.* 418–362 BC), Theban general 119, 120, 198

Epeius, Greek inventor 230

EPHESUS 64, 67–76

Ephesus, Ephesian prince 72

EPHYRA 151, 249, 250, 253, 254, 257–70, *258*

Epicasta *see* Jocasta

Epictetus (*c.* AD 55–135), philosopher, 101

Epicurus (341–270 BC), philosopher 181

Epidaurus 177

Epigoni, attackers of Thebes 114

Epimetheus, Titan 151

Erebus, primeval Darkness 80

ERECHTHEUM (ATHENS) 171, 183

Erechtheus, Athenian king 60, 174, 175, 177, 180

Erichthonius, Athenian king 113, 174

ERIDANUS, River 50

Erinyes, 'Furies' 16, 25, 59, 112, 215

Eris, goddess of strife 145, 222

Eros (i), primeval god of desire 15, 80

Eros (ii) god of desire, son of Aphrodite 79, 80, *83*, 205

Erymanthian Boar, 4th Labour of Heracles 125, *125*

ERYMANTHUS, MOUNT 125, 126

Eteocles, Theban prince 111, 113, 166

ETNA, MOUNT 22

EUBOEA 31, 212

Eumaeus, Ithacan swineherd 239, 240, 245, 246, 248

Euripides (*c.* 480–406 BC), Athenian tragedian 11, 25, 27, 28, 60, 65, 107, 116, 147, 154, 155, 175, 178, 211, 214, 215, 219, 223, 255

Europa, Phoenician princess 108, 185

EUROTAS, River 179, 201, 205, 208

Eurycleia, Odysseus' nurse 238, 245

Eurydice (i), Ciconian princess, beloved of Orpheus 25

Eurydice (ii), Theban queen 114

Eurynome, sea-nymph 22

Eurynomus, flesh-eating daimon 255

Eurystheus, king of Tiryns 114, 116, 117, 122–26, *125*, 128, 129, *130*, 131, 132, 140, 210

Eurytus, prince of Elis 99

Evans, Sir Arthur (1851–1941), archaeologist 190, 191

EVENOS, River 132

Exekias, 6th-century BC Athenian vase painter 69, *70*

Fates 16, 194

Fourmont, Abbé (1690–1746), French antiquarian 207

Furies *see* Erinyes

Gaia, earth goddess 15–17, 32, 54–56, 63, 171, 174

Galba (AD 3–69), Roman emperor 61

Ganymede *aka* Catamitus, Trojan prince 86, 103, 220

Gauls, Balkan tribe 62

GERANIA 91

Geryon, giant 129

Giants 16, *17*, 18, 32, 56, 144, 160, 171, 243

Glauce, Corinthian princess 154, 155, 157

Glaucus (i), sea-god 32
Glaucus (ii), king of
  Corinth 153
GLYKIS LIMEN 259
Gorgons, hideous winged
  sisters 116, 150, 163–65, 253
GORTYN 185, 192, 252
Goths, tribesmen migrating
  west in 4th/5th centuries
  AD 27, 28, 43, 74, 75, 102, 103,
  157, 168, 181, 182, 206, 207
Gouyet, Abbé Julien, 19th-
  century priest 71
Graces, goddesses of allure
  81, 84, 151
Graeae, grotesque
  goddesses 163
GRANICUS, Battle of
  (334 BC) 27
GULF OF PAGASAE 137, 145, 148

HADES, the Underworld 16,
  17, 20, 25, 39, 56, 62, 82, 90,
  105, 111, 113, 131, 147, 149, 152,
  162, 179, 180, 189, 243, 249–51,
  253–59
Hadrian (AD 76–138), Roman
  emperor 43, 76, 157, 181–83
Haemon, Theban prince 114
Haides, ruler of Hades 17, 20,
  25, 36, 37, 38, 39, 44, 131, 163,
  164, 179, 196, 249–51, 252, 253,
  254, 258, 260
HALIARTUS 113
HALYS, River 61
Harilaos Soaps 44
Harmonia, queen of
  Thebes 24, 80, 109
Harpies, half-bird, half-woman
  17, 141
Hatshepsut (1508–1458 BC),
  female pharaoh 190
Hebe, goddess of youth 22, 132
Hecabe, queen of Troy 220–23,
  230, 232
Hecate, goddess of
  necromancy and the
  dead 46, 143
Hector, Trojan prince 220, 221,
  225–27, 229
Helen, Spartan queen 11,
  60, 81, 166, 179, 180, 200–2,
  204–5, 205, 208, 212, 215, 220,
  223, 224, 228, 230–33, 238
Helenus, Trojan prince 221

HELICON, River 26, 257
HELICON, MOUNT 24
Helios, sun god 17, 33, 37, 49,
  80, 86, 114, 129, 140, 151, 155,
  186, 243
Helle, Boeotian princess
  139, 140
HELLESPONT 140
Hephaestus, blacksmith god
  22, 80, 123, 151, 171, 174,
  177, 226
Hera, queen of the gods 17,
  18, 19, 19, 21–23, 33, 46, 47,
  56, 66, 80, 88, 94, 99, 102, 103,
  105, 106, 106, 112–14, 116, 117,
  122, 123, 128, 129, 130, 137,
  139, 140, 152, 154, 159, 160,
  160, 167, 222, 223, 259
Heracleides, 2nd-century BC
  traveller 119
Heracles (i), eldest of
  Curetes 98
Heracles (ii), superhero 9, 12,
  18, 26, 27, 40, 52, 66, 68, 91,
  99–101, 103, 114, 115, 116, 117,
  121–32, 123, 125, 127, 130, 140,
  141, 147, 176, 178, 179, 186,
  210, 221, 229, 255, 257
Hermaphroditus,
  androgynous god 80
Hermes, god of trickery, travel
  and dreams 36, 38, 80,
  87–90, 94, 97, 103, 123, 137,
  147, 151, 152, 160, 161, 163,
  171, 222, 223, 237, 239, 243,
  244, 253
HERMIONE 160, 255
Hermione, Spartan
  princess 60, 215
Herodes Atticus (AD 101–177),
  public benefactor 61, 103,
  158, 181–83,
Herodotus (c. 484–425 BC),
  historian 9, 11, 33, 43, 47,
  73, 84, 102, 159, 173, 177, 190,
  200, 247, 259
Herostratus, 4th-century BC
  arsonist 73, 75
Heruli, Black Sea tribe
  invading Greece in 3rd
  century AD 102, 103, 181, 182
Hesiod, 8th-century BC epic
  poet 9, 11, 15, 24, 46, 66, 80,
  142, 151, 163, 164, 171, 251,
  254, 256

Hesione, Trojan princess
  221, 229
Hesperides, 'Daughters of
  Evening', possessors of
  golden apples 130, 163
Hestia, hearth goddess 17
HIERA 176
Hilaeira, princess 202
HILL OF ATĒ 220
Hippias (d. 490 BC), Athenian
  tyrant 50, 53, 180
Hippias of Elis (c. 460–395 BC),
  philosopher 102
Hippo, Amazonian queen 69
Hippodameia (i), princess of
  Elis 98, 99, 163
Hippodameia (ii), Lapith
  queen 146, 147
Hippolyta, Amazonian
  queen 69, 128, 129, 178
Hippolytus, Athenian
  prince 10, 69, 86, 178, 179
Hippomenes, Arcadian
  prince 196, 197
Hitler, Adolf (1889–1945),
  German dictator 102
Hittites 233, 234
Homer, 8th-century BC epic
  poet 8, 11, 13, 14, 18, 21, 22,
  31, 36, 47, 59, 65, 69, 79, 87,
  90, 91, 112, 140, 153, 154, 162,
  184, 188, 195, 221, 227, 232–36,
  238, 239, 246, 247, 249, 251,
  253, 254, 256–58
Horae, 'the Hours' 19
Hyacinthus, Amyclaean
  prince 10, 201
Hydra, many-headed monster,
  2nd Labour of Heracles
  17, 124, 132
Hyginus (c. 64 BC – AD 17),
  Roman writer 109
Hylas, Argonaut 141
Hymenaeus, marriage god 24
HYMETTUS, MOUNT 171
Hyperboreans, mythical
  northerners 57, 125
Hypermnestra, a Danaid 162
HYPHASIS, River 27
Hypnos, god of sleep 251
Hypsipyle, Lemnian
  queen 140
HYSIAE, Battle of (c. 668 BC)
  167, 168

Iacchus *see* Dionysus

Iambe, Eleusinian servant 38, 40

Icarius, Spartan aristocrat 204, 238

Icarus, high flyer 189

IDA, MOUNT (i), Crete 17, 98, 191

IDA, MOUNT (ii), Troad 81, 146, 214, 219, 220, 222, 222, 223, 230

Idas, Theban prince 202, 203

IGOUMENITSA 260

ILION *see* TROY

ILISSUS, River 40

Ilus, founder of Troy 81, 220, 221

INACHUS, River 160

Ino, Theban princess 107, 139, 140, 152, 244

INOPUS, River 47

Io, Argive priestess 160, 161, *161*

Iobates, Lycian king 153

Iolaus, Heracles' nephew 124, 126

IOLCUS 10, 90, 91, 137–40, 143–45, 147, 149, 152, 154, 155, 179, 195, 202, 224

Iole, Oechalian princess 132

Ion, Athenian prince 60, 61

IONIA/*Ionians* 48–50, 52, 61–63, 73, 75,

IONIAN ISLANDS 247, 248

IONIAN SEA 141, 210

Iphicles, Heracles' brother 116

Iphigenia, Mycenaean princess 66, 212, 213, *213*, 215, 224

Iphitus (i), Argonaut 140

Iphitus (ii), Oechalian prince 131

Iphitus (iii), king of Elis 100

Iris, messenger goddess 19, 46

Isis, Egyptian goddess 28, 50, 161

Ismene, Theban princess 111, 113

ISTHMIA 33, 34, 153, 158

ITHACA 13, 59, 93, 144, 161, 204, 224, 236–39, 242, 244–48, 253

ITHAKI 237, 246–48

Itys, Thracian prince 174

Iulus *see* Ascanius

Ixion, Lapith king 137, 146

Jason, prince of Iolcus 10, 11, 138–45, *143*, 148, 152, 154, 155, 175, 195, 202

Jesus Christ 42, 71

Judgment of Paris 12, 146, 222–23, *222*

Julian (AD 330–363), Roman emperor 62

Julius Caesar (100–44 BC), Roman politician 9, 156, 157, 234, 235

Jung, Carl (1875–1961), psychiatrist, 218

KARNAK 50

KERYKEION, herald's staff 89, 90, 253

KNOSSOS 8, 12, 33, 108, 128, 160, 178, 184, 186–92, 217, 237

Kore, harvest goddess, equated with Persephone 37, 44, 258

KYKEON, cocktail 38, 40

Ladon, dragon 130

Laelaps, tenacious dog 186

Laertes, Ithacan king 236, 237, 239, 242, 245

Laestrygonians, giants 243

Laius, Theban king 109–12

Laocoön, Trojan priest 230

Laomedon, Trojan king 33, 221

LAPHRION 194, 198, 199

Lapiths, Thessalian tribe 137, 146, *146*, 147, 179

LARISSA HILL (Argos) 168

LARISSA HILL (Nafplio) 122

LARISSA 165

LATMUS, MOUNT 72

Leake, William (1777–1860), antiquarian 27, 28

Learches, Boeotian prince 139, 140

Leda, Spartan queen, mother of Helen, Clytemnestra and the Dioscuri 86, 201, *202*, 203, 204, 206, 253

LEFKAS 247

LEMNOS 22, 80, 140, 229

Leon, Calydonian hero 197

Leonidas (*c.* 540–480 BC), Spartan king 206, 207, 208

Leonymus of Croton, 7th-/6th-century BC traveller 228

LERNA 124

LESBOS 11, 26, 203

LETHE, River 257

Leto, Titan goddess, mother of Artemis and Apollo 45–47, 49, 52, 55, 56, 62, 63, 65, 109, 193, 255

LETOAI *see* PAXIMADIA ISLANDS

LETOÖN 46

Leuce, nymph 251

Leucothea *see* Ino

LEUCTRA, Battle of (371 BC) 119, 120, 167, 207

LIBYA 171, 247

LINEAR A TABLETS 190

LINEAR B TABLETS 8, 93–95, 120, 191, 217

Lord Byron (1788–1824), poet 34, 35

Lotus-Eaters, laid-back tribe 240

LUXOR 50, 130

Lycaeus, Arcadian king 23

LYCAVETTUS, MOUNT 171

LYCIA 46, 47, 69, 122, 153, 226

Lycomedes, king of Scyros, 180, 224

Lycurgus (i), Thracian king 107

Lycurgus (ii), ?7th-century BC Spartan lawgiver 207

Lycurgus (iii) (*c.* 390–324 BC), Athenian politician 44

Lycus, Theban king 109

Lynceus (i), Egyptian prince, Argive king 162

Lynceus (ii), Theban prince 202, 203

Lysimachus (*c.* 360–281 BC), Macedonian general 74, 75

Lysippus, 4th-century BC sculptor 27

Macednos, founder of Macedonia 23

MACEDONIA 23, 26

Machaon, Greek surgeon at Troy 229

maenads, female Dionysiacs 25, 36, 59, 62, 107

Maia, nymph, mother of Hermes 88, 89

MALEA 240

MANISA 47

MANTINEA, Battle of (362 BC) 119, 120, 167
MARATHON, Battle of (490 BC) 103, 180–82, 186
Marcus Aurelius (AD 121–180), Roman emperor 43, 44
Marsyas, satyr 47, 48
Mary, mother of Christ 71, 75, 76
Medea, Colchian princess 10, 142–45, 150, 152, 154, 155, 175–77, 228, 243
Medusa, mortal Gorgon 32, 153, 163–65, *164*
Megabyzi, eunuch priests 68
Megapenthes, Argive king 166, 210
Megara, Theban princess, wife of Heracles 114, *115*, 116
Mehmet the Conqueror (1432–1481), Ottoman sultan 234, 235
Melanippe, Amazon princess, 129
Melanippus, Theban hero 166
Meleager, Calydonian prince 131, 140, 166, 194–96, *194*
Melicertes, Theban prince 139, 140, 152, 153
Melissa, 6th-century BC Corinthian queen 259
Memnon, Ethiopian king 91, 228
Menelaus, Spartan king 33, 34, 93, 204, 205, 208, 212, 215, 223–25, 231, 239
Menestheus, Athenian king 180
Menoeceus, Theban prince 113
Mentor, Ithacan noble 239
Merope, Corinthian queen 110
MESSENE 91, 94
MESSOLONGHI 197, 199
METAURUS 10
Metis, Titan goddess, mother of Athene 171, 172
Midas, Phrygian king 48
MIDEA 133, 135, 210
Minos, Cretan king 108, 128, 149, 178, 184–90, 237, 251
Minotaur, half-man, half-bull 12, 33, 168, 178, 185, 186–88, *187*, 190, 191

Minthe, nymph 250
MISTRA 206, 208
Mithridates VI (134–63 BC), king of Pontus 52, 74, 75, 119, 120, 181
Mnemosyne, Titan goddess 16, 23
Moschus, 2nd-century BC poet 185
Mummius, Lucius, 2nd-century BC Roman general 156, 157
Muses, inspirational goddesses 23–27, 47, 49, 62, 145, 171, 228
MYCENAE 8, 59, 93, 114, 133, 134, 166, 183, 190, 204, 210–18, *216*, 224, 231, 233, 237, 246
MYKONOS 46, 52
Myrrha, Paphian princess, mother of Adonis 82
Myrtilus, chariot-technician 99

NAFPLIO 122, 135, 160, 181
Narcissus, Theban prince 86, 117, *117*, 118
Nauplius, king of Nauplia 225, 238
Nausicaa, Scherian princess 244
NAVARINO 88, 94, 95
NAXOS 32, 46, 50, 62, 188
NECROMANTEION 250, 254, 259, 260
Neleus, founder of Pylos 10, 87, 90, 91, 138
Nemean Lion, 1st Labour of Heracles 123
Nemesis, goddess of vengeance 16, 204
Neoptolemus, son of Achilles, Greek hero at Troy 60, 215, 229, 231, 253
Nephele, cloud goddess 137, 139, 140
Nereids, sea-nymphs 12, 16, 32, 145
Nereus, sea-god 16
NERITON, MOUNT 236
Nero (AD 37–68), Roman emperor 61, 102, 103, 157
Nessus, centaur 132
Nestor, king of Pylos 33, 88, 90, 91, 93–95, 224
NILE, River 10, 47, 190

Niobe, Theban queen 12, 47, *48*, 109
Nonnus, 4th-/5th-century AD epic poet 80
NYSA, MOUNT 106
Nyx, goddess of Night 15, 254

Ocean, Titan river-god 16, 22, 31, 37, 66, 129, 163, 243, 249, 253, 256, 257
Octavian *see* Augustus
Odysseus, Ithacan king, Greek hero at Troy 12, 59, 76, 93, 113, 144, 153, 161, 169, 204, 224–26, 229–32, 236–48, *241*, *242*, 250, 253, 255, 257, 258
Oeagrus, Thracian king 24
Oedipus, Theban king 9, 10, 48, 59, 110–13
Oenomaus, king of Elis 99, 100
Oenone, nymph 222, 223, 230
OETA, MOUNT 121, 132
Ogilvie, Robert (1932–1981) 13
OGYGIA 244
Oineus, Calydonian king 166, 193, 194, 195
OLYMPIA 12, 20, *51*, 73, 89, 91, 97, 99–103, 126
OLYMPIC GAMES 26, 91, 96–100, 102, 103, 181, 182
OLYMPUS, MOUNT 14, 15, 18–26, 28, 38, 46, 48, 73, 89, 105, 128, 132, 127, 154, 160, 171, 220, 250, 257
Omphale, Lydian queen 131
OMPHALOS (Delphi) 54, 59, 63
Oncius, Arcadian king 32
ORCHOMENOS 116, 118, 120, 134
Orestes, Mycenaean prince 59, 60, 166, 212–15, 218
Orpheus, Thracian musician 24–26, *26*, 140, 144, 257
ORTYGIA 46
OSSA, MOUNT 18
Ouranus, sky-god 15–17, 78
Ovid (43 BC – AD 8), Roman poet 12, 49, 50, 83, 84

PACTOLUS, River 47
PAESTUM 33
Paionios, 5th-century BC sculptor 103

PALAEPAPHOS 79, 83, 84, 86
Palamedes, Greek hero at Troy
  225, 238, 239
PALIKI 247
PALLADIUM, statue of Athene
  at Troy 220, 230
Pallas (i), Titan 171
Pallas (ii), Athenian noble
  177, 178
Pan, god of the wild
  48, 56, 66, 118, 239
Pandion, Athenian king
  174, 175
Pandora, first woman 9, 23, 151
Pandrosus, Athenian
  princess 174
Panoptes *see* Argos Panoptes
PAPHOS 16, 78–86, *117, 202*
Paphos, Paphian prince 84
Paris, Trojan prince 10, 12,
  81, 146, 204, 205, *205*, 212,
  220, 222, 222, 225, 228, 230,
  234, 238
PARNASSUS, MOUNT 23, 53,
  54–57, 59, 230, 238, 245
PARTHENON (ATHENS) 12, 19,
  19, 43, *146*, 171, 173, 178, 179,
  181–83, 234
Pasiphaë, Cretan
  queen, mother of the
  Minotaur 178, 186
PATRAS 194, 197, 198
Patroclus, Greek hero at Troy
  196, 225–28, 251, 253
Paul (*c.* AD 5 – *c.* 57),
  evangelist 70, 71, 75,
  85, 86, 156, 157
Paulus, Lucius Aemilius
  (*c.* 229–160 BC), Roman
  general 27
Paulus, Sergius, 1st-century AD
  proconsul 85
Pausanias (*c.* AD 110–180),
  travel writer 12, 23, 25, 34, 35,
  43, 59, 60, 67, 79, 80, 85, 97,
  98, 100, 105, 111, 118–20, 134,
  155, 162, 165, 197, 198, 203,
  206, 210, 217, 255, 257, 258
PAXIMADIA ISLANDS 47
Pegasus, winged stallion
  32, 150, 153, 154, *154*, 158, *164*
Peirithous, Lapith king 137,
  146, 147, 179, 258, 259
Peisistratus (i), prince of
  Pylos 93

Peisistratus (ii) (*c.* 625–528 BC),
  Athenian tyrant 42, 44, 50,
  52, 180
Pelasgos Gelanor, Argive
  king 162
Peleus, Phthian king 24, 86,
  128, 145, 195, 222, 227
Pelias, king of Iolcus 10, 90,
  138–40, 144, 145, 147, 154
PELION, MOUNT 18, 24, 136–39,
  145–47, 223
PELLANA 208
Pelopia, priestess 211
Pelopidas (d. 364 BC), Theban
  politican 119
PELOPONNESE 37, 53, 93, 94,
  119, 126, 139, 147, 152, 158,
  160, 171, 194, 203, 207, 215
Pelops, king of Elis 12, 96,
  98–101, *98*, 103, 109, 175, 210,
  230, 255
PENEIUS, River 126
Penelope, Ithacan queen, wife
  of Odysseus 204, 238, 239,
  244–46
PENTELLICON, MOUNT 172
Penthesilea, Amazon
  queen 69, *70*, 227
Pentheus, Theban king
  107, *108*, 109, 113
Periander, 6th-century BC
  Corinthian tyrant
  156, 259, 260
Periboea *see* Merope
Pericles (495–429 BC), Athenian
  statesman 34, 44, 181, 182
Periphetes, brigand 177
PERIPHLEGETHON, River
  249, 250
Persephone, fertility goddess
  of the Underworld 36–40,
  38, 41, 44, 82, 99, 131, 179,
  188, 196, 249, 250, 253, 254,
  258, 260
Perseus (i), Argive prince
  10, 12, 32, 122, 138, 162–66,
  164, 202, 210
Perseus (ii) (*c.* 212–166 BC),
  Macedonian king 27
Persians 9, 34, 35, 43, 44, 52, 61,
  62, 73, 75, 84, 86, 118, 120, 173,
  177, 181, 183, 207, 218
PETRA TOU ROMIOU 79, 86
Phaedra, Cretan princess
  86, 178, 179, 186, 253

Phaethon, reckless
  charioteer 49, 50
PHAGA, MOUNT 111
PHASIS, River 140, 142
Pheidias (*c.* 480 – *c.* 430 BC),
  sculptor 70, 101, 103, 183
Pheidon, ?7th-century BC
  Argive king 167, 168
PHERAE 147, 149
Philip II (382–336 BC),
  Macedonian king
  27, 28, 102, 157, 181, 182
Philip V (221–179 BC),
  Macedonian king 27, 198
Philoctetes, Greek hero at
  Troy 132, 229, 230
Philomela, Athenian
  princess 174, 175
Philopoemen (253–183 BC)
  Megalopolitan
  politician 206, 207
Philostratus the Elder (*c.* AD 190
  – *c.* 230), Greek sophist 136
Phineas, prophet 141, 142
PHOCIS 59, 214
Phoebe (i), Titan 54
Phoebe (ii), princess 202
Pholus, centaur 126, 147
Phorcys, sea-god 32, 163
Phrixus, Boeotian prince
  139, 140, 144
Phrontis, Menelaus'
  helmsman 33, 34
PHRYGIA 47, 69,
Phryne, 4th-century BC
  courtesan 43
PHTHIA 69, 145, 224, 226, 227
PIERIA 23, 25, 89, 254
Pieros, king of Pieria 23, 24
PIMPLEIA 24
Pindar (*c.* 522 – *c.* 422 BC),
  poet 11, 24, 61, 91, 96, 99,
  100, 119, 139, 143, 150, 153,
  169, 173, 239, 257
PISA 101, 212
Pittheus, king of Troezen
  175, 176
PLATAEA, Battle of (479 BC)
  62, 119, 120, 134, 135, 181
Plato (*c.* 427–348 BC),
  philosopher 42, 79, 81,
  180, 181, 183, 251, 257, 259
PLATRITHIAS 246, 248
Pliny the Elder (AD 23–79),
  Roman polymath 73

Plouton *see* Haides
Plutarch (*c.* AD 46–120),
  philosopher 42, 59,
  188, 258
PO, River 50
Podarces *see* Priam
POLIS CAVE 246, 248
Polybus, Corinthian king
  110–12
Polycleitus, 5th-century BC
  sculptor 70, 167, 168
Polycrates (d. 522 BC),
  Samian tyrant 50, 52
Polydectes, king of Seriphos
  163, 165
Polydeuces, Spartan prince
  140, 180, 202, 203
Polymestor, Thracian king 232
Polyneices, Theban prince
  111, 113, 114, 166
Polyphemus, Cyclops
  76, 240–42, *241*
Polyxena, Trojan princess
  224, 228, 231
Polyzelus, 5th-century BC
  Sicilian aristocrat 63
Pontus, sea-god 16
PONTUS, kingdom of
  52, 74, 75, 119, 181
Poseidon, god of the sea,
  horses and earthquakes
  10, 12, 17, 20, 21, 29, *30*, 31–34,
  54, 62, 80, 87, 94, 99, 122, 128,
  138, 150, 153, 158, 165, 171–76,
  173, 179, 183, 186–88, 221, *241*,
  242, 244–46, 250, 251
POSEIDONIA 33
POTIDEA 33
PREVEZA 260
Priam, Trojan king 9, 69, 214,
  220, 221, 223, 226, 227, 231
Priapus, fertility god 80
Procne, Athenian princess
  174, 175
Procris, Athenian
  princess 186, 237
Procrustes, innkeeper *176*, 177
Proetus, king of Tiryns 122
Prometheus, Titan 23, 126, 151
Ptolemy I (367–283 BC),
  Macedonian general and
  Egyptian king 85, 86
PYDNA, Battle of (168 BC) 27
Pygmalion, Paphian king
  83, 84

Pylades, Phocian prince
  214, 215
PYLOS 8, 10, 33, 56, 87–91, 92,
  93–95, 131, 139, 224, 239, 251
Pyrrha, wife of Deucalion 23
Pyrrhus of Epirus (318–272 BC),
  Epirote king 167, 168
Pythagoras (*c.* 570 – *c.* 485 BC),
  philosopher 42
PYTHIAN GAMES 61, 63
Python, serpent 45, 55, *55*,
  56, 62

Quintus of Smyrna, 3rd-/4th-
  century AD epic poet 69

Rhadamanthus, Cretan prince,
  judge of the dead 149, 185,
  189, 251
RHAMNOUS 204
Rhea, Titan goddess 16, 17,
  54, 250
RHENEA 46, 50, 52
Rhesus, Thracian king 226
RHONE, River 144
Riefenstahl, Leni (1902–2003),
  photographer and
  filmmaker 102

SALAMIS 34, 37, 43
SALAMIS, Battle of (480 BC)
  34, 35, 43, 181, 182
Salmoneus, king of Elis
  138, 139, 152
SALMYDESSUS 141
SAME 236
SAMOS 22, 50, 129
SAMOTHRACE 190, 214
SANTORINI 190, 191
Sappho (*c.* 630 – *c.* 570),
  poet 11, 82, 254
Saracens 86
Sarpedon (i), Cretan
  prince 185
Sarpedon (ii), Lycian
  prince 226
satyr, half-man, half-horse
  (later half-goat) 47, 48,
  107, 109
SCAMANDER, River 226, 232
SCHERIE 244, 245, 247
Schliemann, Heinrich (1822–
  1890), archaeologist 134,
  135, 217, 218, 232, 234, 235,
  246, 248

Sciron, brigand 177
SCIRONIAN ROCKS 137
Scylla, monster 32, 243, 247
SCYROS 180, 182, 224, 229
SCYTHIA 69, 129
SELÇUK 65, 71, 75, 76
Selene, moon goddess
  17, 72, 114, 123
Semele, Theban princess,
  mother of Dionysus
  105, 106
SEPEIA, Battle of (494 BC)
  134, 167, 168
SERIPHOS 163, 165
SESKLO 148, 149
Severin, Tim (b. 1940),
  explorer 247
SICILY 22, 63, 66, 90, 119,
  129, 155, 156, 189, 190, 247
SICYON 56, 151, 156, 158,
  211, 212
silenoi, half-man, half-
  horse 107
Sinis (i), brigand 177
Sinis (ii), Greek spy at Troy 230
SIPYLUS, MOUNT 47
Sirens, destructive singers
  23, 144, *242*, 243
Sisyphus, Corinthian
  king 150, 152, 153, 155,
  237, 255
SIWAH 27, 130
SMYRNA 69, 71
Socrates (*c.* 469–399 BC),
  philosopher 49, 61, 251, 257
Solon (*c.* 638–558 BC),
  lawgiver 180, 182
Sophocles (*c.* 497–405 BC),
  tragedian 48, 59, 104,
  110–12, 114, 214
SPARTA (SPARTI) 8, 11, 12, 73,
  75, 93, 119, 120, 131, 134, 140,
  156, 157, 166, 167, 168, 179–81,
  200–4, *205*, 206–8, 212, 215,
  223, 231, 238, 239
SPHACTERIA 88, 94, 95
Sphinx, riddler 10, 17, 50, 62,
  63, 111
Statius (*c.* AD 45–96), Roman
  poet 121, 134
Stesichorus (*c.* 640–555 BC),
  poet 10, 205
Stheneboea *see* Anteia
Sthenelus, Mycenaean
  king 114, 210

Strabo (64/63 BC – *c*. AD 24), geographer 31, 33, 73, 74, 156, 197, 247, 255

Strophius, Phocian king 214

STYMPHALIA 127

Stymphalian Birds, 6th Labour of Heracles 127

STYX, River 131, 224, 249, 251, 254

Sulla (*c*. 138–78 BC), Roman dictator 74, 75, 119, 120, 181, 182

SUNIUM *30*, 31, 33–35, 178, 181

SYRACUSE 155–57

TAENARUM 131, 179

Talos, bronze giant 144

Tantalus, Lydian king 98, 255

TAPHOS 210

TARTARUS 15, 16, 18, 251, 253, 256

TAURIS 213, 215

TAŸGETUS, MOUNT 65, 201, 203, 206

TEGEA 198, 215

Teiresias, Theban prophet 112–14, 243, 245, 246

Telamon, king of Aegina 221, 224

Telegonus, son of Odysseus and Circe 246

Telemachus, Ithacan prince 87, 93, 204, 238–40, 245, 246

Telesilla, 6th-century BC Argive poet 167

TELESTERION (Eleusis) 40, 43, 45

TEMPE 56

TENEDOS 224, 230, 231, 233

Tenes, king of Tenedos 224

Tereus, Thracian king 174

Terpsichore, Muse (of dance) 23

Teucer (i), colonist in the Troad 220

Teucer (ii), Salaminian prince 229

Thamyris, lyre-player 24

Thanatos, death-god 251

THEBES 10–12, 29, 47, 48, 67, 104–14, 116–20, 122, 130, 134, 139, 166, 167, 186, 210, 220, 244

Themis, Titan 16, *17*, 54

Theodosius (AD 347–395), Roman emperor 27, 43, 45, 63, 85

THERAPNE 200, 203, 205, 207, 208

THERMODON, River 128, 178

THERMOPYLAE 132

THERMOPYLAE, Battle of (480 BC) 120, 206, 207

Theseus, Athenian king and hero 10, 12, 33, 69, 112, 114, 128, 129, 132, 138, 146, 147, 169, 175–80, *176*, 182, 186–88, *187*, 190, 195, 204, 231, 257–59

THESPROTIA 250, 258, 259

Thetis, Nereid, mother of Achilles 21, 22, 24, 86, 145, 222, 224, 226, 228

THORNAX, MOUNT 160

THRACE 107, 124, 128, 129, 152, 174, 212

THRIASIAN PLAIN 33, 173

THRINACIA 243

Thucydides (*c*. 455 – *c*. 395 BC), historian 9, 190, 206

Thutmose III (1481–1425 BC), pharaoh 190

Thyades, Athenian female Dionysiacs 59

Thyestes, Mycenaean pretender 133, 210–12

Thyia, early mortal 23

Timotheus (*c*. 446–357 BC), poet 24

TINOS 46

TIRYNS 66, 114, 116, 117, 121–26, 128–35, 140, 153, 166, 178, 210, 217, 221, 233

Titans 16, 18, 23, 46, 54, 106, 130, 151, 157, 256

Tithonus, Trojan prince 221, 228

Tityos, giant 56, 255

TOMI 144

Triptolemus, Eleusinian prince 39, *41*, 44

TROAD 220, 221, 229

Troas, Trojan king 220, 221

TROEZEN 33, 175, 178

Troilus, Trojan prince 221, 224, 225

TROJAN HORSE 166, 220, 230, *231*, 235

TROY 8, 9, 11, 21, 22, 33, 48, 69, 81, 91, 93, 131, 146, 166,

196, 204, 205, 212, 214, 217, 219–35, 238–40, 244, 246, 251, 253

Tydeus, Calydonian prince 166, 194

Tyndareus, king of Sparta 201, 204, 121, 224, 238

Tyro, princess 138, 152, 155

Tyrtaeus, 7th-century BC poet 11

Ulysses *see* Odysseus

VARDOUSIA MOUNTAINS 132

VATHY 237, 246, 248

Vergil (70–19 BC), Roman poet 12, 81

Virbius *see* Hippolytus

VOIDHOKILIÁ 88–90, 93–95

VOLOS 137, 147–49

Walmu, 13th-/12th-century BC Wilusan king 233

WILUSA 8, 233

Wood, John Turtle (1829–1890), engineer 74, 75

Woolf, Virginia (1882–1941), author 218

XANTHUS 46

Xenophanes (*c*. 570 – *c*. 475 BC), philosopher 18

Xerxes (519–465 BC), Persian Great King 9, 34, 233, 234

YEROSKIPOU 78, 83

ZACYNTHUS 236

Zagreus *see* Dionysus

Zephyrus, god of the west wind 201

Zetes, Argonaut 140, 141

Zethus, builder of walls 109

Zeus, supreme god 12, 16, 18–28, *19*, 31, 33, 37, 39, 46, 50, 54, 56, 59, 66, 68, 69, 72, 73, 79–82, 86, 88–91, 94, 97–103, 105, 106, *106*, 108, 109, 112–14, 116, 117, 123, 126, 130–32, 137, 138, 145, 146, 151, 152, 154, 160–63, 171–74, 179, 182–85, 192, 197, 201–5, 211, 215, 220, 221, 226, 227, 228, 237, 241, 243, 244, 250, 251, 253, 257

Zeuxis (b. *c*. 460 BC), artist 102